the complete guide to

living and
working
in Spain

the complete guide to

living and working

in Spain

charles davey

**KOGAN
PAGE**

London and Sterling, VA

Publisher's note

Every possible effort has been made to ensure that the information contained in this book is accurate at the time of going to press, and the publishers and authors cannot accept responsibility for any errors or omissions, however caused. No responsibility for loss or damage occasioned to any person acting, or refraining from action, as a result of the material in this publication can be accepted by the editor, the publisher or any of the authors.

First published in Great Britain and the United States in 2005 by Kogan Page Limited

120 Pentonville Road
London N1 9JN
United Kingdom
www.kogan-page.co.uk

22883 Quicksilver Drive
Sterling VA 20166-2012
USA
—

© Charles Davey, 2005

The right of Charles Davey to be identified as the author of this work has been asserted by him in accordance with the Copyright, Designs and Patents Act 1988.

ISBN 0 7494 4420 7

British Library Cataloguing-in-Publication Data

A CIP record for this book is available from the British Library.

Library of Congress Cataloging-in-Publication Data

Davey, Charles.
  The complete guide to living and working in Spain / Charles Davey.
    p. cm.
  Includes index.
  ISBN 0-7494-4420-7
  1. Spain—Guidebooks. 2. Spain—Handbooks, manuals, etc. 3. Life skills—Spain—Handbooks, manuals, etc. 4. Moving, Household—Spain—Handbooks, manuals, etc. I. Title.
  DP14.D327 2005
  946.083—dc22
                                                        2005011074

Typeset by JS Typesetting Ltd, Porthcawl, Mid Glamorgan
Printed and bound in Great Britain by Cambridge University Press

CHIC OR SHACK?

AFEX®
associated foreign exchange

makes your money go further

You've worked hard for your money, don't lose it in foreign currency transactions.

At **AFEX** we have, over the last 25 years, developed a global reputation for:

- Exceptional client service where your individual needs are important to us
- Offering the best rates of exchange
- A solid and proven security in international money transfers

CALL US NOW ON 0870 735 8486

When living and working in Spain there are many things to consider and foreign exchange probably is not at the top of your agenda. When you agree to purchase a property, you are agreeing to the price in euros, so there is no reason why you should leave it to the last minute and I hope that after reading this you will consider it a lot earlier.

A luxurious 3 bedroom villa, with swimming pool and sun terrace could set you anywhere in the region of €250,000. But how much is it really going to cost? With all the additional charges you should realistically add another 10% to the purchase price, so €275,000. Quite a hefty jump without even considering what impact the exchange rate is going to have on the cost of your property.

Historically over the last 12 months we have seen movements in the euro of over 6% from 1.51 to 1.42 and lower. Long gone are the days when you could get 270 peseta (€1.62) per pound which I remember trading as standard 4 years ago. With this 9 cent movement you are looking at an increase of £11,000 on the original purchase price. With new build properties which can take 2 years or more to complete, the costs can rocket before you can say mañana. If you were to go back four years when the exchange rate was more favourable, it's a difference of £24,000, not exactly spare change and that's when Spanish property was cheaper!

Before you all close this book and give up on the idea of living abroad, there is hope. It doesn't involve winning the lottery or more realistically down grading your property choice to some thing cheaper, hope comes in the form of foreign exchange service providers, and I don't mean your bank. We set up over 25 years ago to help private individuals gain knowledge, understanding and ultimately get a better foreign exchange deal. Commercial rates are not just for corporate companies; they are for people like you and I.

When choosing a foreign exchange service provider, there

are a few things that need to be considered. The first and probably most obvious is the company that is going to give you the best rate of exchange.

From many years of experience in the industry, calling every foreign exchange company is not the way forward. It is extremely time consuming and confusing. Unlike car insurance where you should contact different insurers to get the cheapest quote, where certain parameters are fixed and known, foreign exchange is different.

The rate changes every 2-3 seconds and although this movement is relatively small, over the course of a day the rate can move dramatically. Therefore getting a quote from one company may seem more favourable because you may have been fortunate enough to have called when it was at the high of the day. However, if you had called another company during that same working day, the rate may be at a low. Time really is money in this business.

Further, you will need to find out if the rate you have been quoted, is an indication rate or the actual buying rate and then if it is guaranteed. Confused? I'm not surprised.

It's no good being told the rate is 1.50 when what you are going to get is more like 1.40. A lot of banks tend to only quote indication rates, debit your account and then set the rate once the funds have been transferred which could end up costing you a lot more than envisaged. When you order your currency make sure the rate you are given is guaranteed and ask for a copy of the contract in writing.

A standard transaction is referred to as a 'spot order' or 'spot buying'. You secure a rate and pay the full amount within a short space of time, generally 2-3 working days.

Another transaction which is worth considering is forward buying. This enables you to fix a rate for your currency for a longer period of time without having to pay the full amount in one go. Make sure you have a good idea of when you are going to need the balance as the rate is very much dependant on the maturity date.

Also you can arrange stop loss and limit orders. Basically you set a range in which you wish to purchase your currency. For example the live rate may be trading at 1.43 but you would like to buy at 1.46 but would settle at worse case scenario, 1.41. You account executive would monitor that rates for you and then buy the euros when either levels hit.

If you are completely relocating to Spain, don't close all your bank accounts in the UK. It is worth keeping one account open, especially if you are receiving rental income or pension payments. These can easily be debited from your account each month by direct debit and transferred at the commercial rate for a lot less than if you were to arrange it with your bank.

If you need to open a Spanish bank account, watch out for the charges. Most banks charge an annual maintenance fee of around 20 but don't panic about this. The main charges apply to receive funds into your account. These can be from 0.1-0.6% of the amount you have sent. On €100,000 this could be €100- €600. Check before you open the account as they can be negotiable. Also some foreign exchange companies have agreements with Spanish banks not to charge their clients.

Please contact me to find out more living and working abroad.
Jennifer Saunders, Associated Foreign Exchange (AFEX)
Tel 00 44 (0) 870 735 8486
E-mail Jsaunders@afex.com **Web** www.afex.com

Contents

contract of employment 130; Redundancy 130; Dismissal 131; The
employment of women 132; Workers under 18 132; Disabled
workers 133; Protection against sexual harassment 133;
Discrimination 133; Employee representation 134; Sources of
advice on employment issues 134

Instituto de Empresa 193; Occupational training 193; The Open
University 193; Research 193; Study abroad 193

Preface

How many times have you woken up on a bitterly cold winter morning and wished you were living in the sun? It has become increasingly possible to realize this dream, and indeed thousands of people have done just that.

Within the last three or four years, existing airlines have substantially increased their range of services to the sun, and have been joined by several new players in the air passenger travel market. In the United Kingdom, easyJet has opened up new routes, as have Monarch, Ryanair and MyTravel Lite, with GB Airways and Britannia recently announcing plans to significantly expand services from Manchester. The new players include Globespan flying from Edinburgh and Glasgow, Jet 2 from Leeds/Bradford and Manchester, EUJet from Kent and Shannon, and Thomsonfly from Coventry.

The extent of the expansion in the United Kingdom is underlined by the announcement that a new international airport is to be developed just outside Doncaster (the Robin Hood Doncaster Sheffield Airport), from which Thomsonfly is to operate flights to six Spanish destinations from the spring of 2005. This new airport, only a few minutes from the A1 and from the M18 link between the M1 and the M62, will bring inexpensive and convenient air travel within easy reach of large numbers of people.

In Ireland there are now regular flights to 11 destinations in Spain from Dublin, three from Cork and Shannon. There have been similar developments in Germany, the Netherlands and Scandinavia.

This rapid expansion of passenger travel has been accompanied by, and indeed partially caused by, increased job mobility across Europe. Thanks to European regulations governing a wide range of occupations, the Spanish authorities must now recognize qualifications gained in other EU member states. Anyone from any member state now has the right to live and work in Spain, to have his or her professional qualifications recognized, and to pursue his or her occupation in Spain. A foreign EU national is to be treated by the Spanish authorities on exactly the same footing as a Spanish national. This includes in relation to the provision of help and assistance in finding employment, setting up in business on their own account, and all other matters, such as housing, social security and taxation. Furthermore, many workers and businesses are benefiting from the services of EURES, which assists in job placements for those wishing to work in another EU member state, and provides practical help and advice not just via its website, but also through its team of EURES specialist advisers placed across Europe.

The past decade has also seen a steady rise in the numbers of other English speakers arriving in Spain, most notably Americans and Australians. Whilst it is more difficult for non-EU nationals to work or set up business in Spain, many in the United States and in Commonwealth countries may well find that thanks to their family roots they are able to acquire the same rights as EU nationals (see Appendix 4).

In this book I have endeavoured to set out guidance for those considering a move to Spain in a clear and concise manner. Whilst the British form the largest group of foreigners moving to Spain, and the book is inevitably written with that in mind, I have included information that is pertinent to the nationals of other English-speaking countries, most notably the United States and Ireland. Conscious that this book may also be read by nationals of the Netherlands, and Scandinavian countries, I have included some brief details relevant to them, in particular a short appendix of Dutch and Scandinavian resources for Spain.

This is not a book about buying property in Spain, which I have covered in detail in *The Complete Guide to Buying Property in Spain*. Inevitably, however, much of the subject matter, such as that contained in the chapters on the regions of Spain and on 'settling in', is in large part common to both books.

Secret.

n the glorious **Sierra del egura**…

tarting just 90 minutes from licante and Murcia airports.

Never heard of it?

Exactly.
ww.spanishmountainproperty.com

GETTING A NEW LIFE IN GLORIOUS RURAL SPAIN.

If you think that a month is plenty of time to find the area in Spain in which you want to live – think again – it took Tim Martin four years!

Asked how come? And he says

"There are a lot of pitfalls in forging a new life and I've fallen into most of them!"

I learnt the hard way not to get overstretched- it helps nothing. It is thrilling and courageous to walk a tight rope, but it is a good idea to have a safety net (if you can afford one!)."

So what other useful pointers can he give?

"Well" says Tim *"It seems to me that the more you look into Spain, the more complex it gets – both geographically and socially. Spain is not just one country any more than is Britain. It has its own history, its own values, and its own way of doing things. In country areas especially they are accustomed to doing things their own way and we have to adjust to them – not them to us*

Communication is essential and it's no good saying that you can pick up the language when you get out here. It just doesn't happen unless you are under the age of about twelve. It takes study and practice. If a foreigner came to live in the middle of a small English village he would certainly be looked upon with curiosity and perhaps suspicion until he was able to speak some English.

When you try to speak and you get a funny look it's probably because they haven't heard you: Be bold- Spanish people speak loudly and firmly! And don't be despondent if after having understood perfectly the measured tones of your language tapes, you suddenly understand nothing. They don't tell you how to cope with a local who gives you directions in the equivalent of a hard-of-hearing broad Glaswegian speaker with ill-fitting dentures.

Do your research before you come out. For example – what is your maximum comfortable driving distance to the sea/airports etc; decide on whether you prefer a green landscape – and therefore some rainy days, or do you want wall to wall sunshine and more arid conditions. How isolated you want to be? If you are looking for rural tranquillity – then its charm is precisely BECAUSE it is far away from the Med, the airports, the hypermarkets and the motorways.

In choosing a home it is essential to remember that the style of Inland Spanish homes is often very different to Britain or France.

The Sierra del Segura has good medical facilities, schools and public transport. Even the emptying of rubbish bins and the postal service can actually be better than some urban areas.

Getting back to home searching, I find that having a very broad brief sometimes means that one becomes less flexible because, after a very tiring and expensive search – you can end up forgetting the things you have seen and where you have seen them. The two great enemies are fear and fatigue. It is better to commit to a budget and a life style that is comfortable and convenient to start with and then see how things develop."

What about a few bullet points?

- It's no good asking things like room sizes of houses if you can't buy for three months to a year. The house will have been sold and you will have to start all over again.
- Get the best and most up to date road map before you come out- Spanish roads change a lot.
- Allow twice as much time as you think on mountain routes. Nobody would think of just poping up to Scotland "to see if we like the area", do a few properties in the afternoon and get back to Gatwick for dinner. Spain is BIG.

So –

- Don't cast your net too wide – Spain gets bigger the more you look. And when you do find something you like – have the courage of your convictions: if you buy something because you love it – it is highly   likely that there are many others who will love it for the same reasons.

- Whilst you are looking around, remember that Spanish villages cannot be judged by the road through them. I've seen some marvellous things just by leaving the main road a few hundred meters. Much of Spain is behind closed doors and it is common to find that the residential street with nothing to it actually has a fruiterer a fishmonger and bar!

When asked to sum up, Tim says *"I have made the mistake countless times of going along with helpful locals I've met in bars and hotels, to see a house or some land for sale. Believe me; it invariably evaporates in tears after spending a lot of time and energy. When I finally decided to make use of what I'd learned by opening my agency SPANISH MOUNTAIN PROPERTY SL it still took me a year to get a firm list of properties from people who were serious and able to sell.*

The Sierra del Segura is still fantastic value for money, but it's not the cheapest in Spain. If you go to areas that are exceptionally cheap, there are always good reasons. And if the Spanish are not living there, or want to move out, ask yourself what it will be like in a few years time?

Many Spanish city professionals have second homes here in this Sierra, because its got so many beauty spots. It's already got a thriving rural tourism infrastructure of hotels, restaurants and self catering and its character is well protected. The people are helpful and genuinely like British people."

Sounds brilliant ! How can I do it then ?!

"Get your finances right, get a base, and leap without fear into the wonderfulness of authentic rural Spain!"

The regions of Spain: choosing where to live

SPAIN: COSTAS, MOUNTAINS AND MAIN CITIES

COSTA VERDE

FRANCE

SANTANDER
BILBAO
ANDORRA

SANTIAGO DE CAMPOSTELA
Cantabrian Mountains

Pyrenees

VALLADOLID

ZARAGOZA
BARCELONA
COSTA BRAVA

Sierra de Guadarrama
COSTA DORADO

• MADRID

PORTUGAL

VALENCIA
COSTA DEL AZAHAR

Sierra Morena
ALICANTE
COSTA BLANCA

SEVILLE
Sierra Nevada
ALMERIA
COSTA DEL SOL
COSTA CALIDA

MALAGA
COSTA DEL ALMERIA

CADIZ
COSTA DEL SOL

COSTA DE LA LUZ
GIBRALTAR

Spain is a large country, with a landscape and climate that vary greatly from one region to another. The hottest areas are undoubtedly the Costa del Sol and the Canary Islands, followed by the other Mediterranean *costas* from south to north and the Balearic Islands. On the Costa Brava you will need to heat your home in winter. Note that even in the Costa del Sol, if you live a short distance inland from the coast you will also need heating during the winter.

The waters washing the Costa de la Luz are from the Atlantic Ocean and are much colder than those of the Mediterranean. The North Atlantic coast is cooler still. Here the climate is temperate and humid. Winter weather is cold and wet and much more like the winters in the United Kingdom. Inland Spain, including Madrid, has a definitely continental climate with extremely hot summers and very cold winters. Much of inland Spain is mountainous with cold winters and cool summers. Indeed, Spain is the second most mountainous country in Europe (after Switzerland). Many areas are very arid with only occasional rainfall, though when it rains, the rain is often torrential, resulting in serious flooding.

Property prices and the cost of living

There are so many different factors that determine property prices that it is unwise to over-generalize about different regions. Much depends on a property's exact location within a region, its proximity to local facilities and communication routes, its condition and the views – to mention only some of the matters that influence price. Even the condition of the neighbouring property may have a very significant effect on the price of a property. It is safe to say, however, that the cheapest properties are those in rural areas, particularly the least populated, while coastal areas tend to be among the most popular and most expensive. Indeed, well over 95 per cent of foreigners purchasing property in Spain buy in coastal areas. The cost of living generally is much higher in Madrid and Barcelona, though still lower than in much of Northern Europe, with the price of accommodation, food and alcohol being significantly cheaper throughout most of Spain.

Education

If you have children of school age, you may wish to send them to a British or US school or an international school. There are a considerable number of such schools, with the widest choice being on the Costa del Sol. There are, however, many British and foreign children in state Spanish schools. In some schools this is causing considerable strain for the teaching staff, as well as concern to Spanish parents. Unfortunately, animosities sometimes develop between the Spanish children and those who do not speak Spanish well.

If you wish to send your children to a private Spanish school, there are numerous Catholic schools available, but relatively few private non-Catholic schools. Further details of schools for each region are set out later in this chapter.

Proximity of facilities

If you are elderly or suffer from bad health, you should avoid remote areas and consider settling not too far from centres of medical care. On the other hand, living a little inland may enable you to rent or purchase a larger property and enjoy living without the restrictions imposed on occupants of apartment blocks. You do, however, need to bear in mind the advantages of having shops, restaurants and other facilities around the corner. There are very few retirement homes in Spain, though recent years have seen the construction of a number of retirement developments in Andalusia aimed at Europeans, and indeed the Japanese, particularly on the Costa del Sol. This is surely a field in which some enterprising expatriates will establish themselves in the coming years.

The local population

Inhabitants of different regions have different reputations. Generalizations are dangerous and, in any event, invariably subject to exceptions. That said, the inhabitants of Galicia and Asturias on the northern Atlantic coast are said to be particularly welcoming and friendly. The most important ingredient in settling in any area of Spain, however, is your own determination to participate in the community into which you have moved. In Spain you have the choice of living almost entirely amongst your fellow compatriots, or living in a completely Spanish world, or of opting for a middle course. Whichever direction you follow, the willingness and ability to learn to speak Spanish will stand you in good stead. It will enable you to participate in the local Spanish community if that is your wish, or at least facilitate your dealings with the Spanish administrative authorities. Remember that in some areas, such as the Costa Brava, Costa Dorado and the Costa del Azahar, the main language is Catalan and that Spanish is also the second language in much of the region bordering on the Atlantic coast.

Enrique (Hendrik) Berends
EXTRASPAIN LIFESTYLE CONSULTANTS
Location: Urbanisación El Monte del Casar s/n
Apartado de Correos 8, 10190 CASAR de Cáceres
(10 kms north of Cáceres city on route N630)
Cáceres Province, Extremadura, Spain
GPS SATNAV Coordinates: 39º 32' 30 N, 006º 25' 50 W (wgs 84

WebPages: www.extremadura-country-homes.com
E-mail Direct: enrique@extremadura-country-homes.com
Landline: (0034) 927 290 288
Mobile phone: (0034) 645 130 115
Fax: (0034) 927 291 716

CALL DIRECT from UK at UK telephone rates: 0871 919 7773

Extremadura: Spain's Wild West.
by Hendrik Berends, 2005,

Introduction
Some Europeans interested in Spain, for their own place in the sun or as an alternative full-time residence, are realizing that living on a Costa in a 'foreign enclave' is not their cup of tea. There, the real Spain seems to have been cemented over. By now there is a noticeable tendency to explore Spain's interior as a good alternative to live -even work- in the sun. People are looking to buy a Spanish property at an affordable price and to integrate into Spanish society. In 1994 I retired from the stresses of an international executive living and working in many countries, and chose to live in a small village between Sevilla and Huelva, in south-western Spain. Later, keeping active as a consultant for a European Union export subsidy program for small- to medium-sized Spanish firms, I discovered Extremadura, some 200 to 250 kilometres to the North. From 1998 on I worked throughout this region, falling in love with its huge wide-open spaces, untouched, spectacular nature + welcoming population.

Infrastructure
By now, Extremadura's infrastructure has largely been completed due to years of massive EU development funding, with fabulous roads and motorways, but little traffic. Broadband Internet connections are available throughout. Then there is the high speed AVE (TGV) train that within a few years shall run from Madrid to Lisbon, with various stops in Extremadura. The A-66 North-South motorway from Salamanca to Sevilla is also fast nearing completion, with large tracts of it already opened up.

Name
The name Extremadura comes from the Roman 'Extremo Duero' = on the far side of the river Duero/Douro, which described the Roman Empire's frontier at the time.

Climate
By now, more than 200 water and hydro-electric reservoirs,

some of them among the largest in Europe, have been built. Nautical sports are still in their infancy, a definite growth industry. In older tourist info one finds mention of Extremadura's 'hot, arid climate'. However, that climate has changed, due to the large bodies of water that were created. Extremadura enjoys a dry and salubrious land climate, reaching the high 30's and sometimes even 40's in mid-summer. However, it is a dry heat, which allows for much cooler summer nights than experienced in other, more humid, parts of Spain. Winters are mild, on the whole without snowfall or temperatures below freezing point.

Nature

In a recent column in a British Sunday newspaper, Stuart Winter, The Birdman, writes: I've fallen in love with Extremadura after leading a recent bird watching trip to the region, and seeing an astonishing 19 different species of birds of prey, ranging from the barn door size black vulture, with its 9ft wing span, to the diminutive lesser kestrel. (Sunday Express, March 20, 2005)

Extremadura's nature parks, some of them as yet little known, offer an astonishing variety of flora and fauna. To see pairs of azure-winged magpies screeching after each other, or to go on a fieldtrip to see the bustard, or the golden eagle, is easy. The region's typical landscape, with enormous expanses of Holm- and Cork oaks, is called 'Dehesa'.

Size

The Autonomous Region of Extremadura encompasses a total area of 41,602 km2, almost 8% of Spain's landmass. It two provinces, Cáceres in the North and Badajoz in the South, with their similarly named provincial capitals, are also Spain's largest provinces. Extremadura's capital is Mérida (Augusta Emerita during the Roman Empire).

Population

The region, with 42.000 km2, some 4.000 km2 larger than the Netherlands (16,5 million inhabitants), is home to around 1,1 million. Although the extremeños (inhabitants of Extremadura) have made great strides in providing many kinds of tourist accommodation and attractions, there is an ever-increasing demand for Northern-European type and style hostelries/hospitality. The region is replete with monuments from Roman, Visigoth and Moorish times, with various cities having been designated World Heritage sites.

Living Climate

Living in Extremadura means enjoying clean air, wide open spaces, no traffic jams, little or no polluting industry, some of the best nature reserves in Europe and reasonable pricing. The largest city, Badajoz, has some 160,000 inhabitants. Second comes centrally located Cáceres, with just over 90,000 inhabitants, and designated a World Heritage site for its spectacular, totally intact, medieval centre.

Airports

Madrid (3 hours by road), Sevilla (2 - 3 hours) and Extremadura's Badajoz Talavera Airport, serviced by Iberia. Recently, a UK economy airline started regular flights from London-Stansted to Valladolid, a three hour drive north from Cáceres. Then there is Lisbon Airport, connected by motorway, at approx. 2 to 2,5 hours distance from Extremadura.

Economy

Although many regional small- to medium-sized firms were set up with EU funding, a number of them are still living in a 'subsidized economy', as yet depending on these subsidies without having experienced survival in a competitive world market. Within a few years these EU subsidies will largely disappear and this will signify excellent opportunities for investing/participating in such firms with foreign capital and know-how.

Products

The region is known for its meat products, such as Jamón Ibérico, the tasty thinly sliced Serrano ham. Olive oil, olives, some of Spain's best cheeses with their own Certificate of Origin, many types of delicious fruits, including some of Europe's best cherries (Valley of the River Jerte), the typical smoked paprika, Pimentón de la Vera, essential to Spanish cooking, in its three varieties of sweet, bittersweet and hot, apart from the region's many excellent wines, make up a large part of Extremadura's bounty. Extremeños are justly proud of their region's cuisine. Venison, wild boar and smaller game are on the menu, and the region is famous in Spain for its game.

Investment

Extremadura's prospects from an investor's point of view show one may assume that any investment here might well double in value within the next few years. House prices appreciated on average 17- 20% during the last 12 months. There are still many EU-funded development subsidies available to investors.

Properties

Rural Spain's deficiencies in Land Registry are fast being eliminated, as another sign of the EU's development funding taking hold also here. With some 2 million former inhabitants living outside the region's borders in other parts of Spain or abroad, due to Extremadura's high unemployment until recent times, Extremadura offers many thousands of available properties, from huge farms to small fincas to village houses, many in less than immediately habitable state. A substantial percentage of properties still show deficiencies in Registry, although procedures are becoming more easily available to redress such situations. Sound advice from locally knowledgeable professionals when investigating the purchase of property is still paramount.

Employment

Recent expatriate arrivals are setting up tourist accommodation, cater to the needs & want of other arrivals, or set up a small restaurant, open up a folk music school offering foreign students Master Classes, invest in a winery, cheese factory, or olive oil operation, or take over a producing agricultural smallholding. Their numbers are in the low hundreds thus far, but even when some thousands will make Extremadura their new home during the coming years, all will simply 'evaporate' in the immense space characterizing this enchanting region. They shall do so for many years to come.

Transport links to your home country

Even if you prefer to live in the countryside, you may wish to be within easy reach of Madrid, other major cities and your home country. The proximity of an airport with low-cost flights home and to other destinations can be important. As to the United Kingdom, easyJet, Ryanair, BMI Baby, Monarch, GB Airways, Thomsonfly (from Coventry and the new Doncaster/Sheffield airport), Jet 2 (from Leeds/Bradford), flyglobespan (from Glasgow and Edinburgh) and Iberia have flights to destinations throughout Spain. Málaga is particularly well served with low-cost flights to a good selection of UK airports.

I have listed most major air links with the UK, Ireland, the Netherlands, Scandinavia and the United States later in this chapter. There are also comprehensive lists of flights to Spain in the Appendices.

As to ferries, there is an all-year-round P & O ferry service from Portsmouth to Bilbao (and a car train link from Bilbao to Málaga). The sea voyage lasts about 35 hours. In addition, Brittany Ferries operates a service from Plymouth to Santander throughout most of the year, with a journey time of about 24 hours.

Note that the Spanish mainland and the Balearic Islands are one hour ahead of Greenwich Mean Time (two hours in summer). The Canary Islands operate on Greenwich Mean Time (one hour ahead in summer).

Availability of English-speaking contacts

You may wish to socialize with other English speakers. If you do, there are numerous British and English-speaking contact organizations, especially on the Costa del Sol and Costa Blanca. The Royal British Legion and the Royal Air Force Association have various branches. There are also quite a few English-speaking churches of all denominations. The Anglican Church in particular has several churches on the *costas*. Some areas have sports clubs, women's groups, Conservative and Labour associations, Scottish associations, and amateur dramatic and choral groups.

British/Irish/US goods and services

There are British, US and international schools that offer teaching in English, language schools, libraries and international bookshops at various locations in Spain. There are also numerous local English-language newspapers and magazines and several English radio stations. There are various English (and Spanish) stores selling British, US and Irish food and other products. Iceland has several branches in Spain. There are also many English (and Irish) pubs scattered throughout Spain. Not surprisingly, these are concentrated in the more popular areas. Various companies deliver British groceries and other products, including Life's Little Luxuries (tel: 0190 561 1499; website: **www.lifeslittleluxuries.co.uk**), Expat Direct (tel: 0797 480 7557; website: **www.expatdirect.co.uk**) and Expat Essentials (020 8400 1527; website: **www.expatessentials.co.uk**). Two companies based in Spain are **www.britbuys.com** and **www.Spainsburys.com**. Waitrose products are available via the website **www.sedmax.com/spain**, which has plans to add products from other popular British stores to its site.

A host of US products are available from **www.americangoodies.com**. This company will purchase goods on your behalf from other companies that do not ship abroad, promising that you can declare the _wholesale_ value of the purchase on your customs declaration. There is apparently no annual or sign-up fee.

The regions

Mainland Spain is divided into 17 autonomous regions, with greater developed powers being granted to the traditionally more independent provinces of the Basque country, Galicia and Catalonia (which includes the Costa Brava, the Costa Dorado and the Costa del Azahar). It is the local regions that are responsible for education, health and regional transport. In some regions, most notably the Basque country and Catalonia, there is a constant power struggle between different levels of government, which often makes dealing with administrative problems extremely difficult.

The map shows the 17 regions of Spain, but information is set out in this chapter according to the coastal areas, the names of which should mean more to most North Europeans familiar with Spain than the names of the administrative regions. It is in the coastal areas that the vast majority of those contemplating a move to Spain would wish to settle.

Tarragona Province

Tarragona, or Tarraco, as the Romans named this city, was the Roman capital of the Iberian peninsula.

It is generally overlooked by tourists, despite having some of the finest Roman ruins in Spain. The Romans chose Tarragona as their base for the conquest of the peninsula in the 3rd. century BC and quickly set about the subjugation of the whole Iberian peninsula, this was a direct retaliation to the attack suffered by Rome, when Hamil Barca (after whom Barcelona was named) led his army of elephants from Catalunya over the Pyrenees and Alps and attacked the Roman capital.

The Romans wiped out the Carthaginians as well as the Laeitani peoples and Tarraco, in the south of Catalunya was established as the capital of Tarraconensis, one of the three Roman administrative regions of the Iberian peninsula.

Tarragona was abandoned by the Roman in AD714, when the Muslims arrived, it became a Christian archbishopric in 1089. Today, it is a thriving city of more than 100,000 inhabitants, boasting modern facilities, hospitals, university, shopping malls and a major industrial port. It is the most southerly province of Catalunya 92 kilometres south of Barcelona, located in the centre of the Costa Daurada or Golden Coast. Cambrils, just south of Tarragona, is well known for its yacht marina, one of the finest in the area, with million euro plus cruisers nestling next to the smaller dinghies. There are opportunities to charter fishing boats and catamaran as well as smaller yachts.

The working fishing fleet leave the port early morning and return regular as clockwork around 4pm in the afternoon with the days catch, which makes its way to the many local restaurants. Cambrils is world renowned for its gastronomy, and there are several weeks during the year when the local chefs show off their skills to an eager audience. It is no wonder that the town boasts several michelin star restaurants.

There is a lively upmarket shopping area, with designer shops easily sitting next door to the more tourist orientated shops and those that sustain the day to day needs of the indigenous population.

Outdoor pursuits, such as snorkelling, diving, wind surfing, scuba diving, quad driving, para sailing, cycling, golfing. some of the best courses on the Mediterranean are situated within a few minutes drive of Cambrils- are all easily available.

Tivissa, is just inland by 30 minutes from Cambrils,is a municiplity of four towns, the major one is Tivissa itself and is situated high within the Catalunyan mountains in an area of outstanding beauty, there are golden eagles here, that skirt the local mountains, a huge number of falcons and buzzards, wild boar, deer and other wildlife. The town, itself is an ancient walled Catalan town, that was a base to the Knights Templar, who built the nearby castle at Miravet- that is well preserved and used to celebrate the annual festival of the Knights Templar. The town is steeped in history and boasts remains and ruins that date back thousands of years. It is also famed for its cave paintings from prehistoric times and there are now areas that have been declared world heritage sites by UNESCO.

The outdoor pursuits here, are as one would expect centred around the topography- mountain climbing, hill walking, cave exploration and pot holing. The river Ebro flows close by and is itself respected by anglers from all over the world for the huge (200lb) catfish that thrive in its deep swirling waters. There are charter craft available from points on the river.

The infrastructure in this part of Spain is excellent, the transport system flows, the roads in general are maintained and there are not the hold ups and contraflow systems that dog life in the UK. The trains are clean, cheap and punctual- we don´t have the wrong sort of snow here!

The education system is one of the best in europe, the first language here is Catalan, Spanish is taught as a foreign language, along with french and english how many other 5 year olds speak 4 languages? Health, is always a worry to the uninitiated, but here in Catalunya we have some of the best general and specialist facilities, it has been said that the health system in Spain is second only to France in Europe. There is a certain amount of free health cover, but it is wise to take out a small monthly insurance premium to top up your cover. If you are working your employer will deduct a certain amount of insurance for health from your salary for those who are self employed you will need to take out your own cover, but a competent gestor (this is a professional employed in Spain who is rather like an accountant, but deals with any day to day bureaucracy, gestors are not expensive and can literally save you thousands of euros) will assist you here. Providing you integrate yourself into the system, there is absolutely no problems whatsoever. Property prices in Catalunya generally, are predicted to rise (by the Generalitat- government of Catalunya) by over 100% in the next year and in the Tivissa municipality by over 200%- as the push for and rise in green tourism increases.

The encouragement by the local ayuntamientos (town halls) for the construction of log homes and cabins in the countryside and the grants available towards restoring historic farmhouses and properties is overwhelming. There is only one native English speaking estate agency covering Cambrils and the Tivissa municipality LandBank International. L andBank International is featured in most major property magazines and has property for sale in the beautiful area of Catalunya and also the Teruel Region which was recently featured in A Place in Sun on Channel 4 TV. ..

To find out more about the area www.landbankint.com or their UK associated overseas property agents www.wasinspain.com see their advert in this book.

THE REGIONS OF SPAIN

CANARY ISLANDS

Costa Brava and northwards (including Barcelona)

Costa Brava means 'rugged coast'. Strictly applied, the term refers to the short stretch of rocky coast between Palamós and Begur, east of Girona, pitted with coves that can often only be reached via steep, narrow tracks. In practice, the term 'Costa Brava' is often used to refer to the entire coast from Barcelona northwards to the French border. This spectacular and varied coastline was one of the first to welcome the hordes of tourists from Northern Europe in the late 1950s and 1960s. It has nevertheless attracted relatively few foreign residents, despite the low cost of living, and reasonably priced accommodation. The main significant foreign presence is in some of the resorts to the north of Blanes, which are populated especially by Britons and Germans. Parts of the coast are increasingly becoming a commuter belt for those working in Barcelona, or a popular location for their weekend breaks. The winter climate is rather colder here than on the Costa del Sol or the Costa Blanca, and you will need to heat your home during the winter months.

The coastal strip from Barcelona northwards as far as Callela is very narrow, as the mountains reach almost to the coast. Beyond Callela is a wider coastal plain. It is here, up towards the rocky coast from Palamos, that the main tourist resorts of the Costa Brava have been built, along the wide sandy beaches, such as those at Blanes and Platja d'Aro, or the rather less attractive but very lively Lloret de Mar. The area is highly developed and there is relatively little new construction. Property prices here are accordingly quite high. The coastline further north, beyond the 'rugged' coast and from the mouth of the River Ter, is again home to a number of resorts, including Roses.

The area is also home to a substantial number of important archaeological sites, including the Roman ruins at Ampurias. There is a Dalí museum at Figueres, the birthplace of Salvador Dalí.

Water sports are particularly popular on this coast, as on most of the Spanish *costas*, and there are many marinas and sailing clubs. Scuba diving is also popular. Facilities on land include several golf courses, and the winter ski resorts in the Pyrenees are only an hour away by car. The area is rich in cultural activities and events, not merely in Barcelona but also in Cadaqués (which has an international music festival), Tossa de Mar and Blanes. The region has a number of theme parks and water parks. The best shopping facilities are in Barcelona, Girona and Blanes.

Property prices on the Costa Brava are on average lower than on the Costa del Sol, for example, although there are considerable variations. Coastal properties and accommodation in golf-course resorts are more expensive. A modest three-bedroom villa with a garden is attainable from about 250,00 euros. In Barcelona, prices tend to be considerably higher, especially in the areas most sought after by foreigners, such as in Pedralbes, to the north of the city, where a large apartment can cost 600,000 euros.

Barcelona, a major cultural centre, is by far the largest city in the region and, with a population of 1.5 million, is Spain's second city. Like the rest of the Costa Brava, Barcelona is part of Catalonia, and Catalan is compulsory in all Spanish schools. Most of the population speak Spanish as well as Catalan. Notable museums include the Museu Picasso and the Museu Dalí. You can purchase the *Articket*, giving access to six important art museums for 15 euros. As in the rest of Spain, museums are closed on Mondays (but open every other day, save public holidays). For a little extra you can buy the *Barcelona Card*, which includes access to public transport and discounts in some shops.

Buying property in Spain • Already own in Spain Want a Holiday in Spain

Browsing the internet looking for information about which area of Spain to choose to buy property or visit, learning about the buying & legal processes, or looking for suitable estate agents, solicitors, banks, property management companies, accommodation, flights, car hire, or any other professional service in Spain can be daunting and time consuming.

Not anymore, instead of trawling round endless websites in search of the information you seek simply visit **www.Bluecosta.co.uk – the Complete Spanish Property Package;** being able to see all the suppliers and a snapshot of their services in one website helps reduce the need to trawl hundreds of individual websites and gives you the ability to more easily compare each company before linking seamlessly to specific websites of your choice.

Bluecosta aggregates all the information and services from 100's of suppliers, estate agents, solicitors and businesses operating in the Spanish property sector; providing information and guides on buying Spanish property, contact lists for estate agents, Spanish solicitors, property management companies and a whole range of after-sales service suppliers; everything connected to researching, buying and owning a property in Spain, including how to get there for holidays and business trips.

Purchasing a property abroad not only involves making one of life's major financial decisions, but also requires placing your trust in others to help navigate unfamiliar processes and language barriers in another country.

Nowadays, buyers have lots more information available through magazines. television and via the internet and it can be tempting to take short cuts, but this can lead to problems and we believe overseas property buyers need to use their new found knowledge to conduct positive discussions with reputable professionals to exact the best experience when buying in Spain.

Unlike many other travel & property portals Bluecosta has been designed purely from the buyers perspective and includes everything required to help buyers make informed choices about the areas to consider, estate agents to use, Spanish solicitors and after-sales support services required.

Each company advertising on the website is encouraged to explain how they can help you, detailing what makes them stand out from the crowd before linking you through to their products, or services on their own websites. This helps you to consider and compare how each company might help you before visiting their websites for more detail.

We do not sell property ourselves, nor do we advise in any specific area of the buying, or property management processes. What we do is provide and manage a single website to help you to research, find and compare all the services offered by others in the overseas property industry for Spain.

Ongoing, and to assist estate agents to improve their customer and after-sales services, we offer and supply online communication and progress reporting tools, designed to keep buyers informed of progress during construction of the many new build properties that are so popular throughout the Costa's.

Where your chosen agent doesn't offer this, or their own equivalent service, Bluecosta can provide regular online progress reports for purchasers of new build properties in most areas of Spain.

In addition to retirement, many people buy in Spain either for their own holiday enjoyment, or as an investment to accommodate other holidaymakers. We at Bluecosta recognise this and have included a range of travel services including online search tools to find the cheapest flights, car hire and travel insurance across the internet and through our sister company Bluecosta Holiday Rentals we offer new property owners a FREE property websites to assist in marketing their rental properties to the lucrative holiday trade.

www.bluecosta.co.uk is the Complete Spanish Property Package offering an end-to-end portal service for property buyers and owners in Spain.

British and English-speaking contacts

There are no British or international schools on the coast, though there is one British and one US school in Barcelona, and several English schools following the Spanish curriculum in English. There is a British school in Castelldefels and an international school in Sitges (Escaan). There are many private schools, primarily Catholic, especially in Barcelona, but in these Catalan is likely to be compulsory. There is a business school: the Barcelona Business School. There is no English-language radio station on the Costa Brava, but there is a local free monthly paper entitled *Barcelona Metropolitan*. The paper has an informative website (**www.barcelona-metropolitan.com**), which has a useful section on moving to Barcelona, and details of English-language clubs, societies and associations (see under 'Listings' and also under 'Useful contacts'). The paper contains advertisements from a number of businesses run by Britons and other English speakers. There is also an online English-language newspaper, *CapCreus OnLine* (**www.cbrava.com**), with much information on the northern Costa Brava.

The United Kingdom, Ireland, Australia, New Zealand, Canada and the United States all have consulates in Barcelona. There are few church services in English in this region, though there is an Anglican church in Barcelona, where there is also a Catholic church with services in English, and The International Church of Barcelona (inter-denominational). The British and English-speaking clubs and associations are almost entirely in Barcelona, and include the Rotary Club, Alcoholics Anonymous, football clubs, a Gaelic football club, an Irish Catalan Association, the American Society, the Royal British Legion, Scottish country dancing, Conservatives Abroad and Democrats Abroad.

The only regular showings of films in English are in Barcelona. Many of the larger supermarkets, including in the smaller resorts, have a reasonable selection of British foods. The resorts, including in particular Lloret de Mar and Tossa de Mar, have a good selection of British pubs. There are several English bookshops in Barcelona (see Appendix 1, under 'English bookshops') and also a lending library operated by the British Council. There is a Hard Rock Café in Barcelona, and a warm welcome at Flaherty's Irish pub.

There is a British food shop, *A Taste of Home*, C/San José 38, Sitges (tel: 938 94 98 79; website: **www.sitges-spain.com**). The emergency number for the fire department in Barcelona 932 91 53 53. English-speaking doctors include Dr Mary McCarthy (tel: 607 22 00 40).

Barcelona resources

■ **www.ben.est** – website of Barcelona's City Hall (parts in English);
■ **www.barcelonaconnect.com** – restaurants, bars, accommodation;
■ **www.estudiastrabajas.com** – for student accommodation;
■ **www.bcn-housing-students.con** – for Barcelona Housing Service for Students; for the English version, click on the Union Jack in the bottom right-hand corner.

UK and Ireland travel links

The main airport on the Costa Brava is at Barcelona. There is also an airport at Girona, and airports in Montpelier and Perpignan over the border in France. The main routes for scheduled flights are as follows:

Barcelona: Belfast, Birmingham, Bournemouth, Bristol, Cork, Doncaster/ Sheffield, Dublin, East Midlands (Nottingham), Edinburgh, Glasgow, Leeds/Bradford, Liverpool, London Gatwick, London Heathrow, London Luton, London Stansted, Manchester, Newcastle

Girona: London Stansted, Kent

Montpelier: London Stansted

Perpignan: London Stansted, Birmingham, Southampton

Dutch and Scandinavian air links

Barcelona: Amsterdam, Copenhagen, Helsinki, Oslo, Stockholm

US air link

Barcelona: New York

Other travel information

A new bus line linking Girona airport with Figueres, Castello d'Empuries and Roses has been announced. Blanes is 30 minutes by train from Barcelona. There is a direct high-speed train link (AVE) between Barcelona and Madrid. There is a car train link from Barcelona. There is also a car train link with Málaga. There is a good motorway link from Barcelona to the French border. There are daily ferry services from Barcelona to the Balearic Islands and a weekly service to Genoa in Italy.

Barcelona has an excellent metro system. You can purchase books of 10 tickets valid for use on the metro and on the city's buses and tramways.

Costa Dorado

The 'golden coast' stretches 300 kilometres to the south-west from Barcelona, to the wetlands of the Ebro Delta. As its name suggests, this coastline boasts golden beaches that seem to extend to the horizon. Despite its superb beaches, warm climate, low cost of living and cheap property prices, the region does not have many foreign property owners. That said, the northern half of the coast has a number of resorts popular with foreign holidaymakers and as weekend locations for residents of Barcelona, most notably Sitges, only 40 minutes from Barcelona.

To the south-west of Sitges there are several resorts, for the most part fairly peaceful, such as those at Calafell (with its medieval castle), Comarruga and Altafulla. Torredembarra and Tarragona are rather busier, the latter being well worth a visit to see its Roman remains and medieval buildings, including the city's cathedral. The most substantial tourist centre by far is that at Salou. It has most, if not all, of the features of a Spanish package resort, albeit a little toned down from the excesses of the most popular locations on the Costa del Sol. The resort boasts a noisy nightlife, as is true to a lesser extent of Sitges and Port Ginesta. Not far from Salou is the huge theme park and resort of Universal Mediterrania.

To the south-west of Salou there are a number of small coastal resorts, but access to the beaches is hampered to an extent by the railway line and the N-340, which run along the coast. These have clearly restricted the development of this section of the coast, save around the large busy resort of Miami Playa where there is substantial construction under way.

This is Catalonia, and accordingly you will hear Catalan spoken almost everywhere, although there are many Spanish speakers living here, and most Catalans are bilingual. Catalan is compulsory in Spanish schools in this area.

The Costa Dorado has the full range of water sports available and boasts several marinas. Port Ginesta at Castelldefels was constructed specifically for the 1992 Olympics and has excellent facilities for an extensive range of water sports. There are several golf courses on this *costa*, which also has a number of cultural centres including at Sitges and Calafell. For shopping facilities Barcelona is excellent, but further south Reus and Tarragona have substantial shopping centres, as does Torredembarra.

Property prices are much lower than on the more popular *costas*. Prices of a villa with a sizeable garden start from about 200,000 euros, but inland you may find properties in the region for half that price.

English-speaking contacts

Apart from in Barcelona, the only international school is the Anglo-American school at Castelldefels. In the Spanish private schools your child will receive a Catholic education, and is likely to have to learn Catalan. The numbers of English speakers on the Costa Dorado do not appear sufficient to support any English-language papers, or indeed any churches, Anglican or otherwise. In Barcelona the picture is a little different, with a number of churches holding services in English, including St George's Anglican Church. In Barcelona there is also a monthly publication in English (*Barcelona Metropolitan* – see under 'Costa Brava') and several cinemas showing English-language films in their original version. The larger supermarkets stock various British food items, and at the larger resorts you will find a selection of British and Irish pubs.

UK and Ireland travel links

The main airport serving the Costa Dorado is that at Barcelona, though there is also an airport at Reus. The main routes for scheduled flights are as follows:

Barcelona:	Belfast, Birmingham, Bournemouth, Bristol, Cork, Doncaster/Sheffield, Dublin, East Midlands (Nottingham), Edinburgh, Glasgow, Leeds/Bradford, Liverpool, London Gatwick, London Heathrow, London Luton, London Stansted, Manchester, Newcastle
Girona:	London Stansted, Kent
Montpelier:	London Stansted
Perpignan:	London Stansted, Birmingham, Southampton

Dutch and Scandinavian air links

Barcelona: Amsterdam, Copenhagen, Helsinki, Oslo, Stockholm

Other travel information

There are ferry services to the Balearic Islands and to Genoa in Italy. There is a railway line from Barcelona to Valencia along the coast, with trains stopping at various locations including Miami Playa, Salou, Tarragona, Torredembarra and Sitges. There is also a motorway along the coast (the A-7, and to the north the A-16).

Costa del Azahar

COSTA
DEL AZAHAR

The term 'Costa del Azahar', meaning 'orange blossom coast', refers to the coastal areas of the provinces of Valencia and Castellon. The Costa del Azahar has long sandy beaches, but despite this, only a few Britons have settled here. Germans are present, but in smaller numbers than on the other coasts. For the most part the properties here belong to Spaniards, mostly from Valencia, Spain's third largest city with a population of around 750,000, the inhabitants of which flock to this coast during August.

The Albufera, a freshwater lagoon, lies to the south of Valencia, and at its southern edge you will find the resort of Cullera, the most prosperous resort to the south of Valencia. It is the northern section of this coast, however, that attracts most visitors, especially around the towns of Vinaroz, Benicarlo and Peñiscola, and the resort of Benicasim. Property prices are not particularly cheap, but inland there are farms in need of restoration that can be purchased at low prices, and on the outskirts of Valencia modest-sized houses start from under 100,000 euros. Purchasers should note that many property owners in the autonomous region of Valencia have fallen foul of the Ley Reguladora Actividad Urbanística (LRAU), referred to by foreign property owners as the 'Land Grab Law' (see later in this chapter, in the section on the Costa Blanca).

Valencia has undergone a facelift in recent years and is a popular all-year congress centre with many leisure facilities and a wide range of cultural events. It is to host the America's Cup in 2007 (see the website **www.infoguia2007.com**). Here, and throughout much of the region, the language is Valenciano, a variant of Catalan, though most people also speak Spanish. Twenty new golf courses are planned for the Valencia region, most of them forming part of new large developments.

English-speaking contacts

There are relatively few facilities catering for English speakers, though this is changing. In Valencia there are several British and international schools (including the American School of Valencia, and the British Caxton College), as well as a selection of private Spanish schools offering a Catholic education. There are also two cinemas where English films are shown, and a local English newspaper, *24-7 Valencia* (website: **www.24-7valencia.com**). There is no Anglican church in the region, and indeed no church at all with services in English. There is now a British supermarket in Valencia called Spainsburys (tel: 962 75 11 93; e-mail: info@spainsburys.com; website: **www.spainsburys.com**). You will also find foreign foods at El Corte Inglés, but the range is limited.

UK and Ireland travel links

Valencia: Bristol, Coventry, Doncaster/Sheffield, Dublin, London Gatwick, London Heathrow, London Stansted, Manchester

Other travel information

Valencia is to host the America's Cup in 2007, as mentioned above, and accordingly the airport is to undergo major expansion, including the extension of the runway and the construction of two new terminal buildings. There are scheduled but infrequent flights from Valencia to several European cities, as well as domestic services to Madrid and Barcelona. There are motorway and rail links to Madrid and Barcelona, with a high-speed train link to Madrid under construction. Ferry services operate to the Balearic Islands.

Costa Blanca

For nearly 40 years the Costa Blanca, or 'white coast', has been a favourite holiday destination for British tourists, and is second only to the Costa del Sol as a popular choice for expatriates to settle. There are now a substantial number of complexes dominated by British residents, the earliest being those in Jávea and Altea, and more recently in Gandía in the north and La Manga in the south. This coast has an extensive network of businesses operated by English speakers.

Property prices are lower here than on the Costa del Sol, as is the cost of living. Winters here are extremely mild, and the summers are hot. The region is subject to frequent droughts as rain is in short supply, save in the autumn, when the region is often subjected to extremely heavy rainfall. In 2001 this resulted in extensive flooding that caused substantial damage in Alicante and several of the coastal resorts. There was also serious damage more recently in December 2003, when beach properties in Guardamar del Segura collapsed as high seas washed away foundations.

The northern stretch of the Costa Blanca is the more rugged, with many picturesque and peaceful rocky coves. Inland there are high mountains such as the Montgo behind Denia, and orchards of fruit trees and vineyards lining the valleys. The main population centres are at Denia (which has many amenities, including a marina), Jávea (a seaport with ancient narrow streets), Calpe (an interesting and lively town with a new marina) and Altea (unspoilt and known for its nearby scenery). There are also resorts at Moraira and further north at Ganía, and increasingly new developments are appearing slightly inland in the Jalón Valley. The best-known resort on the Costa Blanca is, of course, Benidorm, to the south of Altea, with its teeming nightlife of clubbing, cabarets, discothèques and open-air concerts. Despite its enduring popularity, property is cheaper here, thanks in part to the continual construction that goes on. Further south there is the slightly calmer resort of Villajoyosa, which also benefits from the proximity of the huge newly built theme park near Terra Mítica. The Costa Blanca also has several water parks. Benidorm Sea Life Park (Mundomar) operates a dolphin therapy programme for disabled children.

The region's capital, about halfway along the Costa Blanca, is Alicante. Few tourists spend long here, and there are not many foreign residents. It has a good range of facilities and plenty of nightlife – especially around El Barrio, the old quarter – along with the disadvantages of a large city, particularly traffic congestion and pollution.

To the south of Alicante the terrain is flatter and much more arid. The rocky coves of further north give way to long, golden sandy beaches. This stretch of the Costa Blanca has only started to undergo development during the past decade, but is expanding rapidly. A considerable number of residential complexes have been constructed, of varying standards, including to the south of Torrevieja. There is a good supply of low and moderately priced properties, thanks to the high level of continuing construction. Torrevieja is a major resort with good amenities and is growing at a pace, its population doubling over the past decade, with many Britons amongst the newcomers. The town is said to be especially beneficial for those with respiratory difficulties or suffering from allergies, owing to the two salt lakes that, together with the sea, surround the resort. It has excellent leisure facilities, including a theatre and casino, and a thriving night scene. Further south is the Mar Menor, one of the most popular resorts in Spain. It is a huge saltwater lagoon protected from the sea by La Manga (meaning 'sleeve') – a narrow strip of land little more than 2 kilometres wide at its widest point and boasting fine sandy beaches that runs parallel to the coast. There are many sporting facilities here, especially for water sports, but including several excellent golf courses. Cycling is popular thanks to the flat terrain. This stretch of the coast has undergone substantial development in recent years, though there are no hospitals here: for this you will need to travel to Cartagena or Murcia (the latter being some distance away).

The Costa Cálida (the 'hot coast') refers to the stretch of coastline between the Costa Blanca and the Costa Almeria to the south. It is rather undeveloped until one reaches Mazarrón, and the resort of Puerto de Mazarrón. Here you will find excellent beaches. Some information on the Costa Cálida can be found on **www.elojoespanol.com**.

The language spoken on the Costa Blanca is Valenciano, a form of Catalan, which is particularly strong towards Valencia to the north, and in the rural areas. The language is keenly supported by the local authorities, though most people also speak Spanish.

Besides the abundant sporting and leisure opportunities, especially water sports, hang-gliding and golf, on the cultural side there are several music festivals, and many local traditional festivals, often accompanied by extravagant firework displays. Most of the facilities, and the vibrant nightlife here, are available all year round. There are also plenty of shopping centres in the main towns, most notably in Alicante, Valencia and Benidorm, as well as a number of hypermarkets, and reasonable facilities serving the main resorts. Carrefour has recently opened a hypermarket in Vinaroz.

Property prices have increased quite significantly over the past decade, though they have not reached the levels common on the Costa del Sol. There is a wide range of different types of property available. Prices are lower on the southern stretch of the coast, and in Benidorm, where you can find properties for under 80,000 euros, the cheapest being the older

TORREALICANTE GRUPO

www.grupotorrealicante.com

THEGROUP

ARCHITECTURE AND DESIGN   DEVELOPMENTS   CONSTRUCTION

SENIOR RESIDENCES   HOTELS   OPERATIONS "KEY IN HAND"

C/ Lo Torrent s/n
03690 San Vicente del Raspeig (Alicante)
Tel. 00 34 96 566 53 47
Fax 00 34 96 566 02 40
info@grupotorrealicante.com

Plaza Deportista Sergio Cardell s/n.
Edif. Residencial Plaza Local 3B
03540 Playa San Juan (Alicante)
Tels. 00 34 96 516 44 25 • 00 34 96 526 12 07
Fax 00 34 96 516 19 41
adimed@grupotorrealicante.com

ASELECTIONOFOURPROPERTIES

FROM £ 151.000 • € 228.500

RESIDENCIAL NUCIA STAR
"We build your quality of life"

Nucia Star

www.nuciastar.com

Situated in one of the most charming places of the Costa Blanca. Using the highest levels of building.

DEVELOPER:
TORRE ALICANTE GRUPO
SALES INFORMATION:
Tel./Fax: 00 34 96 689 63 61
sales@grupotorrealicante.com

FROM £ 104.500 • € 158.000

Residencial Benfis Park

QUALITY & LUXURY FOR YOUR FUTURE

IN THE TOWN OF BENFERRI
(VEGA BAJA - ALICANTE)
2,3 AND 4 BEDROOM HOUSES
ORIENTED TO YOUR COMFORTS,
SERVICES AND COMMUNICATIONS.
SO YOU CAN ENJOY A
NEW CONCEPT OF HOME.
DON,T DEPRIVE YOURSELF FROM LIVING
IN AN EXCLUSIVE AREA.
WE HAVE BUILT IT ONLY FOR YOU.

DEVELOPER:
TORRE ALICANTE GRUPO
SALES INFORMATION:
Urbanización Benfis Park
Calle 10 • Benferri (Alicante)
Tel./Fax: 00 34 965 36 94 73
sales@grupotorrealicante.com

FROM £ 179.000 • € 270.500

EL CONVENT DE LES MONGES
"Les Villes"

Exclusive best quality houses, terrace and spacious gardens

ENJOY **LIFE** IN A
PRIVILEGED ENVIRONMENT

DEVELOPER:
TORRE ALICANTE GRUPO
SALES INFORMATION:
Ctra. Benidorm-La Nucía
Rambla de las Monjas
Tel./Fax. 00 34 96 687 73 59
lesmonges@grupotorrealicante.com

ABOUT US

The Group TORREALICANTE is a group of related Companies that Promotes and develops a wide range of projects with different characteristics and dimensions, especially in the Costa Blanca.

The specialization in each and every phase of the viability studies, design and construction of the resorts are the main points in order to develop projects in different areas.

TorreAlicante is a group specialized in promoting Real Estate Properties and specially, searching, planning and developing lands projects.

HISTORY

The Group TorreAlicante began its activity 15 years ago, just as a property developer for residential resorts and housing in this area.

As our projects came true, our professional team started to grow and support our technical and financial departments, what allowed us to face up to more ambitious Projects.

The Group has adapted to the new requirements as far as the market is concerned, on either design or construction level. It areas have not only improved but also innovated every each day in order to match up to the National as well as the International Real Estate market.

ACTIVITY FIELDS
- Housing Developments
- Tourist Residential Resorts
- Buildings
- Hotels
- Senior Residential Complexes

TORREALICANTE aims at obtaining the most return out of each project according to to the business` philosophy of each project. A highly qualified and professional service is guaranteed. This is our best reference.

THE TEAM

Our team is one of the most valuable points of our group, because of its fundamental assets: professionalism and an enormous interest and dedication to each Project.

The group has an in-house team of professionals such as: architects, designers, experts on marketing, promotion, urban development, economists, lawyers, experts on managing projects for residential homes for the elderly as well as for Hotel developments either on national or international level.

Knowledge, experience and enthusiasm make each Project successful.

Some of our previous Projects as well as the current ones are detailed within the attached dossier.

OUR AIMS are:
VIABILITY
ARCHITECTURE AND DESIGN
IMPLEMENTATION
MANAGEMENT

MARKETING
Land search
Market research and analysis
Requirements of planning and urban development
Conceptual design
Phase development
Analysis of the cost for each phase
Economic-financial research of the Project
Project viability

ARCHITECTURE AND DESIGN

A project starts with an effective design of the architecture, spatial organization, furnishing, finish and decoration. It has to fullfill the customer's requirements and comfort expectations.

Each element of the design should solid reinforce the idea which underlies the global conception of the Project.

A good design also includes flexibility for the future.

The design is the direct product of the interaction among the customer's requirements and aims and the ability and experience of the technical team. Good understanding and a fluently communication are the basis of a Project.

Our projects include:
- Definition of the initial project
- Design proposals
- Evaluation of the proposals
- Definition of the final project
- Analysis of the investment
- Final design and definition
- Selection of the materials and qualities
- Evaluation of the costs for the final design

PLANNING AND COMPLETION

TORREALICANTE is also specialized in carrying out projects of building, planning, contacting, coordinating, controlling costs and developing all kind of constructions.

Planning of schedule of conditions, standard and specifications for the offers.

Analysis and evaluation of proposals.

Negotiation and contracting.

Building implementation, control of the costs and qualities.

Constant supervision on site of every construction element and their development.

Assessment of finished projects, revision of building certifications, adjustements and professional liquidation.

Constant control and supervision of the course of the building, costs, qualities, deadlines and possible changes of the project.

Definite liquidation. Monitoring during the guarantee periods.

Preparation and acquirement of licenses and the required permissions.

COMMERCIALIZATION
POSITION AND PRESENCE AT THE NATIONAL AND INTERNATIONAL MARKET

Analysis and control of the daily commercialisation, follow-up of the carried out business and of the rest of the promotional actions.

Inclusion of our Projects in different official international and national organizations and from this sector.

Organization of different official and commercial events in order to present the product.

Creation of a programme for public relations, press and publicity.

Statistical analysis of the profile of the clients, professional associations, real and potential markets.

Revision of the level of response to the promotional actions.

Periodical revisions of the determined aims and strategies to follow.

Annual marketing plan adapting with flexibility the offer to the demand and positioning continuously the product in the market.

PRODUCTS REPRESENTATION

Regular mailing for potencial and real customers.

Presentation of the product to the professionals of this sector.

Continuous presence in the market by means of being visited by the responsible of Marketing and Sales.

Creation of the annual marketing plan of the product.

Increase and opening of new ways of business.

Information and periodical follow-up from the specialized press

Participation in trade fairs depending on the product and promotional activity

Yearly presentations of the products aimed to the real as well as to the potential market.

Organization of presentations or promotion events to carry out in a determined area.

Follow-up of the carried out promotions

Analysis of the evolution of the product in relation with the market and in comparison with the competitors.

REAL STATE BROKERS

Due to the constant contact to all the involved sectors: financing, investors, sales structures, developers and construction companies, The TORREALICANTE Group is also able to work as a Real Estate advisor. The company has a deep knowledge of the market and also has first hand and comprehensive information about the offer and demand.

Purchase of land for future building
Sale of Hotel buildings
Sale of Residential Homes for the Elderly
Search for Investors for Real Estate transactions

CONCLUSIONS

The TORRE ALICANTE Group, taking into consideration its specialization and experience, is able to carry out all kinds of projects "Key in Hand" apartments built in the early days of the explosion of tourism. A modest-sized villa near Torrevieja, or indeed in La Manga, can cost as little as 230,000 euros, with a two-bedroom apartment costing about half that amount. Further south, near Mazarrón and the resort of Puerto de Mazarrón, you will find reasonable-sized villas for about 180,000 euros. The most expensive properties are in the areas favoured by British house buyers, notably the north-eastern tip of the coast between Moraira and Jávea. Long-term rental property is in very short supply along the Costa Blanca.

Prospective purchasers in the autonomous region of Valencia, which includes the Costa Blanca, should take care not to fall foul of the 1994 Ley Reguladora Actividad Urbanística (LRAU), referred to by foreign property owners as the 'Land Grab Law'. Properties most at risk are those built on rural land, or on other land that has not yet been developed. Property developers have been acquiring agricultural land in the belief that the local authorities will reclassify the land as *urbano*, making it available for development. Under the 1994 law, developers are entitled to a proportion of the land that is adjacent to theirs and can compel the adjacent owners to pay financial contributions towards the cost of building the infrastructure and services of the development. The law was originally introduced to prevent land speculators holding on to property until land prices rose, and thereby effectively preventing development. The wisest course of action is to avoid rural land in this region. The law is presently being challenged in the Spanish courts, and may well be considered by the European Court of Human Rights. Up-to-date information can be found on **www.abusos-no.org** and **www.homecostablanca.com**.

English-speaking contacts

The Costa Blanca has a substantial number of British, US and international schools, including at Valencia and Alicante, with British schools in Jávea (2), Alfas del Pi, Benidorm and Murcia (2), and US schools in Torrevieja and La Manga. Caxton College in Valencia and Shoreless Lake School in Murcia have boarding facilities. There are private (Catholic) Spanish schools in most of the larger cities, including Valencia, Alicante and Benidorm. There are a substantial number of Anglican churches in the region (including at Alicante, Alcocebre, Calpe, Campello, Denia, Gandía, Jávea, La Manga, La Marina, Teulada/Moraira, Benidorm, Orba/Orbeta, La Siesta, Lago Jardin, Los Balcones and Torrevieja), and also Baptist and Evangelical churches (both in Jávea) and Catholic services in English (including at Benidorm).

A considerable number of English-language publications can be found on the Costa Blanca, most notably *Costa Blanca News* (its website at **www.costablanca-news.com** includes a list of English-speaking businesses), *Valencia Life*, *Views Magazine*, *The Weekly Post*, *The Euro Weekly News* and, in Benidorm, *Look What's On*. There is also an English-language radio station, Onda Cero International (94.6 FM), broadcasting full time in English. The Costa Blanca has an extensive range of clubs and associations run by English speakers. These cover sports, theatre (including in Denia, Orba and Jávea) and politics, as well as social groups, charitable organizations, a classic cars club, a yoga group and a Gilbert and Sullivan society. There are a number of cinemas on the coast showing English-language films, including at Calpe, Gata, Jávea Port and Benidorm, and an English library in Altea (tel: 965 84 47 07). Save in Alicante, most supermarkets sell a range of British food products, though prices are often high. There are many British pubs and restaurants, especially in Benidorm and the other main resorts.

Information about English-speaking services on the Costa Blanca is available on **www.costablancasearch.com**. This information includes services in Alicante, Jávea, Torrevieja, Jalón, Altea, Campello, Benidorm, Calpe, Denia and Marina. See also **www.costablancaexpats.net** (with over 300 links) and **www.costablancaworld.com**. The latter is a monthly magazine and information guide for expats. It has a complete list of all schools in the region, and lists of clubs and associations, with contact details. There is an information website devoted to Torrevieja at **www.torrevieja-information.com**, covering rentals, clubs, schools and English cinema.

The United Kingdom, Denmark, the Netherlands, Norway and Sweden have consulates in Alicante. The Netherlands and Sweden also have consulates in Benidorm.

UK and Ireland travel links

The Costa Blanca is served by three airports. Chief amongst them is El Altet, outside Alicante, providing many flights to the United Kingdom and other European destinations. The airport of Manises, close to the city of Valencia, and San Javier Murcia airport, serving the southern half of the Costa Blanca, also have flights to the United Kingdom, in the latter case charter flights. The main routes for scheduled flights are as follows:

Alicante: Belfast, Birmingham, Bristol, Cardiff, Coventry, Cork, Doncaster/ Sheffield, Dublin, East Midlands (Nottingham), Edinburgh,

Exeter, Glasgow, Leeds/Bradford, Liverpool, London Gatwick, London Luton, London Stansted, Londonderry (Derry City Airport), Manchester, Newcastle, Southampton

Murcia: Birmingham, Dublin, East Midlands (Nottingham), Kent, Leeds/Bradford, London Gatwick, London Stansted, Shannon, Southampton

Valencia: Bristol, Coventry, Doncaster/Sheffield, Dublin, London Gatwick, London Heathrow, London Stansted, Manchester

Dutch and Scandinavian air links

Alicante: Billend, Amsterdam, Rotterdam, Oslo, Bergen, Trondheim, Stavanger, Gothenburg, Stockholm

Other travel information

All three airports handle domestic flights, in particular to Madrid and Barcelona. There are regular ferry services from Alicante and Denia to the Balearic Islands, and from Alicante to Oran in Algeria. Unlike many regions of Spain, the Costa Blanca has a developed road network, though the N-332 in particular is subject to severe congestion, especially where it passes through the coastal resorts, and improvements are planned. Public transport is reasonably good. A new bus link has recently opened between Alicante airport and Benidorm. There are rail links from Madrid to Alicante, and a good train service from Denia to Alicante with several stops, including at Calpe. In late 2003, new plans were announced for a high-speed train link from Alicante to Murcia.

Costa de Almería

COSTA DE
ALMERIA

The coastline to either side of the town of Almería is completely unspoilt, but includes a number of popular resorts. To the south-west is Agua Dulce with its marina, and the more modern and busier complexes at Roquetas del Mar, Playa Serena and Almerimar, with a number of marinas and golf courses. To the north of Almería is the rugged and desolate coast of the Cabo del Gato-Nijar natural park, and further north the expanding resorts of Mojácar Playa and Vera, the latter boasting a number of naturist beaches.

This region of Spain is one of the hottest, sunniest and most arid. Average winter temperatures seldom fall below 15°C. Inland, much of the terrain consists of desert, the scene for the filming of many a Western, with a Hollywood-type theme park at Tabernas. Large parts of this desert terrain have proved extremely fertile when watered, and there are now seemingly endless expanses of the region covered in plastic-sheeted greenhouses under which much of Northern Europe's supply of winter vegetables is grown. This has resulted in an additional huge source of new wealth for this very prosperous region.

The population of this area has grown considerably in recent years, in large part due to the arrival of substantial numbers of economic migrants from Eastern Europe and North Africa, working in the expanding agricultural sector. To date, the only resort to see substantial numbers of foreigners is that of Mojácar Playa, where a high proportion of residents are British.

There is an extensive array of water sports available on the Costa de Almería, with scuba diving and sailing being particularly popular. Almería has a good range of shops, but elsewhere choices are more limited, especially out of season. Dining out is generally rather more expensive than on the Costa del Sol.

Property prices are lower than on the Costa del Sol and properties are in good supply, owing to the extent of new construction that is taking place. Two-bedroom apartments start at about 75,000 euros, and villas at about 200,000 euros. Inland you may be able to find houses for about half that amount, though they will probably need significant work carried out.

The area is presently undergoing considerable development in order to participate in the hosting of the Mediterranean Games in 2005.

English-speaking contacts

There are no British, American or international schools on the Costa de Almería. It appears, however, that a new international school is to open in 2005 (probably near Turre), catering for children aged from 5 to 12 and offering a bilingual education with a curriculum based upon the International Baccalaureate. Enquiries should be sent to intschoolsespain@ cs.com. There are, of course, several private (mainly Catholic) Spanish schools in the region. Nursery schools include the Orange Tree Nursery school in Antas (see **www.orangetreenursery.co.uk**). The small numbers of English speakers here do not warrant any English-language publication, but you may find the Costa del Sol publications worth looking at. British food products are available in some of the larger supermarkets, but are expensive. There is also a British supermarket in Mojácar Playa, Mr. UK (tel: 950 47 58 50).

There are Anglican services at Mojácar, Los Castanos, Aguilas, Costacabana and El Agua de Enmediot, Roman Catholic services at Mojácar village church and an Evangelical church at Cuevas. There are several local clubs and societies including bowling, Alcoholics Anonymous, amateur radio, cricket, gardening, archery, theatre, tennis, and branches of the Royal British Legion and Weight Watchers.

Information in English, including details of English-speaking contacts and services, is available on the website **www.elojoespanol.com**, which covers in particular Vera, Garrucha, Mojácar and Carboneras, and also the Costa Cálida, and has a number of chat pages. The website **www.Costa dealmeria.co.uk** is an information and community website with property services, rentals, newspapers and details of local schools, and a link with the local newspaper *The Advertiser*. The website **www.andalucia.com** is also worth inspecting, as it has a section on the Costa de Almería.

UK and Ireland travel links

The largest airport serving the region is that at Alicante, with flights to nine UK destinations and also to Dublin. Almería is smaller, but with services to several UK destinations. Murcia airport also has an increasing number of flights to the UK. The main routes for scheduled flights are as follows:

Alicante: Belfast, Birmingham, Bristol, Cardiff, Coventry, Cork, Doncaster/ Sheffield, Dublin, East Midlands (Nottingham), Edinburgh, Exeter, Glasgow, Leeds/Bradford, Liverpool, London Gatwick, London Luton, London Stansted, Londonderry (Derry City Airport), Manchester, Newcastle, Southampton, Teesside

Almería: Birmingham

Murcia: Birmingham, Dublin, East Midlands (Nottingham), Kent, Leeds/Bradford, London Gatwick, London Stansted, Shannon, Southampton

Dutch and Scandinavian air links

Alicante: Billend, Amsterdam, Rotterdam, Oslo, Bergen, Trondheim, Stavanger, Gothenburg, Stockholm

Murcia: Helsinki, Oslo, Trondheim

Other travel information

You will definitely need a car. Bus and train services leave a great deal to be desired. The road network has recently started to undergo long-needed improvements, and Almería is to have 200 kilometres of new roads and two new highways by 2010. This should go some considerable way towards reducing the region's remoteness, and perhaps improve the rather slow-moving route to the Costa del Sol. There is a ferry service from Almería to Melilla in North Africa.

Costa Tropical and the Alpujarras

COSTA TROPICAL

The most northerly stretch of the Costa del Sol, known as the Costa Tropical, is quiet and unde-veloped. In truth, there is very little space in which to construct, as the mountains of the Sierra Nevada come down very close to the coastline, and in places into the sea. There are a number of small villages along the coast, but only two substantial resorts, La Herradura and Almuñécar. Salobreña is also popular, a whitewashed town topping an outcrop of rock just back from the shoreline, and boasting a 10th-century Moorish castle. There are a number of villas dotted around the hillsides. To the east of Motril, where the beaches are wider, a number of developments have recently been constructed.

Property prices on the Costa Tropical are low, and you will have no difficulty finding a house under 100,000 euros, although prices are considerably higher in Herradura and Almuñécar. There is an international school in Almuñécar in which the UK National Curriculum is taught and pupils take GCSE and A-level examinations.

Inland from the coast are Las Alpujarras, on the lower reaches of the Sierra Nevada. This area is known for its stunning views and tranquillity, and is a popular visiting place for Spaniards seeking some time 'away from it all'. The views here are truly spectacular, but this is very much an isolated and undeveloped part of Spain (the nearest airports are those of Almería and Málaga), with a fiercely cold climate in winter with many routes becoming impassable in wet weather. The town of Trevélez, for example, is said to be the highest in Europe. The area is sparsely populated, with the largest town in the region, Berja, having a population under 15,000. The area's administrative capital, Órgiva, has a mere 5,000 inhabitants.

There are few facilities in Las Alpujarras, though green tourism is rapidly increasing in popularity, and there is of course skiing in the Sierra Nevada further inland. There are very few foreigners living in the area, and, accordingly, few services catering for them, apart from the international school in Almuñécar. Public transport is poor or non-existent. Useful information about the Costa Tropical is available on **www.andalucia.com**, with details concerning Almuñécar and Salobreña. For travel information, see below under 'Costa del Sol'.

Costa del Sol

COSTA DEL SOL

The Costa del Sol, on the south coast of Spain in Andalusia, is by far the most popular area for foreign property buyers, with more choosing to buy here than in the whole of the rest of Spain. There are almost 3 million homes here owned by foreigners, with estimates of the number of Britons resident ranging up to 500,000, with well over 200,000 Germans also choosing to settle here. The Costa del Sol stretches from nearly as far south-west as Gibraltar and towards Motril in the east. It is dominated by the tourist industry, with 9 million visitors a year. The region's capital is Málaga, Spain's fifth largest city, with a population of around 500,000. While much of the coast has an international feel, Málaga is neither a major tourist attraction nor a popular choice with foreign residents. It has retained its Spanish character and its Moorish past – the city was under Muslim rule until the latter years of the 15th century.

The Costa del Sol is an ideal choice for foreigners. It boasts excellent weather, with over 320 days of sun each year, mild winters (average January temperatures are about 16°C). It is easily accessible via the airport at Málaga. It has an extensive range of sports and leisure activities (most notably golf and water sports, but also skiing in the Sierra Nevada, some two hours from the coast by car). In many areas, foreigners make up a substantial proportion of the population, with the British being the most numerous, followed by the Germans and then the Scandinavians. Not surprisingly, in summer the beaches are crammed, and in places traffic is almost at a standstill.

There has been extensive construction of hotels, apartment blocks and a host of different types of housing developments (*urbanizaciones*) over the past 40 years. The region continues to expand: its population is expected to increase by a further 50 per cent over the next decade. The improvement of the road network and other infrastructure has tended to lag behind, and is likely to continue to do so. The region has a considerable number of marinas, theme and water parks and a safari park.

South of Estepona, however, there has been far less construction than elsewhere on the Costa del Sol, save at Sotogrande (about an hour from Málaga airport along the A-7 motorway), where there is a purpose-built luxury development, and many upmarket properties. It is this stretch of the coast, down towards Gibraltar, that is known as the Costa del Golf and is home to a good number of dedicated golf resorts, especially around Sotogrande. The Valderrama Golf Club at Sotogrande is the site of a world championship course. Estepona and San Pedro de Alcántara are expanding, and both have a significant British presence. Inland is the Serrania de Ronda, a series of valleys with very attractive villages where many foreigners have built or purchased substantial properties in which to enjoy the tranquillity of the mountains.

The most popular and expensive location is undoubtedly Marbella with its famous marina of Puerto Banús, the new town of Nueva Andalucía and 'Golf Valley' close by. Farther up the coast are Mijas Costa and the busy town of Fuengirola. In Mijas itself it is estimated that well over 40 per cent of the occupants are foreign. Between here and Málaga are the resort of Benalmádena and the package holiday resort of Torremolinos, the latter being one of the first sites to be developed in the early days of mass tourism, with its noisy nightlife, high-rise blocks and its plentiful supply of a rather unhealthy variety of British cuisine. Benalmádena is newer than Torremolinos, but expanding rapidly with a substantial number of British residents and a good range of facilities. As one passes Málaga, progressing north-east along the coast, the region again becomes far less developed and more tranquil, though the coastal resorts are still crowded during the summer months. Nerja, famous for its caves, is particularly popular with the British, and has a fairly good range of leisure and cultural activities. There are several small- to medium-sized resorts along this stretch of the coast, including Cala de Moral and Torre del Mar. Inland from Torre del Mar the scenery is quite spectacular.

When looking to purchase a property on the Costa del Sol, the golden rule at Fuenplaza Group is to provide their clients with all the relevant information and options to enable them to make the best choice for themselves. They also advise:

Do your homework

Before visiting a real estate agent do as much research as you can. Use the internet and call the agent to discuss your requirements prior to any visit. Ask them to send you information on areas, amenities and any other requirements that you might have. Search their database to see what you can get for your money. Get financial and legal advice before your purchase and make sure that this is from a totally independent party. Obtain information about any potential estate agents, how long have they been around, what is their track record like, will they be around in the future when you are taking possession of your new home, moving again or need further advice.

Choose a real estate agent and not a sales company

Unfortunately not all companies on the Costa del Sol that call themselves estate agents can claim to be real estate agents. Some are merely sales companies with little experience in the Spanish real estate market, taking advantage of what is largely an unregulated profession at the moment. Choose a real estate agent that is a member of a recognized organization and operates under a code of ethics. Also make sure that the salesperson that you deal with is employed by the company and can speak Spanish. Unprofessional sales companies hire low rate temporary staff, that have little knowledge of the local market, or of the language. Such agents will avoid certain properties or developments where they cannot communicate properly with the Spanish vendors therefore reducing the buyer's choice.

Don`t be dictated to

Be careful of companies that organise your visit to suit their own needs. This often starts with a subsidised "inspection trip" and choosing the properties that you will viewing without sufficient input from yourself. Normally a company that subsidises your visit will want something in return, at best this will be your constant attendance during your visit at worst it will be subjecting you to "closing techniques" designed to getting a deposit at all costs as opposed to finding the right home for you. Choose an agent that gives you the liberty that you need to make your own decisions. Make sure that they show you as much about the local area as they do the property, in the long run it will be just as important.

Location location.......

By using a an agent with strategically located offices you will be giving yourself the best chance of finding the home of your dreams in the ideal location for your own personal requirements. The Costa del Sol is made up of a number of towns and areas that each have their own individual identities, Fuengirola, Mijas Costa, Marbella and Estepona for example. By choosing a real estate agent that can offer local expertise along the coast and inland you will be assured that the first important choice, of where you want to be, is not made by any estate agents limited availability of properties.

Off plan v resale properties

Decide for yourself whether purchasing an off plan or a resale property is best for you. As the name suggests off plan involves purchasing a property under construction. This involves an element of speculation and as such the returns can be high in investment terms. Buying off plan generally offers good payment terms during the construction period, but the property may not be ready for up to two years. A resale property, whilst not being brand new, generally means that you will have much more choice in terms of location, property type and of course will be available right away. Beware of agents who may steer you to off plan properties and be reluctant to show resale properties, as they often involve more work for the estate agent in terms of finding the properties and in administration terms during the sale.

Fuenplaza Group

Fuenplaza Group is an English family owned company that has been operating in the Spanish real estate market for just over 25 years. Although they have a quarter of a century behind them they are still regarded as amongst the most forward thinking on the coast. For example, they are founder members and represented on the committee of the Interagency Network Multi Listing Service, a network designed to provide greater client choice and security to real estate on the Costa del Sol by agreeing to work within a strict code of ethics. See www. fuenplaza.com for more evidence.

Operating from 6 offices situated along the length of the Costa del Sol, all Fuenplaza Group's team are bilingual and trained to help you find the home of your dreams, being as informative about the lifestyle and the coast in general as about the properties that you will want to call home. On the contrary to organizing inspection trips they are happy for their clients to design visits to the coast to suit themselves, always with as much assistance as is required relating to travel and accommodation from their call centre staff who can be contacted on 0871 910 3 555.

Fuenplaza Group are genuinely the only real estate company on the Costa del Sol that works within both the Spanish and the expatriate market, because of this they boast a portfolio of over 8,000 properties and new developments designed to provide the client with the widest possible choice and best chance of finding their dream home.

The cost of property on the Costa del Sol is significantly higher than in the rest of Spain, especially in and around Marbella, and has increased substantially in the past few years. The coast is undergoing rapid development, with new residential complexes constantly under construction. The speed with which new accommodation is being built invariably exceeds the creation of the infrastructure required, and in many cases it is some years before important services such as a public transport network, medical facilities and schools are put in place. The cheaper properties (priced at well under 100,000 euros) include many apartments in the older blocks in the busier resorts, such as Torremolinos or Fuengirola, although the standard of these properties is not as high as in the more recent developments. In Sotogrande, on the other hand, apartments start at over 300,000 and villas from 450,000. Marbella tends to be a little dearer still, though both Mijas and Nerja are rather less expensive (especially the latter). Inland, property prices tend to be lower, but there are few amenities, the roads and other infrastructure are poor, and few foreigners choose to settle or buy there. Long-term rentals are difficult to find on the Costa del Sol, though there is an ample supply of properties for short-term letting.

In addition to the many sporting opportunities available on the Costa del Sol, the region has several theme and water parks and a large safari park near Estepona. The region is also home to an extensive range of cultural activities, including annual film festivals in Marbella and Málaga. There is a wide range of shops.

The medical facilities on the Costa del Sol are generally good, with the public hospital in Marbella and the children's hospital El Materno in particular having a reputation for a high standard of care. Marbella boasts a number of private clinics, including some specializing in cosmetic surgery and claiming to be leaders in this field. There are several British-qualified doctors and dentists practising on the Costa del Sol. Recent years have seen the first retirement homes opening on the coast, a new development in Spain.

Useful information about the Costa del Sol is available at **www. andalucia.com**.

English-speaking contacts

There are many English-language speakers established on the Costa del Sol, running an extensive range of different businesses serving the English-speaking communities.

There is a university in Málaga with a plentiful supply of courses in Spanish for foreigners. The area boasts a good number of British and international co-educational schools, especially in and around Marbella (for a detailed list, see **www.andalucia.com/education/schools**, and also the website of the National Association of British Schools in Spain: **www.nabss.org**). The majority of these schools follow the UK curriculum (setting National Curriculum tests, GCSE and A levels), although some programmes of study are based on the International Baccalaureate. The English International School (tel: 952 83 10 58) in Marbella, founded in 1982, provides education for children aged from 3 to 18, and claims to have the best results of the British schools in Spain. The Swans International Primary School (tel: 952 77 32 48) puts an emphasis on learning foreign languages, and in addition to teaching Spanish has a French national teacher to teach French. Other schools include Aloha College (tel: 952 81 41 33), also in Marbella, where the curriculum at sixth form follows the International Baccalaureate; Sunny View School (tel: 952 38 31 64) in Torremolinos; The International School at Sotogrande (tel: 956 79 59 02); and St Anthony's College in Mijas (tel: 952 24 73 16). There are also French, German, Norwegian and Swedish schools on the Costa del Sol. There are a number of bilingual nursery schools, including the Peter Pan Bilingual Nursery (**www.gpeterpan.com** – go to *quiénes somos*, then *English*). There are a number of private Spanish schools. Of particular note is San José College (tel: 952 88 38 58), popular with many foreign residents in Marbella, whose children make up a large proportion of the pupils at the school.

In some areas there are substantial numbers of foreign children in Spanish state schools, placing a great strain on the ability of these schools to cope with the numbers of non-Spanish speakers. In one school in Mijas about half the children are foreign, mainly British, and only 4 per cent of these speak Spanish well. Some Spanish parents are naturally concerned that their children's education is suffering, as the teachers have to spend a disproportionate amount of their time helping the foreign pupils. In some schools there is intense rivalry and hostility between the local Spanish children and the English-speaking children.

The region has a large number of churches of all denominations catering for English-speaking residents. Further details, including contact names and telephone numbers, can be found on the *Sur in English* website, **www.surinenglish.com**, under 'church'. If you intend to join any of these congregations it is worthwhile making contact before you leave, as the minister and the members of the congregation are likely to have much local knowledge that they will be willing to pass on if asked.

There are regular showings of films in English at Puerto Banús. There are branches of Bookworld in San Pedro and Fuengirola (tel: 952 66 48 37), a card shop at Benavista (Rita's), and a second-hand bookshop in San Pedro de Alcántara (Shakespeare), just off the N-340 between Estepona and Marbella. British food can be purchased at most of the region's supermarkets, including at Iceland, and at more specialist British food shops. There are several branches of the Irish store Dunnes in the region and, further south-west in Gibraltar, branches of Safeway, Marks & Spencer, British Home Stores, Mothercare and The Early Learning Centre. The wide range of Britons and other native English speakers in business on the Costa del Sol includes doctors and lawyers, architects and estate agents.

The English-language press is an invaluable source of information, and includes *Sur in English* (website: **www.surinenglish.com**), *Costa del Sol News*, *Essential Marbella*, *Absolute Marbella*, *Andalucia Golf Magazine* and *The Reporter*. There are several English-language radio stations broadcasting on the Costa del Sol, including Onda Cero International, Coastline Radio and Global Radio.

Resources

The website **www.marbellaguide.com** includes a directory of services on the Costa del Sol, and has ads for jobs and also a cinema listing. The site **www.yellowpages.spain.com** covers the Costa del Sol and Gibraltar. A new directory was launched in 2004, **www.freshdirectory.com**, covering businesses where English is spoken.

There is a vast range of clubs and associations run by and for native English speakers. These include the Royal British Legion (eight branches across the region), the Royal Air Forces Association, the American Club (seven branches across the region), the Rotary Club, the Lions Club, Alcoholics Anonymous, Conservatives Abroad, Democrats Abroad and a Labour Group. There are also associations for line dancing, music, amateur theatre, yoga, barbershop singers, surfing, flower arranging, skiing, gardening and even an Achievers Toastmasters Club meeting in Puerto Banús.

British and other non-Spanish food is widely available. There are many English and Irish pubs, especially in the main centres, such as O'Grady's Irish Tavern in Puerto Banús (a somewhat noisy establishment with its big screen and karaoke evenings) and the American Corner (a 1960s bar), also in Puerto Banús. Gibraltar has several British chain stores and other outlets selling products popular in the United Kingdom.

The United Kingdom, Canada, the Netherlands and Norway have consulates in Málaga, and Ireland and Sweden have consulates in Fuengirola.

Employment

Whilst unemployment is generally high in Andalusia, there are sectors in which employers have difficulty filling vacancies, owing to the lack of candidates with the required qualifications and/or experience. This is true for sheet metal and electrical mechanic work, but also for the tourism and hotel industry, and at times the construction industry.

UK and Ireland travel links

Málaga: Belfast, Birmingham, Bristol, Cardiff, Cork, Coventry, Doncaster/ Sheffield, Dublin, East Midlands (Nottingham), Edinburgh, Exeter, Glasgow, Kent, Leeds/Bradford, Liverpool, London City, London Gatwick, London Heathrow, London Luton, London Stansted, Londonderry (City of Derry Airport), Manchester, Newcastle, Southampton, Teesside

Gibraltar: London Gatwick, London Luton, Manchester

Dutch and Scandinavian air links

Málaga: Billend, Helsinki, Amsterdam, Maastricht, Rotterdam, Bergen, Oslo, Stavanger, Gothenburg and Stockholm

US air link

Málaga: New York

Other travel information

The train journey to Madrid takes well under three hours, thanks to the introduction of a new high-speed train. There is also a car-train service between Barcelona and Málaga (and also between Bilbao and Málaga, and Madrid and Málaga), but note that there are restrictions on the length and height of vehicles that may exclude most people carriers and other larger vehicles. Within the region, public transport is limited. There is a train service from Málaga to Torremolinos, Benalmádena and Fuengirola. A new railway line is soon to be constructed from Málaga to Nerja. There are bus links from the airport to Málaga and Marbella. The A-7 toll motorway, the

Autopista del Sol, which runs along the coast, provides a good alternative to the busy N-340.

There are ferry links from Málaga to Melilla, the Spanish enclave on the Moroccan coast, and the Balearic Islands. There is also a ferry service from Gibraltar to Tangier.

Costa de la Luz

COSTA
DE LA LUZ

The 'coast of light' is the Atlantic section of Spain's southern coast, stretching from the southernmost tip of Andalusia at Punta de Tarifa (about 20 kilometres west of Gibraltar) to the Portuguese border. Here the sea is much colder than along the Mediterranean coastline, the currents and the winds much stronger. Despite its warm, sunny climate, miles of stunning beaches and splendid sand dunes, and relatively low property prices, the Costa de la Luz has been far less popular than most of the other *costas*, and the area is only just beginning to be developed.

The Costa de la Luz is split in half by the Doñana National Park, a huge nature reserve in the marshes at the mouth of the River Guadalquivir, boasting many wild animals including cattle, deer and eagles. Entry into the park is restricted, and to drive from the port of Cádiz towards Huelva and the border with Portugal to the west requires a long detour via Seville to the north. To the west of Doñana there is a substantial development at Matalascañas with hotels, villa complexes and golf courses. Further west, towards the Portuguese border, there are a number of smaller developments interspersed between the few coastal villages. Playa de Mazagón, Playa de la Antilla and Fuenebravia are popular. Inland from Cadiz is Jerez de la Frontera, famous for its sherry and its riding school.

The coast south of Cádiz has a number of resorts, including the increasingly popular Novo Sancti Petri near Chiclana, and the rapidly developing complex of Zahara de los Atunes, between Barbate and Tarifa. In the last 20 years the fishing port of Tarifa has been transformed following its discovery as one of the best windsurfing locations in Europe, if not the best.

Apart from water sports, the region has far fewer amenities than the more popular *costas*. There are a good number of golf courses, however, and a Formula 1 racecourse at Jerez. During the winter the resorts here, in contrast to those on the Costa del Sol, tend to be almost deserted. As one would expect, Algeciras, Cádiz and Jerez all have good shopping centres, but elsewhere the facilities are more limited, especially during the winter months. There is a good selection of shops in Gibraltar. The historic city of Seville, with a population of 700,000, is not far away and is well worth a visit. It has excellent shopping facilities, but suffers from traffic pollution, congestion and noise, and stifling temperatures averaging 35°C during July and August.

Property prices on the Costa de la Luz are much lower than on the Costa del Sol. Prices vary, but you will find three-bedroom villas available from about 250,000 euros, with prices lower inland, especially for properties in need of repair.

English-speaking contacts

There are no British or US schools on the Costa de la Luz, or in Seville, though there is a bilingual international school in Jerez following a Spanish curriculum, and another international school further up the coast in Sotogrande. The larger towns have private schools, most of which offer a Catholic education. There are insufficient numbers of English speakers here to warrant an English-language radio station or newspaper. Similarly, there are no English-language church services, nor many films shown in English.

The United Kingdom, the United States and Australia all have consulates in Seville. Useful information about the region can be found on the website **www.andalucia.com**.

UK and Ireland travel links

There are airports at Jerez and Seville, but for the most parts flights are only internal. Most foreigners arrive via Málaga airport, with some, mainly from British airports, arriving through Gibraltar. Resorts to the west are better accessed via Faro airport in Portugal. The main routes for scheduled flights from the United Kingdom and Ireland are as follows:

Jerez de la Frontera: London Stansted

Málaga: Belfast, Birmingham, Bristol, Cardiff, Cork, Coventry, Doncaster/ Sheffield, Dublin, East Midlands (Nottingham), Edinburgh, Exeter, Glasgow, Kent, Leeds/Bradford, Liverpool, London City, London Gatwick, London Heathrow, London Luton,

London Stansted, Londonderry (City of Derry Airport), Manchester, Newcastle, Shannon, Southampton, Teesside

Gibraltar: London Gatwick, London Luton, Manchester

Faro: Birmingham, Bristol, Cork, Dublin, Leeds/Bradford, East Midlands (Nottingham), Edinburgh, Exeter, Glasgow, Kent, London Gatwick, London Luton, London Stansted, Manchester, Shannon

Seville: London Gatwick

Dutch and Scandinavian air links

Málaga: Billend, Helsinki, Amsterdam, Maastricht, Rotterdam, Bergen, Oslo, Stavanger, Gothenburg, Stockholm

Faro: Groningen, Maastricht, Rotterdam, Oslo, Gothenburg

Seville: Amsterdam

US air link

Málaga: New York

Other travel information

There are ferry routes from Cádiz to the Canary Islands; from Algeciras to Tangier and Ceuta, the Spanish-ruled city in Morocco; and from Gibraltar to Tangier.

The North Atlantic coast

NORTH ATLANTIC COAST

The North Atlantic coast, cut off from central Spain by the Cantabrian Mountains, consists of the four regions of Galicia in the far north-west, Asturias, Cantabria, and the Basque Country on the border with France. The region boasts some of the most stunning beaches in the Iberian Peninsula, but the drawback is that they are much cooler than those on the Mediterranean coast. The climate here is temperate and humid. Winter weather is cold and wet and much more like the winters in the

United Kingdom than on the Costa del Sol. Not surprisingly, despite the region's beauty and its low cost of living, very few foreigners have chosen to reside, or to buy a second home, here. In part because of this, the region is far less developed than the eastern coastline. Another factor is that the links to the United Kingdom and to continental European destinations are relatively poor. This coast is a popular tourist destination for many Spaniards during the summer.

Galicia is remarkably different from the rest of Spain. Separated by mountains from the rest of Spain and from Portugal to the south, the region and its population are of Celtic origin and have much in common with Ireland and Brittany. The coastline is rugged and interspersed with small coves, sandy beaches and many natural harbours, often swept by storms and high winds. The land is green and fertile, and the economy heavily centred on agriculture and fishing. Rain is in good supply. The region has also suffered from economic emigration, with many Galicians seeking work in the United Kingdom. On the other hand, the region has seen large numbers of Portuguese working on the black market, with estimates of their numbers being in excess of 250,000. In many inland areas the primary language is Galego. Apart from this language, which has Latin roots close to those of Portuguese, the region has a rich heritage that is definitely Celtic. The local paper is Galicia Nova (website: **www.galicianova.com**). The region is home to one of Spain's most historic and most beautiful cities, Santiago de Compostela. It is known in particular for its Romanesque cathedral, reputedly the burial place of the Apostle St James, which attracts pilgrims from all parts of the Christian world.

Asturias is more Spanish, certainly in its language, although it too shares a Celtic past. The region is green, its coast forming part of the Costa Verde, and pitted with bays and hidden coves. The economy is in large part agricultural, though the cities of Gijón and Oviedo were home to coal mining and shipbuilding. Asturias is known for its gastronomy, strong cheeses and cider. Inland the terrain is mountainous. The people here are fiercely independent, and for 200 years this was the only Christian region in an Iberian Peninsula under Islamic rule.

Cantabria is also Spanish speaking, green and mountainous. It boasts delightful beaches, and popular tourist resorts in and around Santander, one of Spain's busiest ports and a major link to the rest of the world. The region is famous for its prehistoric sites. Its economy relies heavily on farming.

The *Basque Country* has an identity that sets it apart from the rest of Spain. Its people are strongly independent in nature, and the separatist movement

The interior of Galicia is a beautiful area. The scenery is breathtaking, green hills, valleys, winding rivers through gorges and terraced vineyards. The varied landscape ranges from beautiful beaches, the high mountains in Courel, a ski resort in Manzaneda and the winding canyons of the Miño and Sil valleys. The architecture includes celtics forts, Roman bridges, the walled city of Lugo and baths of Orense, and an important Romanesque heritage which gave name to the "Ribeira Sacra" region. The local architecture is varied too, stone houses, the thatched cottages of O Cebreiro and the traditional "Hórreos" (corn drying houses) which vary widely according to the area.

There are many sport activities. Skiing in Manzaneda, hiking, walking, horse riding or mountain biking along the many nature trails. The numerous rivers in Galicia offer fishing, kayaking or peaceful trips in the catamarans that go along the Sil and Miño canyons.

From spring to autumn there are a huge range of activities ranging from gastronomic fairs, music festivals, religious ceremonies and the main "Fiestas" that every village or town hold in honour of their patron Saint. There is a very interesting mixture of pagan folklore and religious rites that take place all over Galicia.

Also many old traditional customs are maintained with a little modern updating to make life a little easier, such the harvesting of the grapes, the subsequent distilling of the traditional "Aguardiente" a strong spirit made with the debris remaining once the wine has been racked or the "Matanza" (pig killing) which still takes place in most Galician village homes.

A whole compendium of things give Galicia its individual identity, it has it's own official language, folk dancing and traditional music together with strong superstitions and legends.

The Galician people are warm hearted and generous. Galicia is the birth place of many important people, politicians, writers, poets and many people all over the world have Galician ancestors due to the massive emigration of previous generations.

GALICIA PARADISE is a small estate agency located in the village of Ferreira de Pantón. Although a modest company it has been one of the first to offer many services, such as its website, advertisements in international property magazines and complete information in English, Spanish, Gallego or French.

It mainly specialises in old rural stone properties due to the area of its influence. But in order to cover the demands of its clients, both buyers and sellers, it is now in a phase of expansion that with the collaboration of other agencies, will cover a much wider area, including Galician coastal areas.

Apart from acting as the intermediaries between the buyers and sellers, it also undertakes some of the renovation work, either supervising and coordinating the work to be done to help the clients achieve their ideal home or in a merely advisory capacity.

One of the things we like to maintain is an individual attention to our clients and for us it is a matter of pride that many of the people we first met as potential clients have now become our friends and we still have close contact with them.

Many of the rural areas in Galicia are becoming abandoned as a large proportion of the previous generation emigrated either to larger Spanish cities or to other European countries and the one thing the people are welcoming here are new families and maybe new business ideas to give the villages a new lease of life. We believe this can be done without damage to the environment and by becoming a part of the local community.

advertisement feature

receives considerable support from the local population, though many remain opposed to the violent tactics of the ETA terrorists. The area centred on Bilbao, the sixth largest city in Spain, is one of the country's most industrialized. Elsewhere the landscape is green and the economy for the most part agricultural, or heavily forested. Spoken only by a minority, the Basque language (Euskera) is forcefully promoted by the regional authorities. Their efforts are not assisted by the complexities of the language. The people have a reputation for friendliness, and for excellent cuisine, centred around seafood.

Property prices are much, much lower throughout the region bordering the North Atlantic coast than on the Mediterranean coast, save in and around the university city of Santander in Cantabria, and the beautiful Basque city and cultural centre of San Sebastian towards the French border, a Spanish equivalent to Biarritz. A sizeable house near the coast, though not on the beach, should cost under 250,000 euros; and inland, houses needing restoration with some land are available for under 60,000 euros.

Facilities on the northern coast are obviously much less developed than on Spain's Mediterranean coastline. Unless you choose to live in one of the larger cities, a car is essential. There is little in the way of leisure services outside the main towns and cities, save during the summer tourist season. As one might expect, various water sports are popular here, including sailing, windsurfing, scuba diving, fishing along the coast, and canoeing and fishing inland. Also popular inland are horse-riding and mountaineering. On the eastern side of the coast, some of the ski resorts in the Pyrenees are within relatively easy reach. Cantabria, in particular, has a number of golf courses.

The local councils of both Bilbao and Santander have websites with partial English versions – see **www.bilbao.net** and **www.ayto-santander.es**.

English-speaking contacts

There are very few facilities specifically catering for English speakers. There is one English school in Asturias, a US school in Bilbao and an international school (Chester College International) at Santiago de Compostela. British and foreign foods are available in some larger stores, and the few specialist shops. As always, the El Corte Inglés department store is worth taking a look at. You will not find the British pubs and restaurants reminiscent of the Costa del Sol on this coast. The English-speaking population is small, and accordingly there is no local English radio station or newspaper. The United Kingdom has consulates in Bilbao and Pontevedra, the Irish consulate is in Bilbao and the US consulate is in La Coruña.

UK and Ireland travel links

The most established links with the United Kingdom are the ferry services to Plymouth from Santander and from Bilbao to Portsmouth. The former takes about 24 hours, the latter nearly 36. The main airport in the north-east is the international airport at Bilbao. There are also airports in Santander and Asturias but these cater for domestic flights only. The Labacolla airport near Santiago de Compostela has flights to several European capitals, including London. The main routes for scheduled flights to the UK are as follows:

Biarritz: London Stansted

Bilbao: Bristol, London Gatwick, London Heathrow, London Stansted

Santiago de Compostela: London Heathrow

Scandinavian air link

Bilbao: Stockholm

US air link

Santiago de Compostela: New York

Other travel information

There are train links between most of the larger cities and Madrid. The line along the northern coast is slow. The road links to Madrid are reasonably good, and work on a major road along the coast is due to be completed within the next 12 months. There is a car-train link from Bilbao to Málaga.

The Balearic Islands

The Balearic Islands are to be found 200 kilo-metres to the south-east of Barcelona. There are three main islands, Majorca, Minorca and Ibiza, and several smaller islands, including Formentera. Catalan is spoken on all three islands, as well as Spanish, with a strong leaning towards Catalan in the inland and remoter areas.

The islands have long been a preferred holiday destination of North Europeans. Of the foreign property buyers here, the Germans are by far the greatest in number, with the British tending to prefer the mainland coast, especially the Costa del Sol. Nevertheless, the British constitute the second largest contingent of foreigners on the islands, followed by the Scandinavians and the Dutch.

While the islands have much in common, there are significant differences, including even differences in their climate (Minorca, in particular, is subject to high winds), and in the extent to which they have been changed by the influx of tourists and foreign residents. In December 2003 a massive coastal clean-up operation was announced. The programme, due to continue for two years, is to involve 15 boats and 22 smaller vessels and satellite equipment to locate the build-up of rubbish, including plastic bags and bottles, to prevent contamination of bathing areas on the islands.

The website for the Autonomous Community of the Balearic Islands is at **www.caib.es** (for English, click on the small flag in the top right-hand corner).

Majorca

Majorca ('ma-yorca'), or Mallorca, is the largest of the islands. It measures about 95 kilometres at its widest point and has a population approaching 700,000, which has seen an increase of more than 100,000 over the past 20 years. There is a substantial foreign presence here, with an estimated 25,000 British and probably a slightly higher number of German residents. The island, also known as the 'Isle of Dreams', is one of the most popular tourist destinations, welcoming over 3 million British and around 4 million German tourists each year. Not surprisingly, San Juan airport is the busiest in Spain and is set to handle in excess of 20 million passengers a year.

Majorca enjoys hot summers. Winters are mild, especially on the coast. During the autumn and winter, especially, rain can be torrential. The island has a very varied terrain with much of the north-west being dominated by the Sierra de Tramontana, a mountain range that boasts several peaks the height of Ben Nevis or above, the highest being Puig Mayor (1,445 metres). Inland the island is unspoilt, tranquil and rugged. On the coast you will find hidden coves with sandy beaches, and cliff faces where the mountains meet the sea. Much of the more accessible coastline is intensely developed.

Recent years have seen a move away from the unattractive high-rise hotels that were so characteristic of the early years of mass tourism on the island, with the local government imposing stricter regulations aimed at preserving the natural beauty of the island. In the near future at least, the island is unlikely to see anywhere near the scale of construction experienced over the past 40 years or so. Indeed, in some areas there is a current ban on further construction. There is a buoyant property market.

The capital of Majorca, and the main administrative centre for the Balearic Islands, is Palma de Mallorca in the Bay of Palma. It is home to nearly half of the island's inhabitants, and a substantial English-speaking community. The city is the main cultural centre on the island. Here you will find an extensive range of facilities and leisure activities including concerts, recitals, plays and exhibitions. There is an extensive range of shops and chain stores, as well as the department store El Corte Inglés. Elsewhere there is a plentiful supply of supermarkets and smaller shops. There is a university at Palma that has a variety of different courses of interest to foreigners, as well as to the local population.

For the past three years, Palma City Council, in conjunction with the Balearic Disabled Federation, has been assisting businesses finance the cost of adapting their premises to better meet the needs of disabled people. In Palma, 80 premises and 6 streets have undergone alterations. It is hoped to extend the programme throughout the Balearic Islands.

The cost of living on the island is the highest in Spain. Property prices are similarly higher than elsewhere, though they vary considerably. The most expensive area is undoubtedly around Calvia, to the west of Palma, and also the area towards Andratx. Much lower-priced property can be found inland, and on the western side of Palma Bay. If you are interested in restoring a house in an inland village, you may be able to pick something up at around 125,000 euros. A two-bedroom apartment in the Bay of Palma is likely to cost around 160,000 euros. Villas on the island start from in excess of 450,000 euros. If you would feel happy living in a primarily British environment within Spain, consider the various developments in the resorts of Magalluf and Palma Nova, which tend to be British dominated. As to rental accommodation, there is no difficulty in finding property for short-term lettings, though the opposite is true of longer-term rentals. Public transport links between the main towns are good, but inland and to the north you will definitely need a car. The standard of the roads between main centres is also good, but this is not true inland.

The island has a huge variety of sporting and leisure activities. Water sports of all kinds are popular, but especially sailing. Golf is very popular – the island boasts five 18-hole golf courses – and also hiking. The island has all the facilities and amenities that you might expect for such a popular holiday destination, including various theme and water parks, and a vibrant nightlife. Majorca also boasts many annual *fiestas*, in particular that of Saint John in June, and Saint Sebastian in Palma each January.

In summer the island is overflowing with tourists, a factor to bear in mind if you are considering purchasing in one of the more popular tourist areas. A further downside of the island's popularity is that it does attract crime. This is on the increase, primarily petty theft, and drunken hooliganism in and around the island's nightspots during the summer months.

You will find useful information about the island on the website of the Balearic Tourist Office, **www.visitbalearics.net**, and also on **www.mallorca web.com**. For employment vacancies on the island, see **www.balearicjobs.com**. The website for Palma local council has a version in English – see **www.a-palma.es**.

English-speaking contacts

There are four British schools on the island, including the Baleares International School and Queen's College, and one US school. There are also a number of private Catholic Spanish schools, but you should note that your child is likely to receive a bilingual education in Spanish and Catalan, as he or she would in a local state school. There is a plentiful supply of doctors who claim to speak English, and indeed many of them do. In Palma you will find The British Medical and Dental Practice (tel: 971 68 35 11) and The European Dental Practice (tel: 971 68 14 39). There is an Anglican Church in Palma (website: **www.anglican-mallorca.org**), with services also at Cala d'Or, Cala Bona, Puerto Pollensa and Puerto Soller. There are also a good number of English-speaking clubs and associations, including bridge, cricket and theatre groups.

There is a cinema in Palma that has one film in English each week. British and some other foreign foods are stocked by the supermarkets, and also by a number of specialist shops. There are a significant number of British-style pubs and restaurants on the island, and a British supermarket just outside Puerto Portals that sells Iceland frozen foods (Nice Price Supermarket, tel: 971 67 75 63; e-mail: sales@nice-price.net; website: **www.nice-price.net**).

The University of the Balearic Islands is based in Palma, and has an English version of its website. The address is **www.uib.es/en**. There is a daily English-language newspaper, *The Mallorca Daily Bulletin*, and one weekly publication, *The Reader*. The free regular publication *Santa Ponça Scene* is worth casting an eye over. There is a British consulate on the island, as well as several other consulates, including those of Ireland, the United States and Germany.

UK and Ireland travel links
The main routes for scheduled flights are as follows:

Palma: Birmingham, Bristol, Cardiff, Coventry, Doncaster/Sheffield, Dublin, East Midlands, Edinburgh, Glasgow, Kent, Leeds/ Bradford, Liverpool, London Gatwick, London Heathrow, London Luton, London Stansted, Manchester, Newcastle, Teesside

In 2004, Falcon Holidays announced that it was to start package holidays to the island from City of Derry Airport, in Northern Ireland.

Dutch and Scandinavian air links
Palma: Billend, Copenhagen, Helsinki, Amsterdam, Enschede, Groningen, Rotterdam, Oslo, Gothenburg, Stockholm

Other travel information
Links with mainland Spain are good, with flights to Madrid, Barcelona and Valencia. There are ferry links to Barcelona, Alicante and Valencia, and also to Marseilles and Genoa as well as the other Balearic Islands. The ferries to mainland Spain take 8–10 hours, but there is a catamaran to Barcelona that takes 4 hours.

Minorca

The second largest of the Balearic Islands, Minorca (Menorca) is 48 kilometres long and 15 kilometres wide. As is apparent from some of its architecture, the capital, Mahón ('Georgetown'), was under British rule intermittently from 1708 to 1782. It is very different from both Majorca and Ibiza, being much less developed and far more tranquil, even during the summer months. The population of the island, at just over 70,000, is a mere tenth of that of Majorca, with around 3,000–4,000 foreign residents, mostly British and German.

Minorca has well over a hundred different beaches and a very mild climate, though it experiences strong winds from autumn well into spring. The island's resorts are concentrated on the south coast, with little development on the rocky northern coast. Water sports are popular, especially sailing, windsurfing and scuba diving. There is only one golf course on Minorca. Mahón, on the east coast, is a cultural centre with events throughout much of the year, though most of the rest of the island has little happening outside the summer months. If you want to party into the small hours, this is not the island for you, and you should try Majorca or Ibiza.

Property prices are cheaper here than on the other Balearic Islands, save in Mahón. Modest villas towards the coast start from about 225,000 euros, and apartments from about 100,000 euros, with prices being lower on the west of the island. If you intend to purchase land on which to build, ensure that planning permission has already been obtained. Here, as on the other islands, the authorities have tightened building regulations and reduced the number of licences being granted. Considerable importance is now given to conserving the island's natural resources.

You will find useful information about the island on the website of the Balearic Tourist Office, **www.visitbalearics.net**, and also at **www. menorcaweb.com**. See also **www.balearics.com**. For employment vacancies on the island, see **www.balearic-jobs.com**.

English-speaking contacts
British and other foreign food items are available from the larger supermarkets and some specialist shops. There is an English lending library in Mahón. There are no British or international schools on the island. There is no British consulate on the island. There is an Anglican church at Es Castell. There is one monthly English-language magazine, *Roquetta*, and a variety of clubs and associations, including a cricket club.

UK travel links
There is a small international airport just south of Mahón, operating scheduled flights to London Gatwick, London Luton and Birmingham.

Other travel information
There are charter flights from several European airports during the summer months. There are flights daily to the mainland and ferry links to Barcelona and Valencia, as well as to Majorca.

Ibiza

Ibiza (Eivissa) is much closer to the mainland than Majorca or Minorca (Valencia is only three hours away by ferry) and is about one-sixth the size of Majorca. It is characterized by stunning beaches, sheer cliff faces and tiny hidden coves. The island is home to nearly 95,000 inhabitants, with the foreign contingent (comprising mainly Germans, and to a lesser extent Britons), estimated at over 15 per cent of the total population. A large number of Spaniards have also moved here. The population of the island has almost doubled in the past 25 years, and fewer than half the island's inhabitants were born on Ibiza.

Ibiza is perhaps *the* most popular holiday destination for young Britons and Germans intent on partying through the night. The raucous behaviour of many of these visitors has been accompanied by drunken violence and by crime. The noisy nightlife is concentrated around the island's capital, Ibiza Town, and San Antonio, and to some extent Santa Eulàlia. Most of the island is peaceful, however, and to a large extent undeveloped, its beauty unspoilt by the tourist-led construction boom of the 1960s.

Average temperatures here are slightly higher than on the other islands: 12°C in winter and 25°C in summer. There is a serious shortage of water on the island. As on the other Balearic Islands, conditions and facilities for water sports are excellent. There is only one golf course. The cultural life of the island is concentrated in Ibiza Town and Santa Eulàlia. The island has two water parks. There is a medical centre in San Antonio.

For the most part, property is more expensive here than on the other islands, with few villas available under 550,000 euros (800,000 euros on the coast). Apartments start at about 180,000 euros.

You will find useful information about the island on the website of the Balearic Tourist Office, **www.visitbalearics.net**, and also at **www.eivissa web.com**. For employment vacancies on the island, see **www.balearic-jobs.com**. There is also an active branch of Friends of the Earth (see its website, in English, at **www.amics-terra.org**).

English-speaking contacts

British and other foreign food items are available from supermarkets and some specialist shops. There is one British school, the Morna International College in Sant Carles. *The Ibiza Sun* is a free weekly publication in English. Its website (**www.theibizasun.net**) includes a list of useful telephone numbers. There are a variety of clubs and associations, including sports and theatre groups. There is an Anglican church at San Antonio, and services also at Santa Eulàlia. The local English-language newspaper is *Ibiza Now* (e-mail: ibizanow@ctv.es).

UK and Irish travel links

There is a small international airport with scheduled flights from Birmingham, Coventry, East Midlands (Nottingham), Kent, Leeds/Bradford, London Gatwick, Manchester and Shannon. There are also many charter flights to a number of UK destinations.

Dutch and Scandinavian air links

There are flights from Amsterdam and Stockholm.

Other travel information

There are many flights during summer months to Germany. At other times you are likely to have to fly via one of the mainland airports. There are ferry services to Barcelona, Valencia and Denia as well as as to Majorca and the small neighbouring island of Formentera.

Formentera

Formentera is the smallest of the inhabited islands of the Balearics, and can only be reached by ferry from Ibiza. The island is almost completely undeveloped. You will find information about the island on the website of the Balearic Tourist Office, **www.visitbalearics.net**, and also at **www. formenteraweb.com**.

The Canary Islands

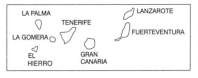

Situated about 100 kilometres off the coast of West Africa (parallel to the southernmost point of Morocco), and colonized by Spain in the 15th century, the Canary Islands are well over 1,000 kilometres from Spain. There are seven islands altogether: the main islands of Lanzarote, Fuerteventura, Gran Canaria and Tenerife, and the three smaller islands of La Palma, La Gomera and El Hierro. Together they enjoy a subtropical climate of all-year sunshine that has made them highly popular tourist destinations for North Europeans ever since the Victorian era. These volcanic islands have an amazing juxtaposition of landscapes, ranging from Spain's highest mountain, Pico del Teide (3,700 metres), on Tenerife, to deserts, jungle terrain and stunning beaches.

Administratively the islands are divided into two provinces: the Province of Las Palmas, consisting of Gran Canaria, Lanzarote and Fuerteventura, and the Province of Santa Cruz de Tenerife, consisting of the islands of Tenerife, La Palma, La Gomera and El Hierro. The website for the Canary Islands' Autonomous Government is **www.gobcan.es**; it has links to local councils.

Property prices here are substantially cheaper than in the Balearic Islands, but more expensive than on mainland Spain. The climate is hotter throughout the year, but there is relief from the high summer temperatures (27°C is not uncommon) thanks to refreshing ocean breezes. A less welcome climatic feature is the occasional sandstorm from the Sahara that can last for several days, causing respiratory problems.

Though part of Spain, and hence of the European Union, the Canaries are not covered by the same taxation and customs regulations. Accordingly, many products, including cars and electrical goods, are much cheaper here than elsewhere in Spain. Overall the cost of living is similar to that in other popular Spanish resorts. Tourism is the main industry on the islands, though there is a significant fishing industry. Vineyards and banana plantations also play an important part in the local economy. There are few job opportunities outside of tourism, and for those wishing to work in that sector an ability to get by in German and Spanish is a definite advantage, perhaps even essential. There is a shortage of water on the islands, which explains the presence of various desalination plants. The islands' population of 1.7 million is concentrated mostly on Gran Canaria and Tenerife. Useful information about the islands can be found on the website for News Canarias at **www.ic-web.com**. The flight time from the UK is about four hours.

Tenerife

The largest island is Tenerife, with a population of around 700,000. It is the most popular of the Canary Islands for Britons buying property. Estimates of the number of foreign residents vary from 10 to 15 per cent of the total population, with the British and Germans being the most numerous. The capital and main cultural centre is Santa Cruz de Tenerife in the north of the island, visited by tens of thousands of cruise-ship passengers each year. The city is known for its extravagant carnival (the largest in Spain), which takes place each February.

The holiday resorts are concentrated along the west coast, which is considered to have the best climate. The most popular resorts are the noisy and bustling Playa de las Américas, Los Cristianos, Puerto de la Cruz and also the calmer resort of Los Gigantes. The beaches are all composed of grey volcanic sand, save for a recent development at Santa Cruz where golden sand was imported from the Sahara. The island boasts all the sports and leisure facilities that one would expect from a top tourist destination, with an emphasis on water sports. It has some of the best marinas in the world. Golf is also very popular, with six golf courses, two of them (Amarilla Golf and Golf de Sur) being championship courses. There is an extensive range of cultural events and activities throughout most of the year, including theatre and musical concerts, primarily in the capital, Santa Cruz. The shopping facilities are excellent and include several large supermarkets, a large El Corte Inglés store in Santa Cruz and even a branch of IKEA.

Geographically the island is split in two by its mountain range. The south is dry and arid. In complete contrast, the north is green with vegetation, including banana plantations, forests and beautiful flora. In the middle of the island the volcano Pico del Teide is said to be dormant, the last eruption being nearly a century ago.

Property prices have risen considerably over the past decade. For two-bedroom apartments, and inland rural properties, prices start at a little over 100,000 euros, and for a three-bedroom villa prices start at about 225,000 euros. There are significant price variations, however. The local authorities are now restricting further development on the island. If you do decide to buy land on which to build, you should ensure that it has planning permission and that you are happy with any conditions placed on any proposed building.

English-speaking contacts

English-language films can be seen at the cinema complex in Los Cristianos, but only during the summer. British and other foreign foods are available in most supermarkets and indeed other shops, but they can be expensive. Pubs and restaurants offering British-style food are in plentiful supply. There are English-language church services for various denominations, including Anglican churches in La Palma, Los Cristianos, Los Gigantes, Puerto Santiago, Playa de las Américas and Puerto de la Cruz. There are three British schools on the island and one private Spanish school. There are four English radio stations to tune into: Power FM, Radio Oasis, Gold FM and Waves FM, and several English-language publications. These include *Island Connections*, *Island Sun*, *The Paper* and *Tenerife News* (which has a useful website at **www.tennews.com** with a number of links). There are also a substantial number of British-run businesses operating on the island, including Mary's bookshop in Puerto de la Cruz and the Book Swap in Las Américas.

UK travel links

There are scheduled flights to the main airport of Reina Sofia in the south of the island (near the Costa del Silencio!) from Birmingham, Dublin,

Edinburgh, Glasgow, London Gatwick, London Luton and Manchester. There are also a large number of charter flights to the United Kingdom.

Dutch and Scandinavian air links
There are flights from Billend, Copenhagen, Helsinki and Maastricht.

Other travel information
There is a second airport at Los Rodeos. This is primarily for inter-island flights and flights to the mainland. There are extensive ferry services connecting Tenerife to the other Canary Islands. Los Cristianos is Spain's busiest port, registering over 1.3 million users a year. On the whole, the network of main roads connecting the larger towns and resorts on the island is good, as are the bus services between the larger population centres.

Gran Canaria

Gran Canaria is the third largest of the islands, but the second most populated, with about 750,000 inhabitants, about half living in Las Palmas de Gran Canaria, the administrative capital of the Canary Islands. The island welcomes even more tourists than Tenerife, with the busiest resorts being on the southern coast, which boasts several long beaches and amazing sand dunes, in particular at Maspalomas. There are a number of more peaceful resorts to the west of the island, where the coastline, like that in the north, is rugged. The centre of Gran Canaria is dominated by mountains and deep valleys with plantations of bananas, sugar cane and mango.

Substantial numbers of North Europeans have settled on the island and there is a significant British community living here, numbering about 11,000–12,000.

The island boasts a huge range of sports and leisure activities, including several theme and water parks. As with other island destinations, the emphasis is on water sports, especially sailing, and several regattas take place each year. There are various marinas, and deep-sea fishing and scuba diving are popular. In addition, there are five golf courses. There is a busy cultural calendar of events in Las Palmas, embracing musical concerts, opera and theatre. The capital, like the island's southern resorts, has a busy nightlife throughout much of the year. There are excellent shopping facilities, including an El Corte Inglés department store.

In recent years the rate of increase of property prices on Gran Canaria has slowed. Prices are still high, however. Two-bedroom apartments start from about 120,000 euros and villas from about 300,000 euros. The more expensive areas are at Maspalomas, Playa del Inglés and San Augustín. If you intend to buy land as a building plot, check that planning permission has already been granted, and that you are happy with any conditions attached to the grant.

English-speaking contacts

There are several British schools and one US school on the island (The British School of Gran Canaria, The American School of Gran Canaria, The Canterbury School, Oakley College and Kent College). In addition to several public hospitals there is a British hospital and several private clinics. English-language publications include *Island Connections* (website: **www.ic-news.com**), *Island Sun*, *The Paper* and *Tenerife News*. English-language radio stations include Holiday FM Radio (13.3 and 106.8 FM). At the time of writing, there were no showings of English films, although there were plans to introduce these. British and foreign foods are stocked in most of the larger supermarkets, although prices can be high. There is an Iceland store on the island. A substantial number of pubs, bars and restaurants on the island, many of them owned by expatriates, offer British fare. There are several other types of British-run businesses. There is an Anglican church in Las Palmas, and services at Playa des Ingles and an Evangelical English church. There is a British Club in Las Palmas with a mixed-nationality membership. The facilities include a library and a snooker room (for details, tel: 928 24 54 51). The British consulate is in Las Palmas, along with consulates for Ireland, the United States, South Africa and Germany.

UK travel links

There are scheduled flights from London Gatwick, London Luton and Birmingham. There are charter flights from the United Kingdom throughout much of the year. The airport is on the east coast at Gando, and several million visitors a year pass through it.

Dutch and Scandinavian air links

There are flights from Billend, Copenhagen, Helsinki, Amsterdam, Eindhoven, Maastricht, Oslo and Stockholm.

Other travel information

There are regular flights to mainland Spain, and ferry services to the other islands and to Spain.

Lanzarote

Lanzarote, the fourth largest island, is the hottest and most arid. It is the least developed of the larger Canary Islands. Arrecife, the capital, is not particularly attractive. The main tourist centres are at Puerto del Carmen, south of the capital, and Playa Blanca, which is further south still, at the southern-most tip. The island is famous for its mountainous volcanic landscape, and numerous extinct volcanoes in the Timanfaya National Park, as well as its white and grey sandy beaches.

Building has been restricted in the past, and this is likely to remain the case as the authorities strive to avoid the overcrowding and the unattractive constructions that are to be seen in parts of Gran Canaria and Tenerife. One-bedroom apartments start at about 80,000 euros and villas from about 340,000 euros.

The population of the island is only about 65,000, with substantial British (about 4,000–5,000) and German contingents.

The island has fewer sports and leisure opportunities than Gran Canaria or Tenerife, but offers an ample selection of water sports, including wind surfing, scuba diving and deep-sea fishing. A major sports complex is due to open within the next few years. The island has a selection of shopping centres.

English-speaking contacts

There are two British schools on the island (The British School of Lanzarote and the Colegio Hispano Británico) and several private catholic Spanish schools. There is a private hospital aimed primarily at the foreign residents, and two public hospitals. There are Anglican services in Arrecife, at Costa Teguise, Playa Blanca, Golf del Sur and Puerto del Carmen, and also Baptist and Evangelical services on the island. English-language publications include *Island Connections* (website: **www.ic-news.com**), *Island Sun*, *The Paper* and *Lancelot* (website: **www.lancelot.es**). English-language radio stations include Power FM 91.5 and 91.7 FM.

UK and Ireland travel links

There are scheduled services from Dublin and London Luton. There are many charter flights to and from the UK. Falcon Holidays is set to start package holidays to the island in 2004 from Derry City Airport in Northern Ireland.

Dutch and Scandinavian air links
There are flights from Billend, Copenhagen, Helsinki and Amsterdam.

Other travel information
There are ferry services to the other islands.

Fuerteventura

Fuerteventura is the second largest island, but one of the least populated, with about 55,000 inhabitants, including significant British and German communities. The island boasts long, white sandy beaches. It is very arid, with little rainfall or vegetation, a substantial part of the island constituting desert. It is undeveloped, peaceful and unspoilt. The main resorts are on the eastern side of the island, to the south of the capital, Puerto del Rosario, and on the Jandía peninsula at the southern tip of the island.

The island has limited amenities compared to Gran Canaria and Tenerife, but an extensive selection of water sports including surfing, windsurfing, sailing, scuba diving and deep-sea fishing. There is one golf course. Public transport is cheap and reliable. Remember that goats have priority on the roads (there are several tens of thousands of them) and that there is a policy of zero tolerance for those who drink and drive.

Property prices on Fuerteventura are lower than elsewhere in the Canaries, but are increasing at a faster rate. Two-bedroom apartments start from about 135,000 euros and villas from about 240,000.

English-speaking contacts
British food items are available in the resort supermarkets, though they tend to be quite expensive. There is no international or private schooling on Fuerteventura, nor are there any public or private hospitals. English-language publications include *Island Connections*, *Island Sun* and *The Paper*. You may find it helpful to consult the website **www.fuerteventuragrape vine.net**.

UK travel links
There are regular charter flights to the UK throughout the summer.

Other travel information
There is a regular ferry service to Gran Canaria.

La Palma, La Gomera and El Hierro

La Palma, La Gomera and El Hierro are the three smallest islands. La Palma has the largest population at about 80,000, with La Gomera and El Hierro having 18,000 and 6,000 inhabitants respectively. There are significant numbers of foreigners living on all three islands, in particular Germans, but relatively few Britons. All three islands have largely avoided mass tourism, with La Gomera and El Hierro being particularly unspoilt.

La Palma is characterized by lush vegetation, thick woodlands, a vast volcanic crater, a mountain range reaching to a height of nearly 2,500 metres (almost twice the height of Ben Nevis) and an active volcano that last erupted 30 years ago. Its capital, Santa Cruz de la Palma, was a port of major importance in the Spanish Empire. The town still has a colonial ambience. La Gomera also has its mountain range, with its highest peaks reaching almost 1,500 metres. It too boasts lush vegetation, including rainforests. El Hierro has the smallest population of the inhabited islands. It is seldom visited by tourists, and agriculture is its main economic activity.

There are relatively few amenities on any of these three islands, with none of them yet possessing a golf course. Trekking, pot-holing and scuba diving are popular on La Palma. Sailing and scuba diving are popular on La Gomera and El Hierro. All three islands have a selection of super-markets, especially La Palma and La Gomera. A limited range of British food items is available on the islands. There are no international or private schools on any of the islands. All three have hospitals, although the cover available at El Hierro, in particular, is limited. In La Palma there is an English-language version of the monthly magazine *Informagazin*.

The cost of housing has risen in recent years on all three islands. The cheapest prices are on La Gomera and El Hierro, where two-bedroom apartments are available from about 90,000 euros. On La Palma prices are still lower than on the four larger Canary Islands.

UK travel links
There are no direct flights from the UK, and for all three islands you will need to fly first to Tenerife or Gran Canaria, save that for La Palma there are flights via Madrid.

Other travel information

La Palma has a tiny airport suitable for small aircraft only. There are daily flights to Tenerife and Gran Canaria, and flights to Madrid, Amsterdam and some German locations. From La Gomera and El Hierro there are flights only to Tenerife and Gran Canaria. There are a number of ferry services linking these islands to Tenerife and Gran Canaria.

Madrid

The Spanish capital is situated almost in the centre of the country, on a high plateau 600 metres above sea level. With a population of 3 million, Madrid is by far the largest city in Spain, the centre of a huge manufacturing area and the wealthiest region in Spain. It is a major cultural centre with an abundance of museums, theatres, majestic buildings, busy nightlife and leisure facilities, and a smooth-running and inexpensive transport system. The city is constantly busy from early morning until the small hours. Despite its excellent public transport network, it suffers from traffic congestion, impossible parking conditions, pollution and noise. As in any large city, petty crime, especially theft, is commonplace, with tourists often the targets. The climate in Madrid can be summed up in one word: fierce. The city has a continental climate, with summers being stiflingly hot and the winters bitterly cold.

The cost of living in Madrid is much lower than in other European capitals. Property prices, though higher here than in many other areas of Spain, are also significantly lower than in London or Paris, with two-bedroom apartments starting at about 220,000 euros. The city has a large population of foreign residents, mainly from Africa and South America, but also several thousand English speakers, mostly British or American, and a significant French population. The latter nationalities tend to favour living in the centre of the city, to the north, or the new towns that have been constructed on the outskirts. For the most part they avoid the suburbs to the south.

On the outskirts of Madrid the leisure opportunities include golf on one of the many excellent courses, and skiing in the mountains close by. Sites worth visiting include the science museum and planetarium and the city's zoo, not to mention the Madrid amusement park, several water parks and Warner Brothers' Movieworld, a recently opened theme park to the south of the capital. Madrid has three museums of world renown in which are displayed many art masterpieces: the Museo del Prado, the Museo

Unusual and Distinctive Properties
CAVE HOUSES

Spanish Inland Properties specialises in the renovation and sale of cave houses in the spectacularly beautiful area of northern Andalusia. Our properties are sympathetically restored from ancient cave dwellings with all modern conveniences and mains services. Cave houses offer an affordable and fun alternative to conventional houses and flats. With one to five plus bedrooms, prices start at around 50,000 euros.

Why not pay us a visit and experience the "oldest and newest" trend to hit the Spanish property market?

To find out more visit:
www.spanish-inland-properties.com
and download your **FREE** copy
of the "Cave Owners Manual".

www.spanish-inland-properties.com

email:
info@spanish-inland-properties.com
Tel: 0034 958739032

THE CAVE HOUSES OF SPAIN

So just what is a cave house?

Cave homes have been around since mankind first appeared. To most of us, life in a cave conjures up an image of a dark, damp, cold hole in the ground with families huddled around smoky fires in fear of the beasts roaming the woods outside.

Since ancient times the people of Andalusia, in Southern Spain, have a long unbroken tradition of cave living, which continues to this day. However, contrary to popular belief, modern cave homes come with all the comforts and facilities of a conventional house and have evolved into unique homes sought after by Spanish and foreigners alike.

Nowadays cave homes are usually a combination of a number of cave rooms with a conventional building to the front. They have all the comforts, facilities and services that you would expect to find in a "normal" house and range from one bedroom holiday homes up to huge fifteen room cave houses large enough for the biggest family or even b&b.

Cave houses are not found all over Spain. They occur only in areas where the rock structure and climate are suitable. The rock in which the cave is dug must be soft to allow excavation with hand tools but the overlying rock has to be strong and impermeable, remaining safe and stable over many years. The area must also be hilly so the cave homes can be built into the hillside. Furthermore there must be low rainfall keeping the cave home dry all year round.

The advantages.

Cave homes tend to be found in areas of Spain that are traditionally Spanish, unlike many areas of the "Costas", which are heavily Anglicised. So, when considering a cave home you must also take its location and the culture of the area into account.

Cave homes, compared to conventional houses of the same size and condition, are significantly cheaper. Savings of 25% or more are easily achievable on a similar conventional house in the same area. Further savings are possible, compared to the coast, because the inland areas in which cave houses are mostly found are relatively undeveloped.

Each cave house is unique in design. Modern cave houses have been developed from homes hand dug a hundred or more years ago. In those days, there were no plans or regulations and so each home was developed according to the needs of the family and the rock surrounding it. So, if you are looking for something uniquely different, a cave home could be the answer.

Warm in winter, cool in summer. Cave rooms built into the natural rock, are significantly less subject to external temperature changes than conventional buildings. The area of northern Andalusia, where many cave homes are found, has an extreme climate. Long hot summers and cold winter nights with temperatures varying from the +40°C of a mid-summer afternoon to the -15°C of the coldest winter night. Cave houses need heating in winter but you certainly will not need air conditioning in the summer, when they are refreshingly cool. As a result there is a worthwhile saving in energy costs.

Cave houses have traditionally been the homes of artisan workers and the modernised cave homes follow this heritage of rustic charm. They have many internal features found in traditional English country cottages; beamed ceilings, irregularly shaped rooms and tiled floors. Externally, with their whitewashed and stone facades, wood beam lintels, shuttered windows and crenellated roof tiles they have an appearance similar to the white village houses so typical of southern Spain.

Ecologically friendly. What could be more ecological than a cave room built into the natural rock? Wherever possible

Thyssen-Bornemisza and the Museo Nacional Centro de Arte Reina Sofía. You can purchase a *Madrid Card*, a pass for 1–3 days costing from under 30 euros to 55 euros. This gives free entry to museums and also serves as a travel pass on public transport, and entitles the holder to discounts in some shops.

As one would expect, shopping facilities in Madrid are first-class, though the selection of British food products is very limited. As always, El Corte Inglés is worth a visit. The emergency number for the fire service in Madrid is 91 588 91 74.

English-speaking contacts

There are two publications serving the English-speaking population: *The Broadsheet* (website: **www.tbs.com.es**) and the primarily US publication *Guidepost* (e-mail: aso.gpost@teleline.es), both free monthly magazines distributed at key points around the city. There are many British and other native English speakers running a host of different types of businesses in the city. These include a small number of doctors and dentists who have set up in practice here. The two public hospitals with the best reputations are Hospital de la Paz and the Hospital Doce de Octubre.

There are several international schools in Madrid, including British schools and one US school, and of course many private Spanish schools, mostly offering a Catholic education. The city's universities include the Schiller International University, which offers a number of business-related degree programmes (website: **www.schillermadrid.edu/**). There are a number of cinemas that show films in English, as well as several bookshops selling English-language books. The city has an Anglican church (St George's), as well as Baptist, Methodist and Presbyterian churches and the international interdenominational Community Church of Madrid. There are also Catholic services in English.

The capital has an extensive array of clubs and associations established by English-speaking expatriates, embracing sports, social groups, theatre, politics, a Canadian association, a South African association, a Scottish country dancing group, a cricket club, a British football team that plays in a local Spanish league, and a Lions Rugby Club. There is even a charity shop run by the British Ladies Association. Friendly watering holes include Finnegan's pub, Café Madrid (metro Opera), and Planet Hollywood in Plaza de las Cortes. There is also a British Benevolent Fund that may be able to assist Britons in times of trouble. For details, contact the British Consulate-General in Madrid

Madrid resources

- **ww.munimadrid.es** – website of Madrid City Hall (some English);
- **www.incmadrid.com**;
- **www.madridman.com** (in English);
- **www.madridconnect.com** (in English; includes bars/restaurants/accommodation);
- **www.madridteacher.com** (in English; jobs/information for teachers of English).

UK and Ireland travel links

There are direct flights to Birmingham, Bristol, Dublin, Edinburgh, Kent, Liverpool, London Gatwick, London Heathrow and London Luton.

Dutch and Scandinavian air links

There are flights to Amsterdam, Helsinki, Oslo, Gothenburg and Stockholm.

US air links

There are flights to Atlanta, Chicago, Miami and New York.

Other travel information

As one would expect, there are direct flights to many international destinations as well as the main provincial airports. The efficient public transport system includes an underground rail network. You can buy books of 10 tickets (with a saving of nearly 50 per cent). Season tickets and discounted passes for young people and retired people are also available.

Barcelona

Information about Barcelona is contained in the section on the Costa Brava.

Welcome to CJSpanishHomes

We are a family-run estate agent, located in the heart of Benidorm. We pride ourselves on having a "no nonsense, no pressure" approach to selling property and offer the personal touch before, during and after your property purchase.

Our extensive portfolio of properties can be browsed using our website, however, should you not be able to find what you are looking for, please let us know and we will be happy to try and match your needs.

As well as working closely with reputable builders to offer you the best in new builds, we also offer a large selection of "resale" properties, both inland and on the coast, for those of you that can't wait to enjoy the Spanish life.

We will look after you

Whether it is on a trip to view houses, or in your exploration of the area - which might lead you to change your mind about where you want to be - we are there to help you find your dream property. ...And when your deal is finalised; we will accompany you to the public notary to ensure everything goes smoothly for you... And afterwards; When your purchase is complete and it's time to begin dealing with Spanish "burocracia" - getting your electricity, water, telephone, satellite or internet connections; finding furniture, cleaners, and much more. We are here to help and offer a full after-sales service to ensure that you settle in with the minimum effort. We will handle all of this personally, and we hope to turn all our clients into friends for the future.

Regional Information

More and more people are finding their home or second home on the southern Spanish costas - not only due to property prices being lower than in the UK, but more to the relaxed and healthy lifestyle in the warmer Spanish climate.

With an average of 320 days of sunshine per year, the beautiful Costa Blanca is one of the preferred areas within Spain.

The Costa Blanca is an area of variation. The scenery ranges from flat salt plains and open curving beaches, to the rugged heights of the Sierra de Bernia and Jalon Valley. Whether you are looking for a beachfront property in a lively tourist area or a quiet "casa de campo" hidden amongst swathes of orchard, you are sure to find your dream home here.

As the area is, in the main, agricultural, there are vast areas of orange, lemon, nispero, avocado, almond and olive trees - not to mention the vineyards - that lend the area a peaceful, beautiful outlook that is a far cry from the industrialised towns with which you may be more familiar.

There is an abundance of fresh fish here too - Alicante and Calpe ports being of prime importance to the fishing industry - and the combination of fresh fish, outstanding fruit and vegetables, olive oil and local wine (at ridiculously low prices) means that the diet here is truly healthy. Particularly if you indulge in the local cuisine: grilled sardines and tomato salads. You will probably not only notice how good everything tastes but your body will thank you for the difference!

It's hard not to take part in an active lifestyle too. The coastline offers many spectacular snorkeling and diving locations, alongside all other water sports such as sailing, windsurfing, fishing, water-skiing and kite surfing. There are many well-marked paths for walking, whether along coastal paths, such as that from Villajoyosa to La Cala de Finestrat, or more mountainous pathways along the Sierra de Bernia and Sierra de Aitana. The view from the top of the Sierra de Bernia is awesome, you can almost see right into the cafes and bars of Ibiza!

The area is also of cultural and historical importance too with many ruins, forts and museums to visit. The architectural blend of Moorish, Roman and Spanish building styles can be truly heart stopping.

For the golf enthusiast there is no shortage of excellent courses to choose from and we are delighted to offer opportunities to buy front-line golf apartments and villas - both new builds and resale's - at some of the most prestigious courses in the area.

So whether you are looking for a holiday retreat, a second home for the winter months or are joining the thousands of Britons leaving the UK to start a happier, healthier life abroad the Costa Blanca has a place in the sun waiting for you!

2 Finding accommodation

Renting a home in Spain

If your stay in Spain is, or may be, only short term, you will clearly wish to rent, at least initially. Indeed, even if you are determined to settle permanently in Spain, renting is a sensible course of action when you first arrive. Purchasing a property in Spain is a serious business. Whilst property prices are generally lower than in the United Kingdom (notable exceptions being in parts of the Costa del Sol), acquisition costs are higher. Similarly, costs when you come to sell are appreciably greater. Choosing the wrong property or the wrong location will be an expensive mistake. Once you have purchased, you may not be able to sell and purchase elsewhere for some considerable time. Accordingly, you should give serious consideration to renting a property before you buy. Even if you know well the area in which you intend to purchase, living somewhere is naturally very different from the occasional holiday, particularly if your holidays have all been during the summer months. Renting, whether of a furnished or an unfurnished property, will give you the time to look around, consider your options and decide whether the area does indeed fit your requirements.

In Spain generally there is a reasonably good supply of property to rent, though in the most popular areas such as the Costa del Sol there is a shortage. Many property owners will only let out their properties for the summer season at very high rentals.

In deciding whether to rent or buy, you will need to consider:

- Your ability to meet the initial purchase costs and the monthly mortgage repayments.
- The size of the property you require. You will probably be able to afford to rent a larger property than you will be able to buy. Further, if your children are nearing adulthood, you may wish to rent a family home now with a view to buying smaller accommodation for your future needs.

▮ The rental market – in some areas, the property available to rent is extremely limited, whereas there is more choice of properties to purchase.

▮ Your job. How secure is it? What are the costs of insurance to cover redundancy, etc? Is your employer likely to ask you to relocate? Will he or she pay relocation costs?

▮ Your age. If you are older than 45, you may not be able to pay off your mortgage before retirement.

▮ Trends in the local property market: a flat on the Costa del Sol is likely to appreciate at a greater rate than a house in the remoter parts of Spain, for example.

▮ How much time you have available to carry out your research. The purchase of a property inevitably calls for more expenditure of time than does choosing a property to rent.

▮ Whether you wish to tie up the capital required for the purchase of your property.

▮ Any implications for your tax position.

▮ Your intentions for the passing on of the property on your death.

I would strongly recommend that anyone moving to Spain should rent initially, if only for a period of a year or so. Renting enables you to familiarize yourself with the locality and the various amenities (or lack of them). It allows you the opportunity to get to know an area and some of the local population. Far better to read in the local paper about protests against a planned new road or other major development whilst you are renting, than after you have sunk your hard-earned savings into what turns out to be a living nightmare. It also permits you to search around for an attractively priced property and to take advantage of any bargain that may come on to the market.

One disadvantage, however, especially in an area like the Costa del Sol, is that prices are constantly rising. If you rent for too long, you may jeopardize your purchasing power.

On the other hand, the property market in the United Kingdom is such that in some cases it may be more advantageous to keep your UK property and rent it out, and rent rather than buy in Spain.

I would also recommend that you do not enter into a rental agreement before arriving at your destination in Spain. Instead, book two weeks or so in short-term or holiday accommodation. If you are intending to rent for only a year or less, do give consideration to a furnished letting.

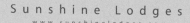

Sunshine Lodges
www.sunshinelodges.com

TRANSPORTABLE LOG CABINS

Round-Log Lodges for Year Round use

Picture in your mind a genuine 'Log Cabin'. The chances are it will be made of round logs. Our lodges create the real 'Cabin feel' and ensure a timeless, rustic look both inside and out.

We can provide you with a beautiful log cabin for a whole variety of uses. From living accommodation, and holiday lets, home offices or studios, our lodges provide a beautiful, natural environment. Our lodges also offer a wide range of standard designs, but we are also able to undertake bespoke design.

Round-log cabins require relatively little maintenance and

will weather far better than some of the less solid designs on the market.

The designs combine the beauty, warmth and character of a log cabin, with the durability and strength of round-log construction. The lodges are built using 8 inch solid, round logs ensuring excellent insulation values. Staying warm in winter and keeping cool in summer, suitable for all year round use.

For further details or for a brochure please contact us at the address or telephone number below

Sunshine Lodges Ltd.
Farmhouse, Braiseworth,
ye, Suffolk IP23 7DS

Tel/Fax: +44(0)1379 871383
email: sales@sunshinelodges.com

www.sunshinelodges.com

TRANSPORTABLE CABINS

To our knowledge **SUNSHINE LODGES** is the sole distributor of transportable round-log lodges to Spain. We have taken the character, strength and superior insulation values of real round-log cabins and transferred them to the mobile home market.

Conforming to the legal definition of a mobile home, our transportable lodges are built to BS3632, the British Standard for Residential Park Homes. This makes them perfect for permanent accommodation, holiday parks, office accommodation, annexes and private holiday lets. Our Transportable lodges can also be relocated without detriment to the building.

SUNSHINE LODGES CABIN CONSTRUCTION

SUNSHINE LODGES use the Swedish cope method of construction. This means the seal recess made in the underside of each log enables it to mate exactly with the one below, leaving an attractive round-log wall. This method of construction also means that each log fits perfectly on top of the one below, ensuring that when the natural settlement of the logs occurs over time the joints are sealed tight. To ensure maximum insulation, insulating material is also used in between each layer of log.

Whatever your requirements **SUNSHINE LODGES** can offer you the highest quality round-log lodges. As a small dynamic company we have the ability to offer you a personal service combined with our manufacturers' (www.windmilllodges.co.uk) years of experience.

The two module lodges are delivered to site in two 10ft wide sections and then bolted together to form a perfect log cabin. Our transportable lodges can be supplied fully fitted out with electrical wiring, plumbing, kitchen and bathroom fittings. These fittings are optional and can also be changed to meet your requirements. We can also supply the lodges fully furnished.

SUNSHINE LODGES offer a range of designs in the transportable twin unit, from a single bedroom lodge to a spacious three bedroom design. Any of these layouts can be altered to cater for individual specifications.

CABIN FEVER......CABIN VIVA!

Quickly becoming one of the Costas fastest growing trends and alternative forms of living for the sun seeker and jetsetter in Spain! Wooden lodges are rapidly becoming the most affordable way to break into the Spanish property market, offering the modern family an opportunity to have their second home abroad within the prime locations and more exclusive areas of Spain. This opportunity alleviates the normal financial burden usually incurred when buying your dream home abroad. With the ever increasing popularity of the Spanish property market, buyers are coming up with evermore ingenious ideas for creating idyllic and clever ways of living and also earning an income in Spain - some, in the form of traditional Scandinavian log cabins as an all year round home, others, with having numerous lodges rented out as holiday lets providing themselves with a substantial income.

This idea, even though it may sound ludicrous to most of us, as we have the perception of log cabins in snow covered mountains, high peaks, white glaciers and weeks tucked under the covers hibernating in front of an open fire, has been a great success! These idyllic retreats have found a home in the mountainous corners of Spain as well as the popular coastal regions, exchanging extreme cold for extreme heat therefore lending itself and its qualities to its new found environment.

UNIQUE OPPORTUNITIES

With prices starting from £30,000 upwards and the prolific increase in specifically designed tailor made country parks (www. breakawayhomes.com) now appearing up and down the Costas, we agree that this form of real estate is definitely becoming the new vogue. This trend is likely to increase because people are realizing that buying one of these luxury log homes offers the individual a unique opportunity to locate/relocate the lodges at their leisure - either at one of these country club sites or utilizing Spain's relatively relaxed laws on transportable buildings, by buying themselves small parcels of land where permission to site their cabins is readily granted by the local town hall. Thus, giving them their own sense of privacy, tranquility, relaxation and peace of mind!

WHY CHOOSE SUNSHINE LODGES?

SUNSHINE LODGES offer a solid range of pine, round-log buildings, which have many benefits over other types of wooden buildings on the market. Although **SUNSHINE LODGES** are not the only importers of round-log buildings into Spain we are the only company to manufacture transportable round-log cabins for use on holiday parks e.t.c.

We also believe that we have the ability to offer a flexible, personal service at a competitive price. With the ability for in-house design, you can be assured that you really can have the log cabin of your dreams! So why settle for a traditional mobile home, when you could be enjoying the surroundings of a solid round-log building?

THE BENEFITS OF ROUND-LOGS

Picture in your mind a genuine 'log cabin'. The chances are that it will be made out of round logs. Not only do round logs create the real 'cabin' feel, they are far more aesthetically pleasing than the heavily machined square log. The round log style gives our lodges a feeling of character as well as making them extremely durable and strong.

SUNSHINE LODGES manufacture the majority of our buildings using 200mm solid round logs, larger than those usually used by our competition, ensuring marvellous insulation properties (roughly the same as a 230mm cavity brick wall). Round log cabins require relatively little maintenance and will 'weather' far better than some of the less solid designs on the market.

We also offer advice on planning and building regulations, and supply all the necessary drawings and literature you need to apply for planning permission.

For further information please visit our website at:
www.sunshinelodges.com

Finding a home to rent

There are many different publications and websites (such as **www.hispa vista.com** and **www.segundamano.es**) specializing in Spain and the Spanish property market, where you will find details of properties for rent, many of them being let by fellow Britons who have already purchased a holiday home in Spain. Once in Spain, you will find advertisements in most of the local newspapers (look under *alquiler*). When answering these advertisements, take precautions. Ask as many questions as you can over the telephone before embarking on what may prove to be a totally wasted visit. You may be responding to an advertisement by an agent who is advertising an attractive but non-existent property merely to persuade readers to ring in. Often they will not supply any information by post, are reluctant to discuss details over the telephone and insist on your attending their offices, when they will only then ask you to pay a registration fee. Reputable estate agents, however, can often prove very helpful.

In the most popular areas, especially in Barcelona and Madrid, but also on the Costa del Sol, where there is relatively little accommodation offered for long-term rental, you will need to check the adverts soon after a newspaper is off the presses! It is also well worth trying the local English-language press (see Appendix 1 and the regional sections in Chapter 1), expatriate websites, church notice boards, etc.

Note that most properties in Spain are let unfurnished, and that 'unfurnished' properties are often mere shells, frequently with no carpets, kitchen units (or even a sink), light fittings, TV aerial, etc.

Visiting the property

Insist on visiting the property at least twice, preferably on different days of the week, at different times and, if possible, in different weather conditions. Watch out for any signs on nearby properties suggesting that noisy and dusty building or renovation works are planned.

Rental contracts

There are two main types of rental contract (*contrato de alquiler*, or *contracte de lloguer* in Catalan). These are the *par temporada* (a short-term or seasonal contract) and the *vivienda* (a long-term contract). A *par temporada* contract covers all holiday lettings and lettings up to a maximum of one year. After the expiry of the letting period, subject of course to any renewal, the tenant must leave. As in the United Kingdom and other European countries, tenants of such short-term lettings have little protection. These lettings are frequently of furnished properties, and the agreement should include an itemized inventory listing the contents of the property.

Protection afforded by Spanish law

The rental market for long-term lettings is subject to regulation by Spanish law, which protects, in particular, the tenant's right to stay in the property and, to a certain extent, the level of rent. Where there is a conflict between the written agreement between the parties and Spanish law, the law prevails.

Unless the contrary is stated, the paragraphs that follow deal with long-term lettings, although much of the practical advice is pertinent also to short-term or seasonal lettings. Note that 'luxury dwellings' – large properties or properties at very high rentals – are not protected by this legislation, and the terms of the written contract will be decisive.

Under the present Law of Urban Lettings (*Ley de Arrendamientos Urbanos*), in force since 1 January 1995, the law provides that in contracts *de vivienda* – that is, rental contracts for one year or more – the tenant has an automatic right to renew the tenancy for up to five years. Indeed, a rental contract is *automatically* extended for a further year if the tenant does not give the landlord 30 days' notice before the end of the anniversary of the contract. Accordingly, if you enter into a two-year agreement with a property owner, you have a right to remain in the property for up to a further three years. During this five-year period the landlord is entitled to increase the rent each year, but only in line with inflation. Once the five-year period has expired, the landlord then has the freedom to increase the rent as he or she wishes.

A short-term holiday rental, *arrienda de temporada*, is not protected by this legislation. A number of the autonomous regions, however, impose their own rules and regulations in relation to holiday and short-term rentals. In Valencia, for example, proprietors of tourist accommodation to let must register the properties with the *Dirección General de Turismo*. Certain minimum requirements are imposed, together with a system of inspection to ensure that the properties are up to standard.

There is nothing to stop you entering into an agreement in English, and this is frequently done for self-catering holiday flats. A landlord wishing to let on a longer-term basis, however, cannot escape the protection granted by Spanish law by granting a tenancy in English, even if the agreement is signed by a UK tenant in the United Kingdom prior to leaving for Spain.

The rental agreement

Read the rental agreement carefully! Consider having it checked over by an *abogado* (lawyer). Agreements can be oral, but you should insist on a written contract confirming the tenancy and setting out the terms. The agreement should include the names of the proprietor and the tenant, the date the tenancy commences and its length. It must also give a description of the property, the level of rent, the amount of the deposit and the purpose for which the property is being let. It is a good idea to register your rental contract with the local housing department.

The deposit (*fianza*)

A deposit of one month's rent is payable on the signing of the rental agreement. The proprietor may be prepared to give you more time to pay this – for example, taking half when you move into the property and half a month later. In any event, ask for a receipt. The deposit is paid as a guarantee of the condition of the property and the other risks taken by the proprietor in letting the property. At the end of the rental, the deposit is returned to the tenant, less the proprietor's costs of rectifying any damage to the property and any unpaid rent.

The deposit can be paid to an agency rather than the landlord. The agency should not release the deposit to either party without the consent of them both. I strongly recommend that you pay your deposit to a reputable estate agent or other agent, rather than to the landlord. An alternative is for the deposit to be held by the housing department of the regional government. Indeed, in some autonomous regions the local laws provide that the owner *must* pay the deposit to the local housing department.

Length of the tenancy

The tenant is not obliged to stay for the five-year permitted maximum, but he or she has a right to stay for the entire period. The proprietor cannot compel a tenant to leave before the end of the agreement except on limited grounds (primarily non-payment of rent and causing damage to the property, but also subletting without permission, disturbing neighbours, etc). In all cases a landlord must obtain a court order before evicting a tenant. This process can take a considerable time. In relation to rent arrears, a tenant will be given time to pay and will usually have to be several months in arrears before an order for possession will be made. The emphasis is on protecting the occupation of the tenant, provided he or she comes up with reasonable proposals to clear the arrears.

Community fees and local property taxes

Proprietors of apartments often insert terms into rental contracts requiring the tenant to pay the annual charges levied by the property owners' collective for the block, and sometimes the property tax (*impuesto sobre bienes inmuebles*, IBI). These fees and taxes can be substantial. While there is nothing to stop landlords trying to recover these expenses from a tenant in this way, the courts take a dim view of such attempts. Judges have struck out many such clauses as abusive, and tenants who feel that they have been unfairly pushed into agreeing to such clauses can often escape liability to pay the fees and IBI. Needless to say, if the fees and IBI are not mentioned in the rental agreement, the tenant is certainly not obliged to pay them.

Maintenance of the property

Maintenance of the property is the tenant's responsibility. His or her liability extends to minor repairs as well as maintenance in order to prevent the property falling into disrepair. The tenant's responsibility covers replacing broken windows, broken keys, paintwork, bleeding of radiators, and replacement of bulbs, fuses and light fittings. The proprietor, on the other hand, remains responsible for substantial works of maintenance and repair.

Improvements to the property

The tenant does not need permission to carry out minor works, such as the fitting of a carpet in an unfurnished property. However, he or she is not entitled to carry out any substantial work or make holes in walls, for example, without the written consent of the proprietor.

The proprietor's right to carry out works

You are unlikely to be able to object to any necessary work that the proprietor wishes to carry out to maintain or improve the property. If peace and quiet are important to you (especially if you are at home during working hours), it would be wise to obtain the proprietor's written confirmation that no works of improvement will be carried out during the tenancy, save with your agreement. This should be recorded on the rental contract.

Insurance

A tenant should ensure that a policy of insurance is in force from the moment that he or she is in possession of the keys. Agreements frequently contain a provision allowing the proprietor to withdraw from the agreement if no insurance is in force.

Subletting

A tenant cannot sublet an apartment without the prior written consent of the proprietor. Even if a tenant is given permission to sublet, he or she remains liable to pay any rent not paid by his or her sub-tenant.

If you are offered a sub-tenancy, you should ensure that the proprietor's written consent has been obtained or, preferably, enter into an agreement directly with him or her. If you do not, and the proprietor becomes entitled to end the tenancy he or she has granted to your landlord, you may well be left high and dry.

Notice to leave given by the landlord

If a landlord wishes to obtain possession of his or her property after the five-year period has expired, he or she must notify the tenant (in writing, from a notary) well before the expiry of the five years. Failure to do so can mean that the tenancy is extended for a further two years on the same terms. Even if the landlord has given the requisite notice, he or she cannot simply proceed to evict the tenant; the landlord must first obtain a court order for possession.

Before you move in

It is essential that a record of the state of the premises is completed before you move in. This is vital if you wish to reduce the risks of a nasty surprise when you come to leave, such as the proprietor blaming you for damage that was already present before you moved into the property. I recommend that you attend the property before you move in, preferably with the landlord or his or her representative, armed with the checklist supplied at the end of this chapter, and go through this document on-site. Check that the cooker and any machines included in the letting are in working order. The landlord may also supply you with an inventory covering any contents. Again, you should check that the inventory is correct before signing it.

I suggest that you use a carbon to make two copies or each make your own copy of the completed document. Ensure that they are identical before both signing them. If only one copy is completed and signed, insist on providing the photocopy yourself. If you give the only copy to the landlord, you may cause yourself considerable problems if he or she loses it or otherwise fails to supply you with your copy.

I also strongly recommend that, on moving in, you take a video of the property. Pay attention to any particular defects, and post the video to yourself by recorded delivery so that you can prove the date when the video was taken. Do not open it unless some dispute arises at the end of the tenancy, in which case open it in front of some third party, such as an *abogado*, who can vouch for the fact that the envelope was previously unopened. If you do notice inaccuracies in the inventory or the checklist of the condition of the property, you should send a recorded-delivery letter to the landlord or his or her agent informing them as soon as possible.

When you come to leave

A further record of the condition of the property should be completed and a comparison made with the previous one, to determine the extent of any damage caused during your occupation. I recommend that you make a video of the premises before leaving. In the middle of the recording, video a significant news item on the television or that day's newspaper so you can prove that it was not taken earlier.

Resolving disputes

In the event of a disagreement with the proprietor (for example, he or she is refusing to carry out a landlord's repair, or refusing to repay the deposit), you should seek advice. Obviously, instructing a lawyer can be expensive and may be out of proportion to the financial value of the dispute. There are, however, various agencies that provide free advice, including those that represent tenants' rights. A starting place is the *Oficina Municipal de Información al Consumidor* (*OMIC*). This agency is charged with handling a wide range of consumer problems, as well as complaints relating to lettings.

You can also refer any problems relating to the renting of accommodation to the *Asociaciones de Consumidores y Usuarios* (Consumers' and Users' Associations) or *Juntas Arbitrales de Consumo* (Consumer Arbitration Boards). People with complaints about short-term or tourist occupation should contact the local tourist office.

Right of first refusal

As a tenant of a long-term letting, you are entitled to first refusal should the proprietor put the property up for sale (this is referred to as the *tanteo y retracto*, the right of first refusal). The landlord should notify you, in writing, of the sale price, and the conditions of sale. If the landlord fails to do this, the tenant has the right to have the sale annulled, and to purchase the property at the price recorded on the contract for sale.

Accommodation for young people: housing initiatives for 18- to 30-/35-year-olds

In certain autonomous communities (including Madrid, Catalonia and the Canary Islands) and some local councils (including Palma de Majorca) there are state-funded advisory services providing legal and practical assistance, and a housing exchange scheme consisting of properties at below market rentals. The scheme is aimed at those aged between 18 and 30/35 who have a salary of at least one and a half times the minimum wage, or who have someone who can guarantee their rental payments. Information is available from INJUVE (tel: 91 363 75 93; e-mail: viviendaempleo@mtas.es).

Short-term, seasonal and student accommodation

INJUVE (contact details above) has reached agreements with local town councils for the provision of short-term rented accommodation to those under 30 with low incomes who are away from home owing to work commitments or studies. Lists of available accommodation can be obtained from local tourist offices. Details of student accommodation, ranging from an entire flat to living with a family, can be obtained from **www.spain exchange.com** or **www.estudiasotrabajas.com**.

CHECKLIST ON MOVING IN/OUT: SPANISH

INQUILINO:

PROPRIETARIO:

PROPIEDAD:

FECHA:

1 = muy bueno   2 = bueno   3 = pasable   4 = pobre

pieza	pintura, techo, vidrio ventana,	suelo, puertas, ventanas, persianas	electricidad	armarios/ módulos	instalación de agua	cerraduras, trabajo en metales
Sala						
Cocina						
Dormitorio 1						
Dormitorio 2						
Dormitorio 3						
Baño						
Cuarto de baño						
Entrada						
Sotano						
Garaje						

CHECKLIST ON MOVING IN/OUT: ENGLISH

TENANT:

PROPRIETOR:

PROPERTY:

DATE OF MOVING IN:

1 = very good   2 = good   3 = passable   4 = poor

room	paintwork, ceiling, window-panes,	floor, doors, windows, blinds	electricity	cupboards/ storage units	plumbing/ toilet installations	locks, ironwork
Living-room						
Kitchen						
Bed 1						
Bed 2						
Bed 3						
Toilet						
Bathroom						
Hall/entrance way						
Cellar						
Garage						

Further information on renting

See **www.civilia.es**. Click on *vivienda joven*, then *alquiler de vivienda*.

Buying a property in Spain

Almost 90 per cent of Spaniards own their own homes, a much higher figure than in other European countries, including the United Kingdom (75 per cent). A significant minority have a second home. There are also an estimated million and a half foreign property owners in Spain. Foreign interest in buying property in Spain continues to rise.

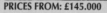

Almeria's secret ingredient

There's something special about the Almeria region of Spain. Top quality accommodation, stunning scenery and beautiful beaches are sure to be a recipe for success.

If you think you know Spain, think again. There is a special region that has been cherished as a well-kept secret among long-term visitors to the country. The region of Almeria is one of the least rainy parts of Europe, the sun shines almost 300 days a year and the average temperature is a gorgeous 27°C in summer and a balmy 15°C in winter. Sound good? You haven't heard the best bits yet! It has long, sandy beaches, great transport links, an 18-hole golf course, and a nautical club. And in the distance you can see the dramatic ridges of the Sierra Nevada mountains, creating a stunning setting. What better place to live or own a holiday home?

That is why reputable developer Blauverd Hàbitat has chosen the area for its latest project. They have more than 20 years of experience, and some impressive projects to their name. This means that you are able to view their previous successes for yourself. Professional property investors always check out a company's track record before putting money into a project, and this is something that is easy to do with Blauverd Hàbitat. Their existing developments include the tasteful Marina Azul, Tamarindo Beach, Dunasol and PlayaSol II in Denia, up the coast in Valencia. All are top quality apartment complexes with unbeatable sea views and facilities.

In Almeria, Blauverd Hàbitat are working to make the most of the area's wild beauty, while providing accommodation that comes up to the high standards you would expect from such a developer.

Their latest project, Vereda Golf has a unique setting next to the beach and the golf course "Playa Serena". This apartment complex comprises two and three-bedroom apartments and penthouses. Most of the apartments enjoy views to the golf course or the sea and have beautifully laid out communal gardens and spectacular shaped swimming pools.

The generously proportioned rooms have a bright, airy feel and are fitted out in quality furnishings. Terraces provide that all-important outside living area for evening sundowners or breakfast in the sunshine.

One of the signs of Blauverd Hàbitat's success and standing in Spain is that a fair number of their apartments are owned by Spanish people themselves, so buying into one of their stunning developments really is a way to experience the real Spain.

When you deal with Blauverd Hàbitat you don't need to worry about hard-sell tactics. Their reputation is everything to them. Their friendly multi-lingual staff are based in an office close to each development, and they are supported by professional staff in their London and Manchester offices, providing excellent before-and after-sales service. You know that when you buy directly from the developer you're getting a great deal, and buying apartments off-plan also has favourable payment plans. What's more Blauverd Hàbitat can help you pre-arrange a mortgage for 70 per cent of the property's price. At every stage of the buying process, Blauverd Hàbitat is committed to making the purchase process as easy and transparent as possible.

Why not take a visit to Vereda Golf or one of Blauverd Hàbitat's other developments? You'll be pleasantly surprised by this special corner of the Spanish costa, and by the high standard of the developments. Providing top quality accommodation is Blauverd Hàbitat's business. But their number one priority is making your dream of owning a home in Spain come true.

Email london@blauverd-habitat.com, or call 020 7224 2202 for your chance to live the dream in Almeria. Apartments at Vereda Golf start at £130,000.

For most people, the purchase of a home in Spain has proved a sound long-term investment, with a surge in prices of 15 per cent a year in Spain since 1998. The purchase of a property abroad, however, can result in serious financial losses and in some cases lengthy and difficult court proceedings. The peaceful holiday or retirement home (or, worse still, your main residence) can turn into a veritable nightmare. You will find comprehensive advice on buying property in Spain (and also on letting out your Spanish property) in my book *The Complete Guide to Buying Property in Spain*, also published by Kogan Page. I have set out below a short set of basic guidelines.

If you decide to purchase in Spain:

1. *Do not expect to obtain a quick short-term capital gain.* In Spain, acquisition costs are high. It is safest to work on the basis that you will need to own your property for several years before you will make a net gain on any sale.
2. *Instruct your own lawyer.* Spanish *notarios* are publicly appointed officials. Their main functions are to draft legal documents, to oversee the transfer of property, to inform the parties of their tax liabilities, and to ensure that monies have been paid. They are *not* representing your interests. Specifically, they do not carry out the important pre-contract enquiries that, for example, a solicitor in the United Kingdom would carry out. Choose a lawyer, or a team of lawyers, who can communicate well in a language that you can fully understand, and who have an understanding of inheritance and tax law in *your* country as well as in Spain. The earlier you instruct your lawyer, the better.
3. *Get to know the area in which you wish to purchase.* Familiarize yourself with the climate. The Mediterranean climate will furnish you with hot summers and mild winters, whereas on the northern, Atlantic coastline the climate is temperate and humid, with cold, rainy winters. Ascertain whether the area suffers from natural disasters. Some Mediterranean areas are subject to flooding. There is no need to automatically exclude these areas, but take special care when making enquiries as to the particular property and surrounding area.
4. *Obtain a surveyor's report.* Lending institutions in Spain generally require only a valuation. A structural survey should prevent you from purchasing a property that is structurally unsound, perhaps dangerous, expensive to restore and difficult to dispose of. In addition, a report often identifies non-structural defects that may not deter you

from your purchase, but may give you ammunition with which to negotiate on the purchase price.

5. *View the property yourself.* Ideally you should visit the property several times, at different times of the day and in different weather conditions. Approach the property from different routes. Try to ascertain why the vendors are selling, and, if at all possible, speak to the neighbours. Look to see whether the boundaries to the property are clearly marked. Is there any evidence of any rights of way being used over the property? Inform your surveyor and lawyer of any concerns you have.

6. *Do not declare at an undervalue.* The authorities in Spain have tightened up on the rules, and are likely to become even stricter in the future.

7. Be particularly wary of timeshare schemes (often wrapped up in other names such as 'vacation plus' or 'holiday ownership'). Whilst there are European regulations governing timeshare schemes, those operating them are sometime unscrupulous and ingenious in side-stepping the regulations.

RMC with you every step of the way

RMC has been trading within the UK and International market for 17 years. Their past experience covers all fields of buying and financing of properties within the UK and abroad.

Inspection Trips:- Inspection trips usually last 4 days whereby our agents are at your disposal on an individual basis. They are there to show you the region, answer all your queries, take you to see suitable properties and ultimately assist you in your choice of home.

A £2,000 deposit secures any available property and a reservation contract can be signed once the sequence of stage payment is agreed.

Finance:- There are 2 basic ways to go about raising capital for your purchase:

- Arrange a second mortgage on your UK home.

- A Spanish bank mortgage can be sorted for 70-75% of the property price. Rates are very competitive and very little personal information if required.

Purchasing Costs:-New home purchasers should allow an extra 10% on the purchase price to cover charges such as I.V.A (VAT), legal fees, connection charges and stamp duty.

Health:-The World Health Organisation refers to this area as one of the healthiest place to live. The Spanish National Health hospitals and doctors are extremely good. Some of them have a working knowledge of English, if not, interpreters are usually available.

- If you are settling over here, National Health cover is automatically provided to employees of Spanish companies, as in the UK. To be covered in the case of an emergency for free, before departing from the UK you should apply for an 'E111' from your local post office for each person.

- Alternatively, some consider private health cover to be preferable. While here, compare the extent of cover and prices of the local private health companies and you will soon find the ideal solution to suit you and your family.

- All pensioners receive free medical care and prescriptions, once they have registered with the Spanish National Health Service.

Pensions:-As we are all now part of the EU there is no problem in transferring any UK pension to be paid direct, free of any charges, into a nominated account in a Spanish bank.

Language:-In most shops, restaurants and professional services you will find English spoken to some degree. However, learning the language is treated with respect and goes a long way. There are language schools, in the area with one to one lessons widely available at about £6 an hour. Some areas offer free sessions for English residents. Utility connections, negotiations with builders and any other important matters can be dealt with by us.

Banking:-Some of the larger popular banks, (e.g. Solbank, Banco Popular Espanol, Deutsche Bank) have at least one multi-lingual member of staff. If you purchase out here through us, an account will be opened with our assistance, able to receive sterling from the UK and convert to euros. Bank accounts opened through us, with your mortgage, benefit from reduced bank charges. Direct debits, as in the UK, can be fixed up to attend to all standing charges when the owners are not in the country.

Tax:-Obviously a complex and highly personal subject on which most people would be taking specialized advice. At the early stages the Spanish tax system is a little similar to the UK in as far as tax bands and allowances go.

If you are coming here to live, we will help you to find a good 'Gestoria' (a professional person/s, at surprisingly reasonable rates) who deals with all your paperwork (taxes, social security etc) involved with living in Spain. Naturally, we only recommend and introduce you to the good ones.

There couldn't be a better way of taking your first step to owning your dream home in the sun than contacting any of our offices. Our friendly, informative and helpful approach, without the slightest pressure, is aimed at helping you decide whether Spain is the place for you. Whether your requirement is a holiday home, a permanent residence, a rental property or just purely an investment, the range of properties is endless from town apartments to individual beachside or golf villas and everything in between.

Your first decision now is whether Spain is right for you, if you decide it is then RMC is there to help you take the first steps towards buying your new home in the sun.

3 Finding a job in Spain

Citizens of EU countries are entitled to live and work anywhere within the European Union. There are no formalities involved in going to search for employment in Spain, other than the possession of a valid passport. Unemployment is high in Spain, though those with expertise in IT, or teachers of English, generally have little difficulty in finding a position.

If you are from a country outside the European Union, you will need to provide your local Spanish consulate with a police certificate confirming that you have no police record, together with a translation. Once the document has been approved, you can make your application for a combined residence and work permit. You must satisfy the *Ministerio de Trabajo* that you have a work contract, and that no competent Spanish person could be found to carry out the work. Employers often handle these applications on behalf of employees. Others often seek the assistance of a *gestor* (see Chapter 7). Non-EU nationals who wish to start a business in Spain will need to prove that they have about $140,000 to invest in Spain and that they will provide employment for Spanish nationals, or nationals of other EU member states.

The Spanish labour market

Despite having the highest level of economic growth in Western Europe, Spain has the highest official level of unemployment. Unemployment rates are highest in Andalusia, but Valencia and the Balearic Islands have rates below the national average. Whilst official unemployment is high, Spain also has the largest black economy in Western Europe after Italy. The most industrialized regions are Rioja and Navarra, whereas Galicia and Extremadura are known for their agricultural production.

As a foreigner, you are already at some disadvantage in approaching Spanish employers even if you speak Spanish to a high level. Furthermore, in recent years there has been considerable immigration into Spain, primarily economic migrants especially from Portugal, Ecuador, North

Africa and Eastern Europe. In 2003 the annual number of immigrants reached 600,000 – equivalent to 14 per 1,000 of Spain's population, the highest in Europe. Accordingly, there is considerable competition for jobs, especially for unskilled or semi-skilled work. Ideally you will find employment before you move to Spain. If you arrive without a job, do not assume that it will be easy to find employment.

One sector in which English speakers are at an advantage is in the teaching of English as a foreign or second language, a sector that employs several thousand native English speakers. Obviously if you have a teaching qualification, especially the PGCE (Postgraduate Certificate of Education), or a TEFL (Teaching English as a Foreign Language) qualification, your prospects of finding work are quite good, though generally the rates of remuneration are not high. Other sectors in which jobs are most in demand are in tourism (though many of these posts are seasonal only), IT, financial services, sales, marketing and construction. In the areas on the east coast of Spain there are many jobs in the service industry, including beauty consultants, hairdressers, restaurant and pub staff, shop assistants, estate agents' representatives, satellite engineers and air-conditioning engineers.

As to salaries, there is considerable variation, with posts in Madrid and Barcelona generally commanding much higher salaries than elsewhere. Those employed in middle management or the professions can expect to earn within the range of 40,000–70,000 euros. Average earnings for manual workers are in the region of 20,000 euros.

Unemployment benefit

Those who are unemployed and from the United Kingdom are entitled to have the Jobseeker's Allowance paid to them in Spain for up to 13 weeks. Similar rules will apply to other EU member states. You must have been registered as a jobseeker for at least four weeks before you left the United Kingdom, and have been available for work up until your departure. You must be leaving the United Kingdom in search of work, and register as seeking work with the Spanish authorities within seven days of your last claim for Jobseeker's Allowance in the United Kingdom. You must contact your Jobcentre Plus office or Jobcentre before leaving, and complete the appropriate forms if you have not done so already to claim benefit. You should be sent a copy of E303 before you leave to enable you to claim benefit in Spain, and form E119 to entitle you to healthcare. If you cannot find employment during that 13-week period, then you will have to return to the United Kingdom if you wish to continue to receive benefit. You are only entitled to claim Jobseeker's Allowance abroad for one 13-week period between periods of employment. Information on transferring your Jobseeker's Allowance is contained in leaflet JSAL 22, available from your local DWP office.

Information on other UK benefits that can be paid in Spain, and on Spanish social security benefits, is contained in Chapter 7.

Finding employment

There are many English speakers employed within the British community, particularly on the Costa del Sol and Costa Blanca, who speak hardly any Spanish, even after years of living in the country. On the Costa del Sol, numerous expatriates are in employment in the tourist industry, the yachting industry, security services, childcare and as domestic staff. Throughout Spain there are a large number of English speakers who teach English as a foreign language, having obtained a TEFL qualification in the United Kingdom, or teachers with a PGCE who teach at one of the many UK or other international schools. However, whilst your chances of obtaining work will be increased by networking amongst other expatriates, or having a teaching qualification, if you are to obtain employment with a Spanish employer a reasonable knowledge of Spanish and a willingness to improve it are essential.

European Employment Services

The European Commission is keen to promote greater mobility in the European labour force in the interests of economic growth and as a means of facilitating political integration within the European Union. European Employment Services (EURES) is a co-operation network established by the European Commission and the national employment services of member states.

EURES's brief is to assist jobseekers who would like to move to another EU country to work or to study. Assistance consists of providing information and advice, and assisting in recruitment and placing of candidates. It is free of charge.

Take a look at the EURES website (**www.europa.eu.int/jobs/eures**) and at the job offers available at **www.eures-jobs.com**. The latter is regularly updated, and you can search by professions and regions. The posts advertised on the EURES portal originate primarily from European Public Employment Services. A blue flag indicates that the employer has a particular interest in taking on workers from other EU countries. From 2005 it is hoped to make all jobs advertised by the different European Public Employment Services accessible from the site, not just those for which the employer has expressed an interest in recruiting a national of a different member state.

The EURES sites include information on living and working in Spain (and other European countries), and a number of useful links. There is also a facility to make your CV available to employers, and to EURES advisers. You can change your CV whenever you wish, using your user-ID and password. Indeed, if you do not regularly visit your page (every 12 weeks), the CV is no longer accessible to employers. You can choose to make your CV anonymous, in which case employers can contact you via the EURES service.

Specific advice and information can be obtained by jobseekers from their local EURES adviser. There is a network of about 500 such experts across the European Union. Contact your local EURES adviser (via your local Jobcentre Plus office) for advice prior to leaving. He or she should be able to establish contact with the EURES adviser in the region in Spain in which you wish to work. In Spain, EURES advisers can be contacted via the local *Oficinas de Empleo*. Some work overseas is also posted on the UK government site **www.jobcentreplus.gov.uk**.

On the Move

On the Move is an interactive programme to provide information and assistance to young people considering mobility in Europe. Its website is accessible via **www.europa.eu.int**. Go to the Ploteus portal and then links.

Oficinas de Empleo

EU jobseekers should register in person with their local office (*Oficina de Empleo*) of the *Instituto Nacional de Empleo* (INEM) or with the regional employment service. This is the most common means of obtaining information about job vacancies in Spain. You are entitled to the same level of help and assistance as a Spanish citizen. Most offices will assist you in finding training courses, and advise on setting up your own business, as well as how best to obtain employment. In some centres you will be able to access various reference books and company listings. Some of the public employment agencies in Spain work hand in hand with partner organizations that offer jobseekers the same type of service without charge. These often offer specialized assistance to particular groups such as the disabled, or students, or sectors of the employment market. For more information, see **www.inem.es** (mostly in Spanish only, although parts are also in English). There is a Guide to Working in Spain that you can download. General help and guidance are also available, including in English, on the government website **www.mtas.es**.

If you have applied to have state benefits transferred to Spain from your home country, you must register with your local employment office in Spain within seven days after leaving your home country.

Empresas de Trabajo Temporal (temporary employment agencies)

You can also make contact with recruitment agencies by sending them a CV and covering letter requesting an appointment. These agencies are only permitted to offer temporary work. They are listed under *trabajo temporal* in Yellow Pages (*Paginas Amarillas*). Some of the major public libraries in your home country may stock these, but the information is also accessible via **www.paginasamarillas.com**. It may also be worth contacting Manpower in your home country before leaving (its UK telephone number is 00 44 207 224 66 88), Adecco (**www.adecco.com**) and Flexiplan (**www. flexiplan.es**).

The media

Scan the classified ads under *ofertas de trabajo* (job offers) in the main newspapers, such as *El Mundo, El Pais, El Periódico, La Razón* and *ABC*, and also the specialist weekly newspaper *Mercado de Trabajo*. The Sunday papers contain the largest recruitment sections. Salaries are seldom indicated in advertisements. Positions for management, professional and technical staff often appear in the *International Herald Tribune*. There are many English-language newspapers and magazines in Spain in which you will also find advertisements for job vacancies.

The websites of the major Spanish newspapers are **www.elmundo.es**, **www.elpais.es**, **www.elpais.com**, **www.abc.es**, **www.larazon.es** and **www.elperiodico.es**. There is also an umbrella website for national and local press at **www.mir.es/oris/enlaces/prensa.htm**. Details of local English-language publications are set out in Appendix 1 and in the different regional sections in Chapter 1.

A number of radio stations, including some that broadcast in English, have job spots. On TV2 there is a regular jobs spot (at 9.30 am Monday to Friday) known as *Aqui hay trabajo*.

The internet

The internet is an invaluable tool for tracking down vacancies and obtaining information. See later in the chapter for lists of potential websites.

Planning ahead and job placements

If you are relatively new to the labour force and have decided that you wish to work in Spain in the future, you should consider applying to complete a traineeship or job placement in Spain. These are often arranged by the larger multinational employers, and provide a perfect opportunity for you to gain some knowledge of Spanish, the local area and job market. Generally, applicants must have completed two years of vocational training, and usually work in Spain for a period of 12 months.

There are also a number of work experience programmes and opportunities for students in certain fields. Many of these are under the umbrella of the International Association for the Exchange of Students for Technical Experience (IAESTE), The Educational and Training Group, The British Council, 10 Spring Gardens, London SW1 2BN (tel: 020 7389 4774; e-mail: iaeste@britishcouncil.org; website: **www.iaeste.org.uk**). Europass and the Leonardo da Vinci programmes under the auspices of the European Union provide young people with opportunities of carrying out vocational training in other member states. Details of these and other schemes can be accessed via the British Council's 'Windows of the World' site at **www.wofw.org.uk**.

Network!

A huge proportion of jobs, both in the more popular coastal areas on the eastern side of Spain and in Madrid and Barcelona, are filled via personal contacts, especially for people who speak no or little Spanish. Networking is vitally important both in respect of finding out about vacancies, and also in ensuring the success of any business enterprise. Make full use of the various foreign chambers of commerce (for the contact details of the American and British Chambers of Commerce, see Appendix 1). Consult the various English-speaking newspapers and websites, and consider placing cards on the notice boards of expatriate organizations, clubs and associations, shops, bars and even churches frequented by other English speakers.

Employment guidebook

Each May a guidebook is published of the companies that offer employment in Spain. It includes a CD ROM that assists in searching for jobs, and is priced at about 16 euros. Further information can be obtained from rmendez@fue.es.

Another source for lists of potential employers is *Kompass Spain*. This includes a list of companies and can be consulted in main libraries and the Spanish Chamber of Commerce in your home country. See also **www. kompass.es**.

American Chambers of Commerce

The American Chambers of Commerce publish trade directories and international databases for different countries, including Spain, providing details of US subsidiaries doing business in Spain. The directory for Spain costs 130 euros and is available either from an American Chamber of Commerce or from **www.americansabroad.com**. You can inspect a section from the Netherlands directory on that same website to give you an idea of the kind of information included.

Unsolicited letters of application

Finally, it can be worth sending well-written unsolicited letters and CVs to companies you are interested in. A surprising number of people obtain employment in this way. Ensure that you carry out some research about the company before you write, and endeavour to demonstrate in your letter your ability to satisfy its likely requirements and to fit in with the organization. Ideally, you should refer to one of the specialist books available on how to present different types of CVs and how to address and set out your correspondence. Always check the company's website for information about the company, to see whether it has a facility for submitting an application by e-mail, and whether it has a standard application form. Look for a link called *trabaja con nosotros* (work for us) or *empleo* (recruitment). Even if you decide not to use the company's standard form, at least take on board the sorts of questions contained on the form, which you are likely to be asked at some point.

Your covering letter

The letter should be brief but should summarize your qualifications and experience. It should explain why *you* are seeking employment with that particular company, and emphasize the strongest points in your favour. If you need a second page, your letter is probably too long. A covering letter must always be handwritten and in perfect Spanish. It should be enclosed with your CV in a *white* envelope. Do not staple your letter to the CV, but use a paper clip.

In Spain, business correspondence is more formal than in the English-speaking world. Open your letter with stock formal phrases such as *Muy Señor Mío* or *Estimado/a Sr/Sra*. The ending should likewise be formal, such as *'En espera de sus noticias. Le saluda atentamente'*, followed by your signature (with your name typed underneath). Always include an international reply coupon if writing from outside Spain, as well as a self-addressed envelope.

Your curriculum vitae

Your CV will determine whether you are to be interviewed. It should be well structured, crisp, clear, concise and 'pleasing to the eye'. It should be written with the particular employer in mind. Two typed A4 pages should be sufficient. The paper should be of good quality and white. You may have a standard CV. By all means use it as a basis, but you should consider it as a working tool, not as a finished product. Consider how best to amend it to attract the particular employer. If your CV is not written in Spanish, you should always have it translated, along with your professional qualification papers. Take a look at the EU's European Standard Curriculum Vitae. It is available in 13 languages and can be downloaded via the EURES website, **www.europa.eu.int/jobs/eures**. Photographs, qualifications and references should not be sent with your CV, unless they have been requested.

The CV should be divided into sections. The first consists of personal details, ie full name, date of birth, address and contact details. The second should set out brief details and dates of your educational and training history, with separate paragraphs for IT and foreign-language training. The third section should deal with your work experience to date, starting with the most recent, and including the names of your present and former employers, dates employed and nature of job carried out. A fourth section can be added containing any information that you consider particularly pertinent to your application, such as a clean driving licence.

Job interviews

Take the time and trouble to prepare yourself. Find out as much as you can about your potential employer. Be prepared to have your knowledge of Spanish tested, and also to be asked questions about your ability to settle in Spain, as well as why you consider yourself to be the ideal candidate for the post. Take with you three or four copies of your CV in Spanish, a translation of your degree and/or other qualifications, your passport and two passport photographs.

Qualifications

A major impediment to working in another member state of the European Union is the difficulty of having one's qualifications accepted in the host nation. EU policy is to make qualifications more transparent, and to integrate the different national educational systems. It has accordingly established a network of National Academic Recognition Information Centres (NARICs) covering all members of the European Union, and indeed some countries in Central and Eastern Europe. The centres provide advice and information to educational institutions, students, teachers and business in relation to the academic recognition of qualifications and periods of study in other member states. Most NARICs do not make decisions as to recognition of foreign qualifications, as this is generally a matter for the individual institutes of higher education, but they provide information and advice. It can take some time (over 12 months is not unheard of), and accordingly you should apply for recognition as soon as you can.

Further information (and links to all national NARIC websites) can be found at **www.enic-naric.net**. The website for NARIC in the United

Kingdom is **www.naric.org.uk**, and further information is also available in the United Kingdom from the Department of Education and Skills (**www.dfes.gov.uk**). The contact details and address relating to Spain are:

Maria Isabel Barrios
Nieve Trelles
NARIC España
Subdirección General de Títulos, Convalidaciones y Homoglaciones
Paeso del Prado 28
E-28014 Madrid
Tel: 00 34 91 506 55 93
Fax: 00 34 91 506 57 06
e-mail: misabel.barrios@educ.mec.es or nieves.trelles@educ.mec.es

It is essential to know how to get your qualifications recognized in Spain. Professions fall into two categories: those that are regulated and those that are not. Regulated professions are those to which access is restricted to those holding the required qualifications. In Spain they include architects, doctors, nurses, midwives, dentists, veterinary surgeons and pharmacists. A full list is available from the Ministry of Education, Culture and Sport (**www.mec.es**).

Other professions are subject to a general system of recognition based on the principle that a person fully qualified in one member state ought to be recognized as able to carry out his or her profession in another member state. Where there are differences between the training received, the Spanish authorities are entitled to require that an aptitude test or a period of work experience should be completed prior to the recognition of the qualification. Application for recognition is made to the government department responsible for the particular activity concerned. Further information is available from the *Subdirección General de Títulos, Convalidaciones y Homoglaciones* at the Ministry of Education, Culture and Sport (see above for address). You will need a certified copy of your academic and professional qualification (with an official translation), and a certified copy of your passport. There is a fee payable of between 40 and 200 euros depending upon the qualification. The process can take over 12 months.

The longer-term objective of the European Union is for citizens to be able to treat both their qualifications and their non-formal workplace learning as a 'common currency' that can be earned in one or more member states but 'spent' in others. The European Credit Transfer System was introduced with this aim in mind, but more recently education ministers have announced plans to establish a European Higher Education Area by 2010 in which degrees should be more easily comparable. Also, in order to achieve improved transparency and recognition of vocational qualifications, a network of National Reference Points is being established in member states in order for comparisons to be made between different national vocational qualifications.

SOLVIT

Member states of the European Union frequently fail to properly implement European directives in relation to the rights of residents from other EU states, especially in relation to the recognition of qualifications. The European Union has now created an official organization to handle such problems, with offices in all member states. You should contact the office in your home country. Contact details are available by telephoning 00 800 678 91011 or on the website **www.europa.eu.int/comm/internal_market/ solvit.**

Dialogue with citizens

A guide has been published by the European Commission to assist EU citizens who have encountered problems in relation to the exercise of their rights to live, work, travel and study anywhere within the European Union. It explains how to challenge unfavourable decisions and how to use each member state's administrative and legal systems to obtain redress. The website is accessible via **www.europa.eu.int**. Go to the Ploteus portal and then links.

Specific job categories

Teaching and teaching English

There are a considerable number of British, US and international schools in Spain offering a range of different subjects, and they periodically recruit staff. Posts are frequently advertised on the website of *The Times Educational Supplement*, and also on the websites of the European Council of International Schools (tel: 0730 268244), **www.ecis.org**, and the National Association of British Schools in Spain, **www.nabbs.org**.

ACADEMIA ANDALUZA LANGUAGE SCHOOL
Languages since 1987

Choosing a new life and wishing to set up in Spain or simple wishing to come to Spain and learn the language and culture, coming to andalusian **Conil de la Frontera** and to **ACADEMIA ANDALUZA LANGUAGE SCHOOL** is a fantastic opportunity to immerse yourself in the local culture, community, history and outstanding natural beauty of the area **"Costa de la Luz"** appropriately named as the "Coast of Light" with white luminous sandy shores of the **Atlantic**. A world apart from the more commercialised Mediterranean coast. West from Algeciras the road climbs almost immediately into the rolling green hills with its famous scattered Moorish villages hidden in the "Sierra" and its fishing villages along the coast.

Conil de la Frontera is located favourably with easy access to everything within the region. A former fishing village with all its original charm **Conil** faces a wide bay of brilliant white beaches stretching for miles to either sides of the town and lapped by a majestic **Atlantic Ocean. Conil** has a wide choice of restaurants and bars with a pleasant climate and low cost of living. The majority of tourists are Spanish so there is an enjoyable, if rather familiar atmosphere, perfect for practicing your Spanish.

ACADEMIA ANDALUZA LANGUAGE SCHOOL is a modern fully integrated Language School suitably located on the brow of **Conil** in a three floor charming traditional town house with panoramic views of the sea from the roof terraces and a plant filled **Patio. ACADEMIA ANDALUZA LANGUAGE SCHOOL** has managed to fuse all of the regions architecture, culture and atmosphere within the institution with a comfortable friendly and welcoming ambience.

ACADEMIA ANDALUZA has been created and staffed by a truly committed and vibrant team providing a professional and courteous service since 1987. Being independent and using up to date technology **ACADEMIA ANDALUZA** is looking to make a real difference being a centre for high standard Language Training Programmes in Spanish and other languages.

ACADEMIA ANDALUZA is open all year round, except for Christmas and public holidays. The School not only provides quality Spanish Language Courses for adults, young people and children from all over the world, but also offers a full Advice Service for Family Relocation or Retirement.

Coming to **ACADEMIA ANDALUZA** and learning the language and culture gives you a window into Spanish life. We will ensure that you will be in a multicultural class, interacting with other students of the same level, age and interest. The teaching staff is fully qualified and highly experienced, constantly challenging the students to develop themselves and further their linguistic abilities.

There are a substantial number of language schools offering tuition in English, with many foreigners preferring to learn English in the warmth of Spain! The demand is such that most qualified teachers, including those with a TEFL (Teaching English as a Foreign Language) or TESL (Teaching English as a Second Language) certificate, should not have too many problems obtaining employment. Indeed, there are a good number of English mother tongue speakers teaching English without qualifications. Some of the schools often prefer their teachers to have attended their own training courses. There are a considerable number of websites providing lists of employment positions, and plenty of opportunities to supplement the quite modest salaries with extra income. You will find language schools under *idiomas* or *escuelas de idiomas* in the Yellow Pages.

The British Council has regular vacancies for qualified language teachers with experience, and for supervisors in its language centres in Madrid, Barcelona, Bilbao, Palma (Majorca) and Valencia (tel: 020 7389 4167; website: **www.britishcouncil.org**). The British Council also keeps a list of language schools throughout Spain.

You will find advertisements of vacancies on the following websites:

- **www.education.guardian.co.uk**;
- **www.tefl.com**;
- **www.tesjobs.co.uk**;
- **www.tesol-spain.org**;
- **www.bilc.co.uk**;
- **www.elfweb.com**;
- **www.developingteachers.com**;
- **www.eslemployment.com**;
- **www.englishclub.com** – a site for English as a second language with information and job offers;
- **www.expatriatecafe.com** – devoted to the teaching of English in Spain;
- **www.madridteacher.com** – established by English teachers in Madrid and lists job opportunities and has information for teachers;
- **www.infojobs.net** – in Spanish but very useful (go to *educación-formación*, the region you prefer and under *'palabra'* type *INGLES*);
- **www.alliancesabroad.com** – includes a programme for teaching English in Spain while learning Spanish;
- **www.spaintutor.com** – puts English tutors and students of English in touch with each other;
- **www.churchtimes.co.uk** – occasionally has teaching jobs abroad.

Language assistants

International agreements permit graduates and undergraduate students to work for an academic year in a school or college as an assistant to the modern languages teaching staff, speaking English to the students and giving information about English-speaking countries. Assistants, who are generally under 30, normally work about 15 hours a week and receive a modest but reasonable level of remuneration. Further information is available from Assistants Department, Central Bureau for Educational Visits and Exchanges (tel: 020 7486 5101).

Translation

It is generally difficult to make a living as a translator. The greatest demand is for technical translation and legal translation. Information on the training of translators is available from the Institute of Linguists (tel: 020 7940 3100; website: **www.iol.org.uk**. See also **www.languagejobs.org**. For jobs in European institutions, see the website of the European Communities Personnel Selection Office (EPSO), **www.europa.eu.int/epso**.

Information technology

Those with qualifications and experience in IT should find no difficulties in obtaining employment in Spain. See in particular **www.tecno empleo.com**.

Secretarial and office work

Word processing experience is essential, and even if you are working primarily with the expatriate community, a good level of Spanish is essential, and in many cases fluent Spanish will be required. A good knowledge of German is a substantial advantage on the popular *costas*. French is less of an advantage, save perhaps in Madrid and Barcelona. The next few years may, however, see a demand for French speakers on the coast as more and more French tourists abandon the Côte d'Azur in favour of the more reasonably priced Spanish destinations.

The yachting industry: recruitment and training

The eastern coast is a major area for the yachting industry. The main agencies for recruitment and training are the following:

- Global Crew Network (tel: 00 44 7773 361959; e-mail: info@globalcrew network.com; website: **www.globalcrewnetwork.com**);
- Yacht Engineers (tel: 00 34 971 28 18 13; e-mail: info@yachtengineers. net; website: **www.yachtengineers.net**);
- Fred Dovaston (tel: 00 34 971 67 73 75; e-mail: fred@dovaston.com; website: **www.yachtjob.com**);
- **www.yachtingpages.com**;
- Viking Recruitment (tel: 00 44 1304 240881; e-mail: info@viking recruitment.com; website: **www.vikingrecruitment.com**);
- Crew Network Worldwide (tel: 00 34 971 40 28 78; e-mail: palma@crew network.com.

Specialist accommodation agents for crew include Crew Accommodation: Homefinders, Majorca (tel: 00 34 64 777 47 25; e-mail: homefinders@ocea.es.

Domestic staff

Agencies include Greycoat International (tel: 00 44 20 7233 9950; e-mail: info@greycoatplacements.co.uk; website: **www.greycoatplacements.co.uk**).

Nursing

See **www.graduatenurse.com**.

Journalism

A number of journalists operate out of Spain. English-language publications in Spain pay only very low rates, and accordingly foreign journalists in Spain make most of their earnings elsewhere, with many also teaching English as a foreign language to supplement their earnings. Spanish VAT is not strictly payable on contributions to magazines, though some publications prefer contributors to charge VAT.

Summer and seasonal work

There is a wide range of summer jobs available in Spain (and a small number of jobs in ski resorts during the winter months). They include sports instructors (especially water sports), crew and service staff for yachts, courier work, hotel and restaurant staff, gardening, representatives of timeshare companies, representatives for tour operators, bar work, shop assistants, fruit and grape picking, and distributing leaflets at major resorts (often relating to timeshares, or nightclubs). One major tour operator that is expanding from its base in Coventry and its new base at the Robin Hood Doncaster-Sheffield airport is Thomsonfly. Websites that are worth taking a look at are **www.overseasjob.com**, **www.summerjobs.com** and **www.resortjobs.com**. A particularly useful book is *Summer Jobs Abroad*, published by Vacation Work.

Au pairs

In return for food, accommodation with a family, and a modest sum by way of pocket money, au pairs carry out housework and look after children. Au pairs report very varied experiences, with some fortunate enough to be treated extremely well but others being expected to work very long hours and subjected to rudeness and cruelty. There are a number of agencies that carry out checks on families before placing you, and are available for you to contact once in Spain. They also often organize language classes in Spanish and other educational or cultural activities, which prevent au pairs feeling too isolated.

You should if at all possible meet the family with whom you are to live before committing yourself. If you are an EU citizen you have the option of waiting until you arrive in Spain. You should not have any difficulty finding a position, as there is a strong demand for au pairs. If you are from a non-EU country you will need a job offer to show to the Spanish embassy or consulate in your home country in order to obtain your visa. A family taking on an au pair must inform the Spanish social security authorities and make contributions on your behalf. This will enable you to obtain healthcare under the Spanish state health system.

Once you start, if you find that you are being poorly treated, leave! Never mind that you signed a contract for six months or a year. It is highly unlikely that an employer is going to take you to court, and even if he or she did, you should have a good defence, as the employer will have almost certainly broken your agreement first by his or her conduct towards you. Au pairs are frequently in short supply, and accordingly an agency should be able to find another position for you. Always have the means to get back home. If necessary, your parents or a third party can pay your air fare back home, and if you are *really* stuck you may able to persuade the nearest British consulate to lend you the air fare home.

Voluntary work

Volunteers generally have to be over 16, or even 18, but usually under 30. The work is often physically demanding (much of the work is on archaeological or conservation projects) and unpaid. Board and lodging are provided (although you may be expected to contribute towards them), and living conditions are frequently fairly primitive. Participants pay their own travel costs, insurance and health cover. Do not bank on having an immersion in Spanish; the common language is frequently English. Handicapped volunteers are often welcome.

General websites in English

- **www.europa.eu.int/jobs/eures.**
- **www.webseurope.com.**
- **www.exposure-eu.com.**
- **www.elsunnews.com.**
- **www.eurojobs.com.**
- **www.jobpilot.es** (in English).
- **www.britishchamberspain.com** – jobs selection worth looking at.
- **www.spainexpat.com** – a very useful site for links to many different sites, including job websites.
- **www.segundmano.es** – a Madrid classifieds newspaper published on Monday, Wednesday and Friday. It has a wide range of classified advertisements. While the paper is in Spanish, you will find, and can place, ads in English.
- **www.overseasjobs.com** – for overseas employment.
- **www.surinenglish.com** – good selection of jobs, especially on the Costa del Sol.
- **www.absolute-marbella.com** – small selection of jobs on the Costa del Sol.
- **www.marbellaguide.com** – selection of jobs on the Costa del Sol.
- **www.costadelsolnews.es** – small selection of jobs on the Costa del Sol.

- **www.costablanca-news.com** – small selection of jobs on the Costa Blanca.
- **www.spainview.com** – information site for freelance journalists.
- **www.spanish-living.com** – includes a selection of jobs, also property and rentals.
- **www.e4s.co.uk** – specializes in employment for students in the United Kingdom and abroad. Carry out a job search for 'abroad'.
- **www.expatexchange.com** – a selection of jobs.
- **www.escapeartist.com** – a selection of jobs and also information and resources for living in Spain.
- **www.tbs.com.es** – *The Broadsheet*. Ads for Madrid, Catalonia, Andalusia, Valencia and Murcia, including rentals and some jobs.
- **www.costadealmeria.co.uk** – an information and community website that gives details of property services, local newspapers, schools and rentals. It has a link to a local paper, *The Advertiser*, that has a selection of jobs, mainly in bars and restaurants.
- **www.justlanded.com** – some jobs.
- **www.wemploy.com** (English and Spanish) – a company that specializes in finding work for expats on the Costa del Sol and Costa Blanca.
- **www.RecruitSpain.com** – a recruitment company helping predominantly UK candidates find employment on the coast.
- **www.tecnoempleo.com** – lists jobs in IT and telecommunications.

Websites in Spanish

- *Instituto Nacional de Empleo*, **www.inem.es**.
- Ministry of Labour and Social Affairs, **www.mtas.es**.
- **www.trabajo.org**.
- **www.infojobs.net**.
- **www.abctrabajo.com**.
- **www.monster.es** – one of Spain's most-used sites for jobs. In Spanish, but you can search instead under **www.jobsearch.monster.co.uk**. Look under 'Search Europe' and go to the region of Spain that interests you.
- **http://www.segundamano.es** – popular Spanish site for a good range of jobs. There are also ads in English for teachers of English. Go to *trabajo* on the left-hand side of the homepage and look under *secciones*.
- **www.infoempleoes** – includes job advertisements and information on training, education and grants.
- **www.todotrabajo.com** – job vacancies and advice.
- **www.tecnoemplecom** – IT and telecommunications.

Working on the black market (*economía sumergida*)

There are large numbers of foreigners and Spaniards working illegally in Spain, especially in the construction, farming and the various service industries, notably tourism. As with other forms of tax abuse, the Spanish authorities have for some time been enforcing the law, and fines have been imposed on numerous employers and indeed employees. Employees working illegally have no rights to health cover or other benefits provided by the state.

Once you have your job offer

If you are offered a job, ensure that you understand the terms of the contract before signing it. Check about relocation expenses, arrangements for accommodation, and what documentation you will require to open a bank account into which your salary can be paid.

Once you have obtained employment, your employer should register you with the social security authorities; it is illegal to work in Spain without being registered, and your employer can be fined upwards of 3,000 euros for failing to register you. The social security authorities will send you a health card (*tarjeta sanitaria*). Your dependants will be covered under your registration. Non-EU citizens must ensure that they obtain a *tarjeta comunitaria*, or permit, at the local *Delegado de Trabajo*, or a police station. You will need your contract of employment, passport, social security card, a medical certificate (which is available from a medical centre and simply states that you have no contagious diseases) and four passport-sized photographs. The permit is issued for one year, after which it should be renewed every five years. Along with the permit you will be given a tax identification number.

Income tax

The vast majority of employees in Spain do not need to complete a tax return, which is generally only required for those earning above a certain limit. Instead, the authorities send employees an assessment of their tax liability each year, and their tax liability is then met by deductions made by their employers from their salaries, with any (usually minor) adjustments made at the end of April each year. Further details in relation to income tax are to be found in Chapter 6.

Your social security contributions

The earnings threshold for social security contributions is 525 euros a month. For an employee on that level of earnings, the contributions are based on a little under 30 per cent of his or her salary. Most of this contribution is paid by the employer. A salaried worker needs to have had contributions paid into the system for 35 years before he or she becomes entitled to the full state pension.

The contract of employment: your rights and obligations

Traditionally, Spanish law has provided considerable protection for employees, including in relation to redundancy and dismissal. In recent years the level of protection has been lowered to increase the flexibility in the labour market. Most *new* employment contracts are now short-term contracts under which employees receive little employment protection. Indeed, the European Economic and Social Committee of the European Union has called on Spain to reduce the number of temporary work contracts issued. Most young people under 25 are employed on such contracts of one year's duration. Employers are entitled to offer subsequent one-year contracts to such employees, up to a maximum of three years. After that, the employer must either offer a permanent position or dismiss the employee, which the employer can do without any financial penalty, provided he or she does so within the three-year period.

The contract of employment

The contract of employment (*contrato de trabajo*) is an agreement between an employer and employee under which the employee agrees to carry out certain tasks in return for a wage or salary. To enter into such an agreement the employee should generally either be aged 18 or above or have the consent of his or her parents or guardian. A contract of employment does not have to be in writing; an oral agreement is sufficient. In Spain, however, the law requires that certain contracts *must* be in writing. These are contracts under which the employee is essentially receiving practical work experience or training, contracts for specific purposes, part-time and fixed-term contracts, contracts under which the employee works at home, and contracts for employees taken on in Spain for Spanish companies abroad.

If a contract does not state its duration, as may be the case with an oral contract, for example, Spanish law assumes that it is of indefinite duration (and hence fully protected, unless there is evidence to the contrary).

Even for contracts of employment for an indefinite duration, employers often insist on a probationary period. To be effective in reducing the employer's obligations, this must be recorded in writing, and must be for no more than two months (six months for technical personnel). During the probationary period the employer (or the employee) is entitled to terminate the contract without giving any reason, and within any period of notice (unless the contract states otherwise). Whilst on probation the employee is entitled to the same rights and subject to the same obligations as if he or she were part of the permanent workforce. The period of probation counts towards his or her length of service.

The terms in the contract

The terms in the contract should include the names of the parties, the start date, the duration (if temporary), the workplace where the employee will work or be based, the employee's professional category or a job description, and the basic wage or salary and additional benefits. It should also record the number of ordinary work hours required per week and the times at which the employee will be required to work, holiday entitlement, and the period of notice required. Lastly, the agreement should identify any collective agreement applicable to the employment relationship.

Protection provided by Spanish law

Spanish labour law provides substantial protection for employees. Should your employer wish to make any of the changes below, you should seek the immediate advice of a trade union representative, or obtain advice from some other appropriate source. There are special regulations governing certain categories of employment, including professional sportspeople, disabled people with a recognized invalidity of 33 per cent or more and who carry out their work in special employment centres, and company directors who in reality own their company. Similarly, there are separate rules relating to artists, commercial representatives who do not work on their employer's premises and are not subject to their employer's hours of work, seafarers and dock workers. Household domestic employees are also governed by different rules (for example, those who work by the hour are entitled to a minimum of 3.59 euros per hour worked, without any further payment for holidays and the 'extra' two months – see below under 'Remuneration'.

An employer is entitled to make changes to the employment contract provided such changes are justified and provided that he or she complies with the requirements of Spain's employment legislation. If an employer wishes a worker to carry out duties of a lower category, the employer must continue to pay the employee the same salary. On the other hand, if an employer requires an employee to carry out duties of a higher category for more than six months in a year, or eight months in two years, the employee is entitled to request a promotion.

As to relocation, Spanish law provides that for a transfer requiring a change of residence, or when there is a temporary move lasting for more than 12 months in a three-year period, the employer must give the worker 30 days' notice of the move. The employer is also required to compensate the employee for the costs incurred. The employee is not obliged to accept this change, and can instead elect to terminate the contract, in which case he or she is entitled to receive 20 days' compensation for each year worked (up to a maximum of 12 monthly payments).

In relation to other significant changes in the contract involving remuneration, working hours, timetable and shift patterns, and work performance, an employer is obliged to give employees 30 days' notice of the change and pay compensation for any costs incurred. Again, the employee is not obliged to agree, and can choose to leave, in which case he or she is entitled to receive 20 days' compensation for each year of his or her employment (subject to a maximum of nine monthly payments).

The Spanish state guarantees the payments to workers, including compensation for dismissal or termination of an employee's contract of employment, and wages still owing when an employer becomes insolvent or bankrupt or enters into an arrangement with creditors.

The minimum wage

Spanish law provides for a minimum wage (*salario mínimo interprofesional*, SMI). It is unlawful for employers to pay less. In 2004 the SMI for all workers was 460.50 euros per month (15.35 euros per day). This daily rate does not include Sundays or holidays. The SMI for part-time employment is reduced pro rata. There is a minimum annual salary (including bonuses) of 6,447 euros. There are also General Wages Councils in various sectors of the economy that fix adequate salary levels for different groups of workers.

Remuneration

Remuneration is provided for in the contract of employment, but may also be the subject of collective bargaining. In addition to a basic salary, workers often have fringe benefits related to length of service or consisting of bonuses, profit-sharing, distance and transport bonuses, workplace bonuses for difficulty of work, unsocial hours, dangers involved or for quality or quantity of production.

Employees must be paid at intervals not exceeding one month, and be given a clearly itemized payslip. The employer is required to deduct tax and social security contributions.

Salary is usually paid by way of 12 monthly payments. In addition, employees receive at least two extra payments per annum: one at Christmas and the other generally in the summer. Entitlement to these additional payments, known as *pagas extraordinarias* (but in fact they are *normally* paid), should be provided for in your contract of employment. Casual or temporary workers who have been employed by the same employer for less than 120 days are entitled (apart from the minimum daily wage) to a proportionate part of the payment for Sundays and public holidays. They also receive the two additional payments, equivalent to 30 days' salary. This is subject to a minimum of 21.80 euros per day (in 2004).

The average monthly salary is about 1,500 euros. (An IT professional can expect to earn a little over twice this amount.)

Working time

Spanish law lays down a number of stipulations in relation to working time. The maximum working week is limited to an average of 40 hours per week over a 12-month period. Employees should not normally work in excess of nine hours per day, except where this has been agreed as part of a collective agreement. Employees younger than 18 may not work for more than eight hours per day. Working time must be distributed fairly evenly throughout the year, unless a more irregular distribution has been agreed as part of a collective agreement.

Workers must receive at least 12 hours' rest between one working day and the next, and a minimum weekly rest of 1½ days of uninterrupted rest (two uninterrupted days for those under 18). When a working day exceeds 6 hours, workers must be given a rest period of at least 15 minutes. Employees aged less than 18 must receive a 30-minute break once a working day exceeds 4½ hours.

Women workers receive up to one hour off work for feeding a child under nine months of age (this time can be taken by the father instead, if both parents are working). Both men and women have an entitlement to a reduction in their work time of between one-third and one-half if they have direct responsibility for a child under six or a disabled person or member of their family in one of a prescribed set of circumstances.

As to overtime, the law provides that this is voluntary, unless the subject of an agreement to the contrary, or is to carry out emergency work. Overtime is limited to 80 hours per year. Employees under 18 may not carry out overtime at night, and overtime at night is also subject to substantial restrictions for adult employees.

In Spain the working day is generally 9.30 am to 1.30 pm and 4.30 pm to 7.30 pm. However, foreign businesses and a growing number of Spanish companies expect their workforce to work from 9.00 am to 6.00 am with an hour for lunch.

The basic normal working week is 40 hours, and there is entitlement to one month's holiday in addition to 14 statutory holidays. Employees should be paid an additional 40 per cent for overtime, with double time on Sundays and statutory holidays.

Holidays

Employees are entitled to time off of a minimum of 30 calendar days. This entitlement cannot be replaced by a financial payment. Employers are required to give an employee at least two months' notice before the dates allocated for time off. Disputes as to the timing of holidays can be resolved by application to the courts.

There are up to 14 public holidays a year, including Christmas Day, New Year's Day, 1 May (Labour Day) and 12 October (the Spanish National Day) – see Appendix 8 for a fuller list. Public holidays that naturally fall on a Sunday are moved to the Monday. The autonomous regions have power to replace some of the public holidays (save those listed above) with public holidays of their own.

When a public holiday falls on a Tuesday or a Thursday, employers often declare the previous or subsequent day a holiday also, thereby giving employees a long weekend.

If a company shuts down during the summer, its employees are required to take their holiday entitlement at the same time.

Retirement and pensions

Relatively few Spanish employers offer a pension scheme over and above the state pension. Payments to a company pension are deductible up to a maximum of about 9,000 euros per year (though the limit is higher for older employees). There is no compulsory retirement age.

Travel expenses

Travel expenses to and from your workplace are deductible against tax.

Restrictions imposed by employers

In Spain, most employers do not permit their staff who are employed full time to take on another post, although they are unlikely to object to employees teaching on a part-time basis. As in other countries, employees owe a duty of confidentiality to their employers in relation to information that they learn in the course of their employment, including trade secrets and client lists. Contracts often include restrictive covenants that prevent an employee from working with another company in the same type of business within a defined geographical area and for a fixed period of time. Employers are entitled to protect their interests in this way, but often such clauses are too onerous and may not necessarily be enforceable. You should take legal advice if you are considering setting up on your own, or working for another employer and suspect that you may be in breach of such a provision.

Leave

Employees are entitled to paid time off for marriage (15 days) and the birth of a child (2 days). The same applies to a death, accident or serious illness or hospitalization of blood relations or relations by marriage up to second degree (2 days, or 4 if they have to travel), moving house (1 day), and for unavoidable public duties (such as jury service).

The mother or father of a child born prematurely, or who must remain in hospital for any reason following the birth, is entitled to one hour off per day during this period. The parents may reduce their working day by up to a maximum of two hours, with a proportional reduction in wages.

A legal guardian responsible for a child under six or for a person who is physically or psychologically disabled or partially sighted or with hearing difficulties but who does not him- or herself carry out paid work is entitled to a reduction in working time. This is subject to a proportional reduction in wages of between one-third and half for the duration.

Sickness leave

Employees are protected when they are unable to work and need medical care as a result of an illness or accident, whether or not work related. To benefit when suffering from a common illness, the employee must have paid 180 days' contributions during the five years immediately prior to taking absence due to illness. Sickness benefit is payable for up to 12 months only, with a possibility of a six-month extension.

Maternity and paternity leave

A woman is entitled to maternity leave of up to 16 consecutive weeks, with an additional two weeks per second child and subsequent child in the case of multiple births. A mother must take 6 of these weeks immediately after the birth, but can choose when to take the other 10 weeks. If both parents work, they have the right to elect for the father to take some time off after the birth.

A mother is also entitled to up to 16 consecutive weeks' leave if she adopts or fosters a child under six years of age, with a further two weeks for each subsequent child in the case of multiple adoption or fostering. The time off is to be taken either from the administrative or legal decision on fostering, or from the court judgment establishing adoption. The right to 16 weeks' leave also applies where adopted children are over six but are disabled, or where they have particular difficulties socializing or are foreign and have particular problems integrating into Spanish social and family life. Where parents are adopting or hoping to adopt a child from abroad, they are entitled to take up to 4 of these 16 weeks prior to the decision that will allow them to adopt a child, to permit them to travel.

Employers receive various reductions in their social security contributions in relation to employees taken on to replace women on maternity leave.

Extended leave of absence

Workers who take an extended leave of absence, and who have been employed for at least one year, have a right to be given priority over a period of between two and five years should a vacancy arise. Employees are permitted to take extended leave to care for members of their family. This is for up to three years for each child, including adopted and fostered children. There is also a right to extended leave of absence to look after a blood relative or relation by marriage (up to the second degree) who is unable to look after him- or herself, or work. This is limited to one year. Employers receive reductions in their liability for social security contributions in respect of staff taken on to cover for those taking leave to care for family members.

End of the contract of employment

The end of the contract of employment can come about as a result of mutual agreement, according to the terms originally agreed in the contract, the expiry of the contract for a fixed term or a given purpose, resignation, or death or serious invalidity or retirement. It can also arise as a result of natural disasters, redundancy, dismissal or constructive dismissal (where an employee justifiably leaves his or her employment in response to unacceptable conduct on the part of the employer).

Redundancy

If an employer wishes to make an employee redundant on economic grounds or because of a material change in his or her business, the employer must adopt the procedure prescribed by law. The employer has to present his or her case for a redundancy to the employment authorities by presenting a restructuring plan, and the employee must be given the opportunity to respond to the employer's case for dismissal. The employee may only be dismissed if the plan is approved by the employment authorities. If dismissed, the employee is entitled to 20 days' salary for each year of his or her employment, up to a maximum of 12 months' salary.

Dismissal

An employer can dismiss a worker for continued albeit justified absences, or for poor performance, but is required to pay compensation equal to 20 days' salary for each year of service, up to a maximum of 12 months' salary.

An employer is entitled to discipline employees for misconduct including physical or verbal abuse, fighting, theft, disobedience, drunkenness, breach of confidence, etc. Disciplinary action can include written and verbal warnings, and, in the case of continued breaches or a single serious breach, dismissal. The employer must give written notice of the dismissal, stating the cause and the date of dismissal.

The employee who is dismissed and who wishes to challenge his or her employer's action has the right to invoke a conciliation process. Indeed, this is a prerequisite for bringing a claim before the Social Court. Requests for conciliation should be made within 20 working days (only Sundays and public holidays are excluded for the purposes of calculating this time limit) of the dismissal. This time limit is very short, and accordingly advice should be sought from a trade union representative, lawyer or other competent adviser as soon as possible after dismissal, or before if dismissal is threatened or anticipated.

Efforts are initially made to reach a compromise and to settle the employee's claim. If no agreement is reached, then the employee must bring a claim to the Social Court. This should be done as a matter of urgency, as the time limit is 20 days *from the dismissal*. The application can be lodged by the employee him- or herself, or by a lawyer. If an agreement is reached, the employer and the employee must both abide by it. If either party breaches the agreement, the other may bring legal proceedings to enforce the agreement.

If an employer is found to have unfairly dismissed an employee, he or she is liable to pay damages amounting to the pay the employee would have received from the date of the dismissal to the date of the final hearing. The employer must also pay damages for future losses consisting of 33 days' salary per year of employment up to a maximum salary equivalent to three years six months (for someone with over 35 years' service).

The law provides for lower levels of compensation for those in positions of management, though in practice employment contracts for higher-paid staff often contain a provision for enhanced levels of compensation for breach of contract, above the levels referred to above for other employees.

The employment of women

Women receive an allowance of 1,200 euros per year and a reduction of 1,200 euros of income tax per year if they have children under three years old and are self-employed or employees. Entitlement is limited to those who are registered with the social security authorities or have a corresponding Mutual Insurance scheme. Application is made on Form 140, which is available from any offices of the *Agencia Tributaria* (Tax Agency), to where it must be returned once completed.

When employing women over 25, employers benefit from a reduced liability for social security contributions, with the liability reduced further in the case of women over 45, and a further reduction again for those over 55. There is an additional reduction when employing a woman from an underrepresented group, and also reduced liability for social security contributions for women who are self-employed.

Notwithstanding the above provisions, women still face considerable difficulty, especially in obtaining part-time work. The European Union has asked Spain to increase the number of part-time contracts, which would go some way towards reducing the marked differences in unemployment between the sexes.

Workers under 18

It is illegal to employ children under 16, and is a criminal offence, though an employer is still required to pay the child for any work performed. Parental consent is required for the employment of those aged between 16 and 18. Workers under 18 may not work at night (ie between 10 pm and 6 am), work overtime, or be engaged in any employment considered unhealthy, requiring heavy labour, or dangerous.

Disabled workers

In Spain, physically and mentally handicapped people are protected in the Constitution. This protection has been given concrete form in the Act on the Social Integration of the Disabled. This provides for subsidies to ensure minimum levels of income and for assistance with the cost of transportation. A disabled person is defined as someone who has a disability assessed at 33 per cent or above. Employers must not directly or indirectly discriminate against disabled workers. Public authorities or commercial businesses employing more than 50 workers are required by law to allocate at least 2 per cent of their posts to disabled workers. In addition, the Spanish authorities provide subsidies to employers in relation to disabled workers, reductions in their social security contributions, and assistance in the provision of vocational training.

The state grants a subsidy of 3,906.58 euros and a 70 per cent reduction in employer's social security contributions for the employment of a disabled woman aged under 45, and a 90 per cent reduction for older women. Reductions are also applicable to part-time female employees. In addition, employers can apply for a payment of 901.52 euros for alterations to the employee's job and for training. The employer can also set an amount equivalent to these two subsidies against corporation tax.

Protection against sexual harassment

If you are a woman and believe that you have been subject to harassment on the grounds of your sex, you have a right to bring a complaint. This should be addressed to the *Instituto de la Mujer* (Institute for Women) or to the Institute's *Centros de Información de los Derechos de la Mujer* (Women's Rights Information Centres), with offices in Madrid, Santander and Seville. There is also a national 24-hour help line for women, available free of charge. Advice and information are available on legal and practical issues (tel: 900 19 10 10; 900 15 21 52 for the hard of hearing).

Discrimination

Spanish law prohibits sexual and racial discrimination, and also discrimination on the grounds of age, marital status, language, religious and political beliefs, trade union membership and disability.

Workers from other member states of the European Union are entitled to the same rights and benefits as Spanish nationals. These include the right to school education and to employment training courses, and access to public or subsidized housing. Spain may not impose unnecessary hurdles or conditions on access to employment or any rights or benefits that indirectly discriminate against nationals of other member states.

Employee representation

All employees have a right to join a trade union, and also rights to participate in decision-making via personnel representatives and works committees.

Trade unions

Whilst less than 15 per cent of the Spanish workforce is unionized, the trade unions in Spain exercise considerable influence in wage negotiations. The two main unions are the *Union General de Trabajadores* (*UGT*) and the *Comisiones Obreras* (*CCO*).

Work disputes

Employees can be represented either by a personal representative (companies with fewer than 50 employees) or by a member of a Works Committee or by a trade union representative if the trade union is active either in the company or in the relevant industrial sector.

Spanish law imposes a restriction on the right of workers to collectively withdraw their labour (ie to strike). Those who do not wish to participate in a strike have the right not to do so. Those who are responsible for essential safety and maintenance may be required to work through the strike. In Spanish law, a contract of employment is considered to be temporarily suspended during a strike. Workers will not be paid, and are not entitled to unemployment benefit.

Sources of advice on employment issues

Advice on employment rights and the General Wages Agreements can be obtained from trade unions and also from the Social-Labour Office, Administrative Information Subdepartment, Agustinde Bethercourt 11, 28071 Madrid (tel: 91 553 62 78).

5 Starting and running a business in Spain

Setting up a new business in your home country is fraught with difficulties. Most new businesses fail in the first 12 months as a result of a variety of problems associated with inexperience, lack of planning, changing market conditions and plain bad luck. A major problem is lack of liquidity or cash flow, caused by overly optimistic sales forecasts and the underestimating of start-up costs. Non-EU nationals intending to set up business in Spain must provide investment funds of at least 120,000 euros and create work for Spanish or other EU citizens.

Those seeking to set up business in Spain face additional hurdles:

■ You will be operating in a foreign land in which, to begin with at least, there will be more unknowns as a result of not being in your native surroundings. Furthermore, your business may not prosper unless it has a broad enough appeal to attract the local Spanish population, and/or other non-English speakers.
■ To a greater or lesser extent you will be operating in a foreign language. Even if your clientele is mainly English speaking, your suppliers may not be, and your dealings with public officials and bodies will be in Spanish.
■ Taken together, the taxation and social security burden on businesses is higher than in the United Kingdom.
■ Bureaucracy is acknowledged by the Spanish themselves to be very burdensome for businesses.

It is vital that you carry out substantial research before committing yourself. There are many Britons and other Europeans in Spain who have had to face financial ruin due to the failure of their business project, in many cases because of lack of planning and a refusal to appreciate that their plan was doomed to failure from the outset.

A substantial number of businesses rely on the expatriate British and other English-speaking communities, including bars, English bookshops, local newspapers, financial advisers, estate agents, suppliers of UK and US food and other produce, security, and services relating to the yachting industry. Nevertheless, as a foreigner, you, or your business partner, will need to speak Spanish to a reasonable level or at least have a business adviser who is fluent in both languages. Your adviser must be familiar with matters of finance and have (not merely claim to have) substantial experience of advising businesses in Spain.

There are various agencies that provide help and assistance in establishing a business. Prior to leaving the United Kingdom, you could contact the Spanish Embassy (Commercial Office) at 22 Manchester Square, London W1M 5AP (tel: 020 7486 0101) and/or the Legal Department of the Spanish Embassy at 24 Belgrave Square, London SW1X 8QA. A number of government booklets are available in English, including 'A Guide to Business in Spain', 'Forms of Business Organisations' and 'Labour Legislation'. Take a look at the Spanish government website **www.investinspain.org** and also the websites of the British and American Chambers of Commerce in Spain: **www.britishchamberspain.com** and **www.amchamspain.com**. The Chambers organize seminars, conferences, discussions and workshops, and are vital sources of information and contacts for those carrying out business in Spain. The British Chamber is based in Barcelona at Calle Bruc 21, 08010 Barcelona (tel: 933 17 32 20; e-mail enquiries to the director, Sarah-Jane Stone: britchamber@britchamber.com), but also has representation in Madrid, Bilbao and Zaragoza. Assistance can also be obtained from Barclays Bank (**www.barclays.es**) or Lloyds TSB Bank (**www.lloydtsb.com**). Barclays has branches in Madrid, Barcelona, Bilbao, Seville and Valencia, but following its recent acquisition of Banco Zaragozano, Barclays is set to treble its existing customer base and branch network in Spain. Lloyds TSB has branches in Madrid, Barcelona, the Canary Islands, Bilbao, Marbella, Majorca, Navarra and Seville.

Once in Spain, you should contact the local Spanish chamber of commerce. The main office in Madrid is *Consejo Superior de las Camaras de Comercio, Industria y Navegación*, C/Velazquez 157, E-2802 Madrid (tel: 91 590 69 00: website: **www.camerdata.es**). Ask what other help and assistance is available. In some areas, chambers of commerce run courses in English on how to set up a business.

To counter the difficulties of dealing with bureaucracy, all provinces now have a one-stop centre for businesses (*ventanilla única*) at which all the documentation required of a new business can be submitted together, and from which you can obtain advice about administrative requirements. The address of your local office can be found at **www.ventanillaempre sarial.org**.

According to a recent conference in Seville, the start-up costs for a small or medium-sized business in Spain amount to only 1,500 euros, far below the European average cost of 5,120 euros. Furthermore, the average time for the setting up of a business in Spain was one of the shortest, with an average of only 15 days being required. These figures, however, are averages and in reality, as a foreigner, you are likely to find that the costs and time required are greater, although with the correct professional advice you are likely to find it easier to set up business in Spain than, for example, in neighbouring France.

You should find a competent chartered accountant and/or commercial lawyer to advise on what form your business should take, to assist with the necessary formalities and to advise you on your standard contract terms. He or she can also advise you about the latest financial and other support available to businesses (there is an extensive array of subsidies, grants and tax incentives). It is vital that you choose someone with experience of doing business in Spain (see Appendix 1 for details of some practitioners). An essential source of help and advice is the *gestor* (see Chapter 7), who is well qualified to guide you through the bureaucratic nightmares and help with much of the paperwork that you will be required to complete. His or her charges should be relatively modest.

Whilst any citizen of an EU country is entitled to live and work in Spain, a self-employed person, or *autónomo*, must also obtain a permit, as well as pay into the Spanish social security system, though on a different basis from an employee. A number of occupations – from doctor to hairdresser – are subject to specific restrictions and regulations, so you will need to make enquiries of the relevant professional body. It is fair to say, however, that such professionals now find it very much easier than in the past to have their qualifications recognized, and to establish themselves in Spain. Self-employed people from the United Kingdom who may need to have their experience certified should contact the Department of Trade and Industry for a guidance pack (Certificate of Experience Unit, DTI European Policy Directorate, Bay 211/212 Kingsgate House, 66–74 Victoria Street, London SW1E 6SW; tel: 020 7215 4648).

If you undertake two or more unrelated part-time jobs, you will find yourself having to submit different sets of paperwork for each, and you may find yourself paying social security contributions in respect of each.

In order to establish yourself, you must:

■ Register at the local police station or *Delegación de Trabajo*. To do this, you will need your certificates establishing your professional qualifications, your passport and a photocopy, four photographs, and your lease (*ecritura*) for your business premises.

■ Register at the *Hacienda* for payment of the *impuesta de actividades economicas* (a licence, but in reality a tax on economic activity). This tax is only payable when your turnover exceeds 600,000 euros, but you still need to register and obtain your code).

■ Register at the local office of the social security authorities as a self-employed person. Monthly contributions start at a little over 200 euros.

■ Obtain a licence for the opening of any business premises.

I would strongly advise that you instruct a *gestor* at the outset, as he or she is likely to save you a considerable amount of time and unnecessary stress. The following vehicles are available for the running of a business:

■ As a sole trader (*empresa individual*). As in the United Kingdom, a sole trader is personally liable for the business's debts and losses. You must of course also join the relevant trade association.

■ In partnership. Again, partners remain personally liable.

■ As a limited liability company (*sociedad limitada*). It is now possible for one person to form such a company. Should the business fail, the owners' liabilities are limited to the value of their shares in the company. In practice, however, it is likely that an owner will have to give some personal guarantees, for example to the company's bank, or to its landlord if it operates from rented premises. For this option, share capital of 3,000 euros is required.

■ As a *sociedad anónima* (SA). This is equivalent to a plc (public limited company) in the United Kingdom. Liability is limited to the amount of capital each investor puts into the company. Share capital of 60,000 euros is required.

■ As a branch of a foreign company.

You should seek legal and financial advice before deciding which option to adopt.

If you are contemplating the purchase of an existing business, insist on working in the business for a while before you sign anything, so that you can form your own views as to the accuracy of the turnover figures and learn the ropes prior to taking over the business.

Taxation of business

Social charges

If you are self-employed and do not employ anyone else, your social charges will cost at least 200 euros per month from the outset, and can rise to a ceiling of around 2,600 euros per month. There are penalties for late payment. Once you employ others, your social charges contributions will start to escalate. The employer's contributions are high. You should assume that once you have taken these into account and the additional two months' salary payable at Christmas and in the summer, the average total monthly cost of an employee will approach nearly twice his or her monthly salary.

Remember that it is the employer's responsibility to register his or her employees, and that employers can be fined for failure to do this. Take advice on the type of contract to offer *before* employing anyone. Remember that it may not be easy to dismiss an employee without having to pay compensation. A self-employed person is not entitled to unemployment benefit should his or her enterprise fail.

Business tax

Business tax (*impuesto sobre actividades económicas*, IAE) is payable by all businesses with a turnover in excess of 600,000. All companies and all those who are self-employed are nevertheless required to register, even if their turnover does not reach this level.

Company/corporation tax

The principles of corporate taxation in Spain are the same as in the rest of the European Union. The standard rate of corporation tax (*impuesto sobre sociedades*, IBI) is 35 per cent, but 30 per cent for small and medium-sized businesses, both partnerships and limited companies; a large proportion of enterprises fit into this category. Businesses in the Canary Islands pay a maximum of only 5 per cent, however. Tax evasion is widespread, and the government is committed to making major changes to the corporate tax system.

When deciding on investing in the business by purchasing substantial assets, such as a computer system, you should note that not all the costs are deductible against tax in the year in which they are purchased. The cost of such assets will be spread over a number of years and only a proportion will be deductible against tax in the year of purchase. You may wish to consider leasing equipment, whereby tax deductions are more in line with your expenditure. You should, of course, keep records of your various expenses, in order to have these deducted against the business's revenue.

VAT

All businesses are required to register for VAT (*impuesto sobre el valor añadido*, IVA), to charge VAT at 16 per cent on all supplies of goods and services, and to account to the tax authorities for these sums every three months.

Business premises

As elsewhere, a great deal of business property in Spain is leased. Like the residential tenant, the business tenant benefits from a degree of protection under the law, including a right to the renewal of his or her business lease. This right is subject to exceptions and the completion of the necessary formalities, and you should take advice from a lawyer and/or *gestor*. It is likely that the landlord will restrict the kind of business activity that may be operated from the premises. For any business premises you will also need a *licencia de apertura*, a licence permitting you to open your business. The cost of these varies, but it can be as little as 150 euros.

Bank finance

Having a business plan, in Spanish, is essential if you are to obtain a bank loan to finance your business. You will need to provide an assessment of the demand for your product or service, likely revenue, assets being introduced into the business, your fixed and variable costs and some cash flow forecasts. Banco Bilbao Vizcaya Argentaria (BBVA) has recently launched new fixed-rate loans for small and medium-sized businesses. As loans are at historic lows, it is perhaps a good time for businesses to agree fixed rates to limit future financial costs.

State aid and other assistance

There are various subsidized loans, grants and subsidies available from the European Union and central, regional and local government, particularly in the less prosperous regions. In addition, there are several tax incentives and allowances in the early years of a business. Five companies have recently established a small and medium-sized businesses modernization programme: the Spanish bank Bankinter, the Spanish company Informática El Corte Inglés (the information technology subsidiary of the Spanish retailer El Corte Inglés), the US computer maker IBM, the Spanish software developer SP and the Spanish telecommunications company Telefonica. They have together initiated a programme for promoting the use of high technologies in small and medium-sized enterprises in Spain. The initiative is aimed at companies with 1–250 employees and with an annual turnover of 40 million euros or less (95 per cent of all Spanish companies). The scheme provides software, hardware and telecommunications technologies.

Insurance

It is mandatory for businesses to have insurance cover for their vehicles, health insurance for their employees and property insurance. The notification period for claims is very short.

For further information on establishing a business in Spain, contact UK Trade and Investment, Kingsgate House, 66–74 Victoria Street, London SW1E 6SW (tel: 020 7215 5000) or take a look at the websites **www.uk tradeinvest.gov.uk** and **www.ukinspain.com**.

6 Income tax and social security contributions

Liability to pay Spanish taxes

You are considered resident in Spain for tax purposes if:

- you spend 183 days or more in Spain during a calendar year; or
- your main centre of business is in Spain; or
- your spouse and dependent children (assuming you are not legally separated) usually live in Spain and have residence permits.

In the latter case it is open to you to argue that you are not resident in Spain, but this would only be possible in rare cases.

Income tax (*impuesto sobre la renta de las personas físicas*, IRPF, or *La Renta*)

Income tax rates and social charges have increased substantially over the past 10–15 years. In the past, tax evasion was rife and the authorities did little to enforce tax legislation. The climate has changed, however, and the authorities now can and do impose steep fines for non-payment.

The vast majority of salaried employees in Spain do not need to complete a tax return. This is generally only required for those earning above a certain limit (in the region of 23,000 euros). Instead, the authorities send employees an assessment of their tax liability each year, and their tax liability is then met by deductions made by their employers from their salaries, with any (usually minor) adjustments made at the end of April each year.

Annual income tax declarations must be filed between 1 May and 20 June. This applies to residents and non-residents. You are required to pay either the whole amount, or 60 per cent when filing your tax return, with the balance to be paid by November. Any delay in submitting the form, even a very short delay, will result in a surcharge of 20 per cent. Those with worldwide annual income of less than 8,000 euros need not make a tax declaration or pay income tax unless they are self-employed. Pensions are taxed on the same basis as salaries. There are three different income tax forms depending on the type of income you receive. They can be obtained from tobacconists for a minimal fee or from your tax adviser or local tax office (*hacienda*).

Whilst the forms are accompanied by explanatory leaflets, most people who need to file tax returns find it helpful to obtain assistance, at least for their first Spanish tax declaration. Help is available from your local tax office, where staff may speak sufficient English, or from a tax adviser. A fiscal representative will provide you with basic advice and lodge your tax return for as little as 70 euros.

The tax year for income tax runs from 1 January to 31 December. There are generous allowances, after which tax of 15 per cent is payable on the first 4,000 euros, rising to 45 per cent for taxable income over 45,000 euros. The income tax of a married couple is based on their joint incomes, whereas those of unmarried couples are assessed separately. The income of dependent children forms part of their parents' income for tax purposes.

If you have income from various sources, you should seriously consider seeking advice from a financial consultant with knowledge of the tax system of your home country as well as that of Spain. If you are a non-resident, and have income derived from sources in Spain, you are also required to file an income tax declaration. Non-residents who are property owners must, by law, nominate a fiscal representative who is resident in Spain to represent them vis-à-vis the Spanish authorities. You can find information about income tax and other taxes at **www.aeat.es**, though little of this is available in English.

Besides a personal allowance there are a host of different tax allowances and deductions, including:

■   social security contributions;
■   a special deduction for disabled persons that may be claimed by the disabled person him- or herself or by his or her parents or dependants;
■   for children, with additional amounts for children under three;
■   for persons aged 65 and older;
■   for those working away from home;

- contributions to private pension plans up to a maximum of between 8,000 and 24,250 euros depending upon age;
- child support payments made pursuant to a court order;
- mortgage payments;
- a proportion of the costs associated with purchasing and renovating a principal home;
- charitable donations.

Income from Spanish property, even rental paid into your UK bank account, is subject to Spanish income tax. In 2003 the government reduced the proportion of rental income subject to income tax to 50 per cent in an effort to encourage the rental market. If you are a non-resident, however, you are liable to pay income tax of 25 per cent on *all* your property rental income; the reduction introduced in 2003 applies only to residents. Residents and non-residents are entitled to deduct numerous expenses against rental income, including maintenance, security, cleaning, mortgage interest (only on Spanish loans), local taxes and insurance. In practice, many residents pay little tax on their rental income.

Income tax on imputed income from property

The Spanish tax authorities impute an income to your property (other than your principal residence, which is exempt) generally calculated at 2 per cent of the *valor catastral*. The sum is included as income in your income tax declaration, and then taxed at the individual's rate of taxation. For non-residents the tax is fixed at 25 per cent, making a tax of 0.5 per cent of the *catastral* value.

Social security contributions

Spain's social security system has a similar range of benefits to other West European states, covering old age pensions, unemployment, sickness, injuries at work, maternity, etc. Social security contributions are substantial, though nearly 85 per cent of the cost is met by employers. Social security contributions are levied on all salaries in excess of around 450 euros, with employee's contributions amounting to about 6 per cent and employers' to nearly 40 per cent. Information (in Spanish) on benefits and contributions is available on the website of the *Instituto Nacional de la Seguridad Social* at **www.seg-social.es**.

Participation in Spain's social security system is compulsory. If you are working in Spain temporarily, whether as an employee for a company based in your home state or on a self-employed basis, you can continue to pay social security contributions in your home country whilst claiming benefits in Spain. You seek reimbursement of medical expenses from the Spanish authorities. The latter then recover these sums and any other medical costs incurred from your home state.

Welcome to Southern Catalunya, a country within a country. Its capital is Barcelona. It also has its own Regional Government, language, customs, wine and food, which has allowed it to maintain quite a separate cultural identity within Spain. The climate in this area is still divided into seasons. The hottest months are July and August, with winter covering December through to February. There are many coastal bays and villages along the Costa Durada, which offer long stretches of sandy beach, calm warm seas, and traditional Catalan food - fresh fish, rice dishes, seafood, and local cooking. Also along this coastline is the Delta E'bre where the River Ebro meets the Mediterranean Sea. Here is one of the most important places for bird watching

The main town of this area is Tortosa. The city is situated on the River Ebro and is the capital of the Southern area of Catalonia. This city provides interesting historical sites, popular festivals and fairs, good accommodation in the historical Castle of "La Zuda", good restaurants and designer label shopping. The River Ebro is one of Spain's most celebrated waterways. It enters southern Catalunya from Aragon and is a fisherman's paradise with Red Mullet, Perch, Carp and the famous Catfish in abundance. Many fishermen come here to try their hand at landing some of the 100 pound or so Catfish.

Leaving the River Ebro behind we move inland through the mountains to the Terra Alta region. This region is home to around 13,000 citizens divided among the 12 villages of La Pobla de Massaluca, La Fatarella, Vilalba dels Arcs, Batea, Corbera D'Ebre, Arnes, Le Pinell de Brai, Horta de Sant Joan and Gandesa. This particular area is famous for the last major clash of the Spanish

Civil War, the battle of the Ebre, which lasted from July to September 1938. It was the single most violent encounter of the war leaving about 21,000 dead, including British soldiers.

Further in land is Horta de Sant Joan also known as "Picasso's Paradise" is an inland village in the Terres de l'Ebre. It has stunning scenery with the famous Massif of the Ports Mountains as a backdrop. Picasso stayed twice at Horta, which gave him such inspiration he is quoted as saying "everything I know I have learnt in Horta". The work, which is about 240 paintings, can be viewed in reproduction in Horta's Picasso Centre. A visit to any of these villages provides stunning landscape, historical architecture, local food and many leisure pursuits including walking, fishing, canoeing, cycling, horse riding, rock climbing and animal watching, the most common of which are Ibex, wild boar, and birds of prey. For the more gentile there are picnics by the streams, having a coffee in one of the many local bars, people watching or even a glass or two of wine.

So why come to Southern Catalonia? For a lot of people it offers them the opportunity to experience what rural Spain is all about and integrate in village life. It must be said, it is not easy to pack up and move to another country, adjustment is hard and dreams can fall through. Here at Catalunya Property Services we have been through those experiences and 3 years on are able to pass on to our clients the knowledge we have learned. We offer our clients a very high standard of professional service. We aim to meet the needs of our clients before, during and after purchase. We will give every assistance in the sales process with as much help and advice within our means.

7 Settling in

The new Spain

Over the past 40 years Spain has undergone a transformation. In the early 1960s Spain was a poor country with a mostly peasant population. With intensive foreign investment and membership of the European Community, the past 20 years especially have seen rapid economic growth. Spain is now wealthy. It boasts a substantial industrial sector (it is one of the world's largest car producers) as well as healthy agricultural and tourist industries, and has one of the highest standards of living in the world.

The tourist industry has continued to grow, with over 50 million visitors to Spain each year. The market has changed, in that many of those travelling to the Iberian Peninsula are not looking for the package holiday of sand and sun, but are increasingly visiting cultural and historic sites, inland Spain and the northern coast. Much of the agricultural sector has changed out of all recognition, with acres of land now devoted to the mass production of fruit and vegetables for the North European market, most striking in the endless stretches of plastic sheeting on the Costa de Almería.

With increasing prosperity has come improved education at all levels, as well as a shift away from traditional values and horizons in favour of greater individuality and freedom of expression. The past 20 years have also seen the availability of divorce (illegal until 1981), increasing participation of women in the labour market and in decision-making, one of the lowest birth rates in the industrialized world, and accordingly far smaller families than previously.

Spain has also undergone tremendous political changes since the death of Franco in 1975. The return of the monarchy in the form of King Juan Carlos was accompanied by the creation of a new constitution based on compromise, the right to form trade unions, the election of democratic governments, entry into the European Community and, in 1982, membership of NATO. King Juan Carlos and the royal family have proved extremely adept at winning the confidence of the nation, and the monarchy is very popular, with an estimated record 25 million watching the televised marriage of Crown Prince Felipe and his future Spanish queen, Letizia Ortiz.

Whilst Spain is almost entirely Catholic, the Church holds far less sway than in the days of Franco. Major changes have been introduced despite opposition from the clergy, not just in relation to divorce, but also abortion and even the official recognition of same-sex relationships. Not only is the influence of the Church declining, but it is having major problems recruiting new entrants, and the number of priests has declined markedly.

The political and administrative system

Spain is a parliamentary democracy. Though the king is head of state, his government is responsible to parliament. The *Cortes Generales* (the Spanish parliament) is made up of two houses or chambers, the *Congreso de los Diputados* and the *Senado*. The most important assembly is the lower chamber, the Chamber of Deputies, which draws up state budgets and controls government action. Voting is by direct secret ballot of those over 18 years of age. National elections, and indeed elections for regional and local councils, are held every four years. A key plank in the Spanish Constitution of 1978 has been the creation of the Autonomous Communities with extensive responsibilities – 17 regions and the two autonomous cities of Ceuta and Melilla in North Africa. Each of these has a separate regional government and parliament.

Cultural differences

Family and children are of great importance in Spain. In contrast to most of the English-speaking world, it is common for children to stay at home until they are 30 or older. Once married, Spaniards have found it difficult to persuade the courts to release them from each other, though recent changes to the law have made divorce far easier. The family is still of paramount importance in Spain. Traditions remain implanted in the country, with many structural organizations tending to be rather patriarchal.

Mealtimes are of major importance in Spain: they are occasions for family gatherings. Spaniards are very proud of their gastronomic inheritance, though foreigners have a rather mixed reaction!

Whilst many people in other Western countries are preoccupied and over-stressed with their work, the Spaniards have a greater emphasis on working to live, rather than living to work. Spaniards prefer a more relaxed lifestyle.

Within Spain there are significant cultural differences. Many Castilian native speakers look down on their compatriots from Galicia and the Basque Country, and indeed on those from the Castilian-speaking south, which is generally considered backward. There are also signs of hostility towards the growing numbers of British in Spain. Some Spanish state schools have large numbers of native English-speaking children who have little Spanish, and, understandably, Spanish parents feel that their own children are being held back, and that teachers are spending a disproportionate time helping foreign children. There is also an increasing irritation at the unwillingness of many British to speak Spanish, and at the growing prominence of English. In 2004 the local council in Fuengirola, on the Costa del Sol, introduced legislation requiring all external restaurant menus and signs to be written in Spanish. Apparently nearly 500 establishments had no street menu in Spanish. Failure to display a menu in Spanish is punishable with a fine of 50 euros, with persistent offenders facing court proceedings.

Culture

Spain has an immensely rich cultural past, having been influenced by many different factors throughout its tempestuous history. It has inherited an extensive historical and artistic legacy and boasts a huge number of monuments recognized as being of major historic importance. In recent history a considerable number of Spanish painters and writers have risen to fame. Spanish cinema too has had much success both in Europe and on the world stage. These factors, and the untiring efforts of the *Instituto Cervantes*, have contributed to the growing recognition of the Spanish language across the world.

The Spanish are a people who love to celebrate. In addition to national festivals such as those at Christmas and Easter, every town and city has its own patron saint whose memory will be celebrated over several days. Some of the most famous include the *San Fermines* in Pamplona, the *Fallas* in Valencia and *San Isidro* in Madrid.

Despite the dramatic changes in Spain over the past 30 years, bullfighting remains immensely popular and very much part of Spanish culture, although there are some signs of a growing but small number of Spaniards opposed to what is undoubtedly an extremely cruel form of entertainment.

Spanish bureaucracy and the *gestor*

One aspect of life in Spain that is only just beginning to change is the seemingly limitless enthusiasm of Spanish government agencies for generating paperwork and creating every conceivable kind of hurdle to undermine the smooth running of their daily contact with the public. Procedures that in other countries can be carried out speedily, or by post or telephone or over the internet, require personal attendance, often necessitating a return journey of several hours followed by hours of queuing at different counters, usually at opposite ends of the official building.

Help is at hand, however. To deal with this nightmare of administrative bureaucracy the Spaniards have created the profession of *gestor*. Licensed to advise and represent Spaniards and foreigners, he or she can greatly ease the burden of your everyday dealings with the state. The *gestor* can provide you with invaluable advice, or, better still, can handle these procedures on your behalf. His or her fee is modest. After you have spent several days pulling your hair out, you will wonder why you did not use the *gestor*'s services in the first place and spend your time in some more worthwhile pursuit. Whilst initially you may wish to rely on your lawyer for matters relating to your purchase, you should make enquiries amongst the expatriate community and any Spanish friends as to any *gestors* they would recommend.

In recent years, some municipalities in areas with large numbers of foreign residents have set up specialist foreign departments with staff who speak English and other foreign languages, and who can help you with administrative problems. Note also that many different forms are available from tobacconists, where queues are much shorter than in government buildings.

Your right to stay in Spain

Citizens of the European Union are entitled to live and work in any of the member states. No special documentation is required for your first 90 days. As of 1 March 2003, certain categories of citizens of the European Union who wish to stay in Spain for more than 90 days do *not* need to apply for a residence card. These new regulations cover employees, the self-employed, students, and dependants of EU nationals who are themselves EU nationals. This exemption does not apply to the majority of EU citizens who have retired or who have independent means, and who must accordingly still apply for a residence card. Those who are not required to obtain a residence card may still do so if they wish to have proof of their residence status.

Applications for a residence permit are made to the local *Comisaria de Policía* or to the *Oficina de Extranjeros*. You should take with you a valid full passport and three passport-sized photographs. If you are retired, or not otherwise earning an income, you will need to produce evidence that you have the resources to support yourself. Proving that you have a level of income equivalent to the Spanish retirement pension, for example by producing past bank statements, is sufficient. You will also need to produce evidence of health insurance or registration with the Spanish state system. For children and other dependants you will need their birth certificates.

Non-EU citizens intending to remain in Spain for more than 90 days must apply for a special entry visa from a Spanish consulate before arriving in Spain. Applications can be made for residence permits, which will normally be issued for the term of your contract of employment in Spain, or for two years. On expiry of this residence permit you can apply for a five-year permit. When you apply for a residence permit you will be provided with a receipt to prove that you have made an application. This serves, in effect, as a temporary permit. It is valid for two months only, but can be renewed if you have not received your permit within this time.

You should carry your residence permit with you at all times, as it is a form of identification and can also be requested at any time by a police officer. Failure to carry it can result in a fine. Those who are not required to obtain a residence permit should carry their passport. The residence card entitles you to travel to any part of Spain, including the Canary Islands and the Balearic Islands. On the card you will find your NIE (Foreigner Identification Number). This is your tax number, and is used on all official forms. You should note that all persons resident in Spain for more than 182 days in a calendar year are regarded as residents, and required to pay income tax on their worldwide income.

Further information on residence permits is available on **www.mir.es**, the website of the Ministry of the Interior.

Citizens of the various English-speaking countries (including the United States, Canada, Australia, South Africa and New Zealand) may well be entitled to live in any country of the European Union by virtue of their Irish roots (see Appendix 4).

Retiring to Spain

Spain is a popular location for people who are retired or planning their retirement. It is hardly a surprising choice, given the weather in most regions, and the lower housing costs. In most cases the sale of a home in the United Kingdom will enable you to buy a very comfortable home in Spain and still have a substantial surplus. It is important, however, to be realistic, for it is retired expatriates who are the most likely to return home. Consider what you are likely to miss about your home country. Are you likely to feel at home in Spain? How you will manage with the Spanish language? How you will cope with advancing age, possible illness and the loss of a partner? Consider also that retirement, nursing homes and day care centres are few and far between in Spain, and there is as yet no equivalent to such services as 'Meals on Wheels'.

If, after considering these matters, you are determined to make the move, there are several areas, in particular parts of the Costa del Sol, where much of what you may miss about life in the UK is duplicated, including cricket, the great British pub, British food and Anglican church services. Details of what is available in each region are set out in Chapter 1. The most popular areas tend to be the most expensive, but you may find them more conducive to making a home and developing a feeling of belonging.

There is no problem with receiving European state and private pensions in Spain. As a retired person, you are entitled to use the Spanish health system on the same basis as a Spanish citizen. Indeed, as a retired person you are entitled to reimbursement in full of medical expenses. In the United Kingdom, further information is available in leaflet SA29 available from the Department for Work and Pensions (DWP) (tel: 0191 218 7777). In addition, there is a practical guide produced by the European Union: *Your Social Security Rights When Moving within the EU*, available on the internet at **www.europa.eu.int/comm/employment_social/sec-prot/scheme/guide-en.htm**. You should obtain form E121 from the social security authorities in your home country to enable you to register with the Spanish health services (the local office will be listed in the yellow pages under *Seguridad Social*). If you have not yet retired, you should obtain form E106. In either case, take the form to the local health office in Spain, which should provide you with a Spanish medical card (*tarjeta sanitaria*).

One matter that UK nationals need to consider is exchange rate fluctuations. The problem will, of course, disappear when the United Kingdom eventually adopts the euro. In the meantime, you could move some of your investments to Spain. Alternatively, you could just accept that there is a risk that sterling may suffer modest falls in value, and discuss with your financial adviser how quickly you could move your investments if it was felt that sterling was likely to become particularly weak. Issues relating to inheritance are covered in Chapter 12. Advice to pensioners is available from various organizations, including Help the Aged (see also under 'Welcome to Spain', later in this chapter).

Payment of other UK benefits whilst living in Spain

The principle of free movement of labour within the European Union requires that citizens of member states should not be impeded from living and working in other member states. Accordingly, citizens of EU countries should not lose any of their rights to welfare benefits by moving to Spain. Those currently in receipt of an old age pension, invalidity and disability benefits, widow's benefits or benefits received as a result of an accident at work, or an occupational disease, are entitled to have their benefits paid to them irrespective of where they choose to live. The relevant benefits should be paid gross and include any increases. Incapacity benefit will only be paid to those who have paid Class 1 or Class 2 and 4 National Insurance contributions.

If you have not yet retired, your existing entitlement to a UK pension will be frozen and you will receive a reduced pension from the UK authorities when you reach retirement age. For those approaching retirement, it may be worthwhile making voluntary payments to bring your National Insurance contributions up to the level entitling you to a full pension. You should contact the Pension Service's International Pension Centre (part of the Department for Work and Pensions; tel: 0191 218 7777) and the Inland Revenue's Centre for Non-Residents (tel: 0845 070 0040). Ask for up-to-date information and advice, including whether you should pay Class 2 or Class 3 contributions. The former is the more expensive option but entitles you to incapacity benefit.

As to unemployment benefit, those out of work are entitled to have the Jobseeker's Allowance paid to them in Spain for up to 13 weeks. You must have been registered as a job seeker for at least four weeks before you left the United Kingdom, and have been available for work up until your departure. You must be leaving the United Kingdom in search of work, and register as seeking work with the Spanish authorities within seven days of your last claim for Jobseeker's Allowance in the United Kingdom.

Offshore Money Managers

Correduría de Seguros S.L.

OMM – a Regulated Firm

With over 18 years experience in the retired expatriate market in Spain, OMM was the first to obtain approval from the Spanish regulatory authorities for advising clients on all aspects of offshore finance and investment. OMM has representatives throughout Spain and holds Professional Liability Insurance for its regulated activities.

Offshore Investment Advice

Our main area of expertise is in advising on the best ways of holding accumulated capital so as to maximize the returns whilst keeping the exposure to risk at a level acceptable to each individual client. Minimum exposure to tax, whether Spanish or UK, is nearly always a high priority — as is the generation of a suitable level of income to supplement pension income.

Tax-Efficient Investments

With the EU Savings Tax Directive in July, tax-residents will either have their offshore cash declared to Hacienda or be taxed at source. However, Spain has introduced some very substantial tax concessions on profits from specialized offshore bonds which can result in an average tax rate of well under 5%. OMM, as a regulated brokerage, is able to advise on these.

Equity Release

A further area of expertise is Equity Release from Spanish properties. Spanish property owners are liable to Spanish Inheritance Tax on death. Registering a debt against a property reduces its assessable value for IHT by the amount of the debt. In most cases it is possible to reduce this liability by around 90%. A regular income is also possible, enabling a property owner to get substantial benefit from the capital otherwise locked up there.

Free Consultation

In the first instance, please call us on **+34 95 283 09 16**, fax us on **+34 95 283 67 36** or e-mail us at **info@offshoremoneymanagers.net**.

We will then put you in contact with a local representative.

You must contact your Jobcentre Plus office or Jobcentre before leaving, and complete the appropriate forms if you have not done so already to claim benefit. You should be sent a copy of E303 before you leave to enable you to claim benefit in Spain, and form E119 to entitle you to healthcare. If you cannot find employment during that 13-week period, then you will have to return to the United Kingdom if you wish to continue to receive benefit. You are only entitled to claim Jobseeker's Allowance abroad for one 13-week period between periods of employment. Information on transferring your Jobseeker's Allowance is contained in leaflet JSAL 22, available from your local DWP office.

Attendance Allowance and Disability Living Allowance are not normally payable once you move abroad permanently (though this is being reviewed). If you are living in Spain but remain liable to pay UK income tax and National Insurance, you or your spouse is entitled to claim Child Benefit from the UK authorities. This is not means tested.

For further information on payment of sickness benefit, see leaflet SA29, 'Your Social Security, Insurance, Benefits and Health Care Rights in the European Community'. You can also contact the Department for Work and Pensions (International Services) at Longbenton, Newcastle upon Tyne NE98 1YX (tel: 0191 225 4811; website: **www.dwp.gov.uk**). You should also consider obtaining the guide 'Social Security for Migrant Workers', available from the Department for Work and Pensions, Pensions and Overseas Benefits Directorate, Tyneview Park, Whitley Road, Benton, Newcastle upon Tyne NE98 1BA (tel: 0191 218 7777). It is also available from **www.europarl.eu.int/factsheets/4_8_4en.htim**.

Entitlement to Spanish state benefits

For those not in receipt of benefits when they move to Spain, but who subsequently become entitled, the rules are different. Generally, you are insured by the country in which you work and pay tax and social contributions. Those who work in more than one EU country are governed by the rules of the country in which they live. Contributions that you have paid in your home country (or any other member state) should be taken into account in determining your rights to benefits in Spain. Accordingly, if you lose your job in Spain you are entitled to claim unemployment benefit from the Spanish authorities, who will take into account the National Insurance contributions you have paid in the United Kingdom or other EU country. Unemployment benefit is currently around 340 euros per month (fixed at 75 per cent of the minimum wage). You should ask your Jobcentre Plus office or Jobcentre for the forms you would need to enable you to make any claim in Spain. Unemployment benefits are administered by *Instituto Nacional de Empleo* (INEM) (tel: 915 76 89 02; website: **www. inem.es**).

The level of other benefits, and of pensions, is determined by your salary level (subject to minimum and maximum rates). Note that at present, only those who have contributed for 15 years are entitled to a Spanish state pension. It is also becoming increasingly common for Spaniards to take out a supplementary private pension. Contributions are tax deductible.

Maternity benefits (*baja por maternidad*) are paid to expectant mothers who are entitled to payments equal to their full salary for 6 weeks prior to the birth, and for an additional 10 weeks that may be taken before or after the birth. Entitlement is restricted to those who have paid social security contributions for at least 180 days over the previous five years. There is also provision for paternity leave.

Pensions, invalidity, sickness, maternity benefits, etc are administered by *Instituto Nacional de la Seguridad Social* (INSS). The latter can be contacted by telephoning the *Centros de Atención e Información de la Seguridad Social* on the free number 900 16 65 65. See also the website **www.seg-social.es/ inss**.

Importing your belongings

There are no restrictions on EU citizens bringing personal belongings into the country (for motor vehicles, see Chapter 10), although you are required to have an inventory that can be produced to customs officials. Non-EU nationals intending to reside in Spain are required to pay VAT on any possessions that they bring into the country and that they have owned for less than 6 months, and on all belongings brought into the country 12 months after their residence began (there are some exceptions). To import personal belongings, non-EU nationals are required to make an application to the head of the customs office (*La Dirección General de Aduanas*) in the area in which they will be living, to allow the goods to enter Spain free of duty. Reputable international removal companies are familiar with the various procedures and should advise you of the necessary details, although application forms are available from Spanish consulates. You are required to make a detailed inventory, in duplicate, of all your possessions, with translations in Spanish, and pay a deposit equal to about half the estimated value of your belongings. You then have 12 months in which to obtain a residence permit and to produce this to the customs officials, together with a request for the return of your deposit. Failure to apply in time results in the loss of the deposit! Those non-EU citizens with a second home (*vivienda secundaria*) should follow the same procedure, but have two years in which to apply for the return of their deposit.

Spain has similar restrictions to the United Kingdom in relation to importing such items as drugs and firearms. There are also regulations relating to the importing of animals, animal products, plants and items with a possible military use. If in doubt, you should ask for advice from Spanish customs.

Pets

A new European regulation (no 998/2003) governing the movement of pets across Europe came into force from July 2004. Those wishing to take a dog or cat to Spain from the United Kingdom or any other member state, or from a non-EU listed country, must now have their animal identified with a microchip, vaccinated against rabies and issued with a Pet Passport. The non-EU countries from which you can import pets to Spain include the US mainland, Canada, Australia, New Zealand, Norway and Gibraltar. Ferrets travelling to Spain must have either a passport or a valid export health and rabies certificate issued prior to 1 October 2004 showing that it has been microchipped and vaccinated.

In the United Kingdom, passports are issued by Part 2 Local Veterinary Inspectors. Further information is obtainable from the Pets Helpline at the Department for Environment, Food and Rural Affairs (Defra) (tel: 08459 335577). There is also a website explaining the procedures at **www.defra. gov.uk**, which contains useful information in relation to the European Union generally, but in particular the United Kingdom, Ireland and Sweden.

You must travel with your pet or meet it at the port of entry. Dogs and cats under three months old and unvaccinated can be imported into Spain. They must have a passport and have remained at the same location since birth without contact with wild animals that are likely to have been exposed to rabies, or be accompanied by their mothers and still dependent upon them.

The requirements for bringing a dog or cat into or back into the United Kingdom from Spain have not changed as a result of the new European regulation. In brief, you will need to have your pet fitted with a microchip and then vaccinated against rabies. You will then have to arrange to have a blood test to check that the vaccine has been effective and obtain a Pet Passport. *However, you will have to wait a period of six months after the blood test before your pet can enter the United Kingdom.* The whole procedure takes about eight months, so you will need to plan ahead. Check with the centre that is to test your animal's blood how long it is currently taking to return results (there is wide variation). I have been told that the Institut für Virologie, Frankfurter Strasse 107, D-35392 Giessen in Germany (tel: 00 49 641 99 38350) returns results reasonably quickly. Just before leaving (24–48 hours prior to departure), you will need to have your pet treated for ticks and tapeworm.

There are relatively few companies that have made arrangements permitting them to bring pets into the United Kingdom (see Appendix 3). More routes are anticipated in the coming years and you should contact Defra (see above) for information.

Similar rules apply to the importation of ferrets into the United Kingdom: that is, they must be microchipped, vaccinated against rabies and issued with a passport, and be treated against ticks and tapeworm. This should be recorded on the passport. In the case of ferrets, however, there is no need to wait six months. As to pet rabbits and rodents (such as guinea pigs, hamsters, rats, mice and gerbils), there are at present no requirements for these pets when entering Spain or returning to the United Kingdom or any other EU member state (or Norway), not even in relation to rabies. The European Union may impose regulations in the future, however. The new regulation also covers other animals including birds (other than poultry), ornamental tropical fish, most invertebrates, and reptiles. At the time of writing, the rules to be passed under this regulation were not yet available. Up-to-date information will be posted on the Defra website.

There is no limit on the number of pets that can be moved from one EU country to another. The regulations and a Pet Passport can be downloaded from the EU website via **www.defra.gov.uk**. The Pet Passport contains details of the owner and of the animal, including the date it was micro-chipped and its vaccination record and blood details.

As a transitional arrangement, UK PETS certificates were issued up until 30 September 2004 and they will remain effective until their expiration, and accordingly your animal can enter both the United Kingdom and Spain with a valid PETS certificate. If you already have a previous PETS certificate, you can change this for a Pet Passport. Take your pet's vaccination record to your veterinary surgeon and the date that it was microchipped in order for him or her to record the details in section III of the passport.

In addition to vaccination against rabies, you should vaccinate your dog against hepatitis, parvoviris, leptospirosis, distemper, kennel cough and also leishmaniasis. Cats should be vaccinated against feline leukaemia and feline enteritis. Health insurance is available in Spain at under 100 euros per year for a dog and at around 50 euros for a cat.

Spanish law provides that within Spain, dogs must be registered with a tattoo in their ear or a microchip in their neck. Tattooing is carried out under an anaesthetic, though the animal may be sore for a while afterwards. A microchip can be inserted painlessly. I have been assured by several vets and breeders that the microchips do not irritate a dog. One disadvantage of the microchip is that it is possible to remove it without leaving an immediately obvious trace (for example, if your dog is stolen). Removal of a tattoo, on the other hand, would involve cutting an animal's ear, which would make it difficult for the thief to sell it. Even if your dog is identified in either of the above ways, ensure that it also has a nametag with your contact details.

Fierce breeds are subject to strict regulations, including American Staffordshires, Rottweilers and Staffordshire Bull Terriers. You will need a special licence to keep such dogs. They must be muzzled and you must have appropriate insurance cover.

Taking and transferring money to Spain

There are no restrictions on transferring money to Spain, though it is advisable to keep records in case you need to prove that the money does not arise from income earned in Spain. Those travelling to Spain carrying more than 6,000 euros in cash (*efectivo*) are required to make a declaration on entry into Spain, stating the purpose for which the money is being brought into the country. Residents wishing to travel abroad with more than 6,000 euros in cash are also supposed to make a customs declaration. You can obtain the form from the bank from which you obtained the cash. If you wish to carry more than 30,000 euros you are required to fill in a different form and to seek authority from the *Dirección General de Transacciones Exteriores*. Permission is generally granted.

Once you have a Spanish bank account, it is easy to make transfers from your UK account into your Spanish account. UK banks normally tell you that it will take up to five working days. In practice, the transfer in euros may be credited to your Spanish account more quickly than this, but in some cases it can take longer. Under new European regulations the receiving bank is not allowed to make a charge for receiving sums in euros. Your UK bank may make a charge of £20–£30 per transfer, irrespective of the amount. Changing to a Spanish bank that is part of the same group as your UK bank may significantly reduce the charge. Ensure that you obtain the commercial rate for transfers. This is much more favourable than the tourist rate. Bank charges generally also vary and it accordingly pays to shop around.

There are no restrictions on transferring money out of Spain, but you will have to declare all transfers over 600 euros on a 'B' form, stating the identity of the recipient and the purpose of the payment. The Spanish government requires this information in its efforts to restrict money laundering, and to prevent tax evasion. A resident who receives transfers from abroad is similarly required to inform his or her bank of the identity and address of the sender and the reason for the payment.

A Spanish bank account

You will need a Spanish bank account, probably a current account (*cuenta corriente*). Non-residents can open a non-resident account (*cuenta extranjera*), though you will need a certificate from the local police confirming that you are not resident. The account must be closed once you become resident in Spain.

You will be provided with a chequebook (*talonario*), although cheques are not used with the same frequency as in the United Kingdom. Note that post-dating a cheque is ineffective: it can be drawn on immediately. Many Spaniards ask for cheques to be made out to the bearer (*portador*), ie the equivalent of cash, to avoid having to declare it for tax purposes.

Residents have 15 per cent of interest earned deducted direct for tax purposes, though you can recover this if you are not liable for tax on these sums. Bank charges in Spain are higher than in most other European countries, even for routine operations. Commission on transfers out of Spain vary tremendously. If you are likely to make regular transfers abroad, a bank's charges for this service should be one of the factors you consider when deciding upon your choice of bank. Becoming overdrawn or exceeding an overdraft limit without prior agreement is a serious matter in Spain and should be avoided! As with other banks, notify your Spanish bank immediately of any loss or suspected theft of your chequebook or card – you are responsible for any loss until you do.

Buying a property in Spain? Make sure you save money on your dream home...

If you are planning on buying your dream home in Spain, there are a number of considerations you will have to make before taking the plunge.

A crucial element of any overseas property purchase for a UK resident, and one that is often overlooked, is the exchange rate between Sterling and the currency of your chosen destination, in this case the Euro. This will directly affect the amount, in Sterling, that you will pay for your Spanish property.

So what are your options?

You basically have two options to buy the currency that you will need to pay for your overseas property: You can use your high street bank or you can turn to an experienced currency trader such as Moneycorp.

High street banks are not geared up to providing the kind of professional assistance needed when individuals are faced with moving large sums of money overseas, as it is not an area they choose to specialise in for private individuals. Currency dealers, however, are experts in the currency markets and spend their time monitoring exchange rates' They will provide you with information and solutions to help you to make the most of your Sterling.

In most circumstances, a specialist currency dealer's exchange rate will be better than the equivalent rate from a bank, and certainly a great deal better than the tourist rates often sold to unsuspecting clients. A currency trader will also be able to offer you a variety of simple market tools that can help you both avoid the risk of an adverse currency movement, or help you make the most of any favourable rates that may occur.

The services offered by a currency trader are free of charge – all you will pay is a small transfer fee, which will be lower than you would pay the bank. Funds to the majority of countries will usually arrive on the same day.

Regular overseas payments

Currency specialists will also be able to assist you with transferring any smaller regular overseas payments you may have once you have decided on your property, such as mortgage payments and pension transfers. This enables you to fix an exchange rate on monthly overseas payments for up to two years, so you know exactly what you'll be paying, for a nominal transfer fee.

Although the process may sound daunting, by calling a currency trader, you will receive personal guidance through the buying process and are likely to save a considerable amount of money on your overseas property purchase.

Rosanna Stimson is an Account Manager at foreign exchange specialists Moneycorp. To speak to a member of the Private Client Division, please contact **+44 0 20 7589 3000** or email **enquiries@moneycorp.com** or visit **www. moneycorp.com**

Complaints about banking services should first be addressed to the local manager. If he or she does not resolve your complaint to your satisfaction then you can take the matter to your bank's *defensor del cliente*. This frequently results in a decision in the client's favour. If you are still dissatisfied you can take the matter to the Bank of Spain's *Servicio de Reclamaciones*.

A bank statement is *el extracto*, a current balance is *saldo actual*, a standing order is *domiciliación*, an overdraft is *giros en descubierto*.

Household insurance

You should insure your property for its full worth, taking into account the value of the land, but also the cost of demolition and rebuilding. Similarly, with contents you should insure their full value if you are to be certain of having a claim met in full. Your insurers need to know if the property is vacant for much of the year and if you are letting the property. If this is the case, the premiums will be higher, but failure to notify your insurer of the situation will result in the disallowance of relevant claims.

Claims normally have to be submitted within a very short time of an incident, so you should check the terms of the policy. Thefts and break-ins also have to be reported to the police as a condition of the policy, usually within 24 hours.

Communications: the telephone and postal system, fax, and the internet

The Spanish postal service is extremely variable, and deliveries of mail in Spain are often slow. Deliveries to Europe can take anything from two to seven days, and mail to the United States anything from five days to nearly two weeks. Those who live near Gibraltar will find that mail to the United Kingdom posted there arrives more quickly than if it is posted in Spain.

The post office operates a domestic express and tracking service that carries a guarantee of delivery within 48 hours anywhere in mainland Spain. Mail from the United States will take about 7–10 days. For express delivery from the United States the post office's Priority/Express mail is good value and reasonably fast. Another alternative is UPS.

Post office services include registered post (for which compensation is payable for lost or damaged items), postal insurance, and a facility for providing proof of delivery (*aviso recibo*). At main post offices, staff will package parcels for you at a modest cost. An extensive range of banking services is available through post offices by virtue of an agreement with Deutsche Bank.

Post offices in Madrid and the main cities are generally open from 9.00 am to 10.00 pm or even later from Monday to Friday, and on Saturday mornings. Elsewhere, opening hours are more restricted, with many post offices still closing at 2.30 pm and mail received after 1.00 pm having to wait until the next day. It is often possible to collect parcels after the post office has closed. Queues in Spanish post offices are notorious, but note that stamps can also be purchased at shops licensed to sell tobacco.

It is worth considering having a PO box (*apartado de correos*). This can mean that you receive letters several days earlier than if they are sent to a conventional address. The cost of having a PO box is modest, and in any event you will need to visit the post office to collect any large parcels, as in most areas these are not delivered to homes. Try to post letters at a main post office, and in particular avoid using postboxes.

The Spanish telephone operator Telefonica lost its state monopoly about 10 years ago, and telecommunications in Spain have since changed dramatically, with more choice, lower prices and shorter delays. A mobile phone can be operational within 24 hours of its purchase. Public telephones are still difficult to find in remoter areas. If you need to use one, ask at a hotel or restaurant. Most newsagents have a fax facility. The number for the local police is 1092 and that for the operator is 1004. A reverse-charge call is made by first telephoning 1009 for Spain, 1008 for the European Union and North Africa, and 1005 for the United States and elsewhere. For directory enquiries, telephone 11818 (you will need to know the town in which the person lives) and for international information 11825. If you wish to take your UK mobile phone to Spain, contact your service provider. It can be quite expensive. Telephone cards are available from tobacconists, post offices, petrol stations and supermarkets.

Telephone directories are provided free for your own area, and for other areas can be purchased at a modest cost from the provincial office of Telefonica. The White Pages contain useful information about a wide range of matters as well as instructions in English on how to use the telephone (see also **www.paginas-blancas.es** and **www.paginas-amarillas.es**).

On the whole, Telefonica remains more expensive than other telephone companies. You should compare prices and consider using more than one provider to enable you to choose the least expensive options for different destinations and times of day pertinent to the calls that you make. There is the usual range of telephone facilities, including caller identification (*identificación de llamados*), call waiting (*llamada en espera*), three-way calls (*llamada a tres*), answerphone (*contestador automático*) and call diversion (*desvio*). Telephone bills should be paid promptly, as your line can be cut off without warning for non-payment.

Public telephones are available in many different public places, but also in bars, cafés and restaurants. Instructions on use are available in English (see the language selection button underneath the display). Telephone cards are available from post offices, and also from newsagents and tobacconists. The SOS phones on motorways and main routes are free for emergencies and breakdowns.

Spain has lagged behind the United Kingdom in the spread and popularity of the internet. That said, its use has grown rapidly in recent years, and most large businesses, government departments and local councils have websites providing a vast quantity of information. Some basic internet vocabulary is included in Appendix 7.

Television and satellite

There are several Spanish television channels, but many foreign residents prefer to receive English-language programmes. There are several ways in which to obtain UK television and radio programmes via satellite. A number of channels can be received free of charge using a receiver that you can purchase from a dealer or electrical retailer. Some Britons in Spain receive BBC 1, BBC 2, ITV, Channel 4, Channel 5 and Sky by using a receiver available from specialists and a card from the United Kingdom. This is, in fact, unlawful, as licensing and copyright laws restrict the use of the card to the United Kingdom. Note that British and US televisions will not work in Spain, where the PAL-BG standard is used.

Digital television is available from Canal Satellite Digital (**www .csatellite.es**) and Via Digital (**www.viadigital.es**). English-language satellite television can be received anywhere in Spain, with a wide range of stations being available, and stations also in other languages, including Dutch and Swedish.

Overlooking the importance of the foreign exchange rate can be one of the major causes of stress for overseas home buyers. Foreign exchange specialist, Currencies Direct, answers some frequently asked questions on the subject.

Q: If I'm buying a property in Spain, how should I arrange for payment?
A: Traditionally, you would approach the bank to arrange the transfer of funds overseas. However, this isn't always your best option. As an alternative to your bank, foreign exchange specialists are able to offer you extremely competitive exchange rates, no commission charges and lower transfer fees.

Q: Why is it important to watch the exchange rates?
A: Unfortunately, no one can predict the exchange rate as many factors constantly affect the strength of the pound. Exchange rates are constantly moving and there is no guarantee that they will be in your favour when you need your money, so it is vital that you protect yourself against these movements. A lack of proper forward planning could potentially cost you thousands of pounds, reducing your spending power abroad.

Q: How can I reduce my risk of losing out because of exchange rates?
A: There are many options available through foreign exchange specialists including spot deals, limit orders and forward buying. Which option is best for you will depend on your timing, circumstances, and foreign currency needs. A foreign exchange specialist will be able to talk you through the options and help you to decide which is best for you.

Q: What are the advantages of buying euros in the UK as opposed to sending sterling directly to Spain?
A: If you send sterling directly to Spain you are at the mercy of the Spanish banks and have no control over the exchange rate given. However, by purchasing euros in the UK you are in control of the rate you receive as you are able to compare rates between the banks and other foreign exchange providers.

The railway system

The railway system is known as RENFE (*Red Nacional de Ferrocarriles Españoles*). The TALGO is a fast, comfortable inter-city train, but has been outclassed by the newer AVE (*alta velocidad española*), a high-speed train reminiscent of the French TGV, linking Madrid with Seville, Madrid with Barcelona, and Barcelona with the south of France. High-speed links between Madrid and Málaga and Madrid and Valencia are due to be completed in 2005. You can transport your car by train from Barcelona to Málaga, Bilbao to Málaga and Madrid to Málaga by train, although note that there are restrictions on car length and height which exclude most people carriers.

There is an extensive range of different train tickets, and it can be difficult to determine the most economic. Train fares are reduced on *días azules* (blue days). Children aged 4–12 travel at half price, younger children travel free. Information on fares is available on **www.renfe.es**. Tickets are available from travel agencies as well as online.

Welcome to Spain

If you wish to integrate fully into Spanish life, and especially if you live in the more rural areas, you must make contacts amongst the local Spanish community. Even if you are the only English-speaking family, you are probably not the only newcomers in the area – there are many Germans and Scandinavians, as well as those Spaniards who leave Madrid in favour of a home in the countryside.

There are steps you can take to ease the transition to your new home and environment. Prior to purchasing, or indeed renting, you would do well to introduce yourselves to your immediate neighbours in order to ask them about the property and the neighbourhood. Once you have moved in, renew the acquaintanceship. You have the perfect pretext in that you are new to the area and can ask them for information or advice about the area or alterations and improvements that they have made to their property.

There will be local sports and cultural associations in which you can participate. If you have children at the local school, you will find that they soon make friends. This will bring you into contact with other parents in the area, some of them keen for their children to establish links with

English-speaking people in the hope that this will help them in acquiring what remains by far the most important world language.

Most villages have regular festivals. Each local school will have its annual events. Integration inevitably requires participation. If you are in a village, do carry out some of your shopping locally. Do buy and look at the local newspaper. It is not only about becoming part of the community, but it may be the first notification you have that, say, a new motorway is planned that will directly affect your daily life and/or the value of your property. On this note, some expatriates have taken an active part in campaigning on local issues. Foreign residents have the right to vote in municipal elections, and in some areas the British and other foreign residents form a potentially significant group of the electorate.

A guide on cultural institutions (*Guía de Servicios Culturales*) is available from Ministerio de Educación, Cultura y Deporte, Centre de Información y Atención al Ciudadano, Sección de Información Cultural, Plaza del Rey, 1 E-28071 Madrid (tel: 91 701 70000; e-mail: informa.admini@sgt.mcu.es).

There are many English-speaking associations throughout Spain, especially in the more popular areas. They are mainly British, but include US, Irish, South African, Canadian and Australian clubs and associations and some that are specifically Scottish or Welsh. They range from churches and religious groups to cricket clubs, women's groups, organizations offering activities for children, and retired servicemen's associations. There are also various UK and joint cultural centres and groups – most notably the British Council. Friendships are often quick to form amongst the expatriate community. Whatever your age and circumstances, you may find others' help and advice indispensable, including in relation to finding employment. You may, however, be reluctant to immerse yourself completely amongst expatriates. One possibility is to participate in the joint Anglo-Spanish groups.

Advice for those seeking to retire in Spain is available from Age Concern, Astral House, 1268 London Road, London SW16 4ER (tel: 020 8765 7200). Age Concern has several offices in Spain, including in the Federación Age Concern España, Apartado 7, 07180 Santa Ponsa, Mallorca (tel: 971 23 15 20; e-mail: federation@ageconcern-espana.org. A full list of its offices in Spain can be found on **www.acespana.org**.

Formalities

In many ways the Spanish remain more formal than the British and other Anglo-Saxons. This is most apparent in business and other correspondence. It is common to use the formal *usted* (you) when talking with a stranger, rather than to immediately employ the informal *tu*. Remember that women do not change their name when they marry, so a husband and wife bear different surnames. *Don* or *Doña* often precedes a person's name. Someone whom we would refer to as Mr Richard Smith, whose mother's maiden name was Jones, would be referred to as Señor Don Richard Smith Jones. When introduced to someone it is polite to reply '*encantado/a*' (pleased to meet you). Avoid calling on someone or telephoning during the siesta.

When addressing letters, the road name is written first, followed by the number: 45 Barcelona Street would be written Calle Barcelona 45.

Speaking and learning the language

In many parts of Spain it is very easy to live in an almost totally English-speaking environment in which you rarely have to speak a word of Spanish. However, if you are truly to settle, you really do need to have some understanding of the language. Indeed, it is essential if you wish to obtain employment with a Spanish employer. It is important, too, if you are to handle emergency situations confidently and for your dealings with the various administrative bodies.

In fact, Spain has four languages: Castilian (the language generally known as 'Spanish'), Basque, Catalan and Gallego, the language of Galicia. These are all distinct separate languages, although all derived from Latin, save for Basque, the origins of which are the subject of some academic dispute.

Castilian is the first language of the majority of Spain, including Madrid, and is also (broadly) the language spoken in the 20 or so Spanish-speaking countries throughout the world. Though derived from Latin, the language has obvious Arabic influences, as is apparent from many place names that have Arabic roots. Castilian has a variety of regional accents, and that of the northern Spanish is said to be the easiest for foreigners to follow. It is also the language of Andalusia, and hence of the Costa del Sol and the Costa de la Luz, and also of the Canary Islands.

Catalan is spoken by about 9 million people, mostly in Catalonia, Valencia and the Balearic Islands, and is spoken across the social spectrum.

It is the language of Barcelona and the Costa Brava, Costa Dorado and Costa del Azahar, and to a lesser extent the Costa Blanca.

Basque is limited to the eastern end of the North Atlantic coast. It is notoriously difficult to learn. Legend has it that after seven years of trying to learn to speak Basque the Devil was only able to say 'yes' and 'no'. When he realized that he had confused the two words, he gave up!

Gallego is understood by most of the 2.75 million inhabitants of the north-western corner of Spain. However, today it is primarily the language of the rural areas, and Castilian Spanish is dominant elsewhere.

There is no doubt that Spanish is a much easier language than French, the traditional choice of foreign language for most of us in our schooldays. There is, of course, no better place to learn it than in Spain itself. There are many different courses. A detailed list can be found at The Spanish Directory: Learn in Spain at **www.europa-pages.com**. Many courses will be in target language only (Spanish), with no English spoken. The best-known organization is the *Instituto Cervantes*, which is akin to the British Council or *L'Institut Français* for France, and runs courses in all the main cities in Spain and also at centres in the United Kingdom. There are (expensive) total immersion options available in which you spend a period of time in a Spanish family, attending courses during the day. (For further information on learning Spanish, see 'Spanish – learning the language' in Appendix 1.) In addition, the provincial governments and local city councils run Spanish courses for immigrants that are quite often free of charge.

One useful tool, once you have reached a reasonably fluent level, is a bimonthly magazine and cassette known as *Puerta del Sol*. For the serious student there are many qualifications that can be gained. Study for O-level and A-level Spanish is possible via correspondence courses with the National Extension College, as is the external degree in Spanish Studies at London University. The Open University has courses for complete beginners up to a diploma in Spanish, in which the level of language is equivalent to that learnt at a traditional university. There are various examination centres in Spain, although you should check with the individual examining body.

The best way to advance your Spanish is obviously to use it. Making Spanish friends will prove invaluable to this end, and those who have a Spanish partner clearly have a huge advantage. You should make full use of the Spanish media. Watching and listening to television is a must, but ensure that your viewing is *selective*. Avoid the most difficult programmes to follow, such as chat shows (everybody always talks at the same time!) and Spanish television series. Translations of English-language films or television series are invariably in standard Spanish and you seldom have to cope with the difficulties of regional accents. You will also be more familiar with what is being shown pictorially (such as courtroom scenes, police investigations, lifestyles, and so on). The programmes will, accordingly, be easier to follow (and enjoy) as well as to learn from. DVDs are generally in multiple languages, and are an ideal tool in that you can watch them in your own language before seeing them in Spanish.

Obviously, you can learn more by adopting a systematic approach. For example, the same words appear frequently and it is helpful to make a note of them. If you record a programme, you can replay it to hear something that you have missed. News bulletins are also worth watching: newsreaders tend to speak clearly and are accordingly easier to understand. News is repeated throughout the day, so if you did not pick something up the first time around, you will have another opportunity to do so, perhaps listening to a different newsreader.

Radio is inevitably more difficult to follow. However, time in your car could be usefully spent learning the language and, if you are not listening to Spanish-language tapes, consider a news channel, especially on long journeys. Consider listening to the BBC News or, preferably, a local English radio station that has local and national news. This will give you an idea of the main news items and help you to follow them on Spanish radio.

You will find that many people try to speak to you in English. You should politely persist in speaking Spanish. They may well be simply trying to impress a third party and it may be that their knowledge of English is limited to only a few words. If so, it will not compare to your own level of Spanish after you have been in the country for a while.

If you wish to study the language prior to moving to Spain, consider the courses run by the *Instituto Cervantes*, which has centres in London, Manchester and Dublin. These are cultural centres where you can also learn more about Spain and Spanish culture, see Spanish films and meet Spanish people living in the United Kingdom or Ireland.

Your neighbours and you

The key to minimizing problems is always to attempt to establish a good relationship with your neighbours from the outset, whatever their nationality, even if you are going to keep them at arm's length. At some point you may well need each other – especially if you live some distance from shops and other facilities. If a dispute does arise, do your utmost to settle disagreements without recourse to the courts, perhaps asking a third party (such as an *abogado*) to act as arbiter. Litigation may only fuel animosities and leave both sides with substantial legal bills.

You have no right to complain about a nuisance that is no more than a norm for the neighbourhood (such as church bells that have been rung for centuries, but which might lead to mental instability if you were unwise enough to purchase the house next door). This is merely a characteristic of the neighbourhood, and one that you are obliged to accept. For abnormal nuisances, however, there are rules and regulations governing such matters as noise and pollution.

The time of day

To most other Europeans, the Spanish day is two hours or more behind that in the rest of Europe. Lunch takes place at about 2.00 pm (or even an hour later in Andalusia) and dinner from 10.00 pm. Spaniards go to bed later than the rest of Europe. Literally, the expression *mediodía* means midday, but is invariably used to refer to about lunchtime – ie from 2.00 pm, during which a siesta is often taken. Most shops open at 9.00 or 10.00 am and close at 1.30 pm for lunch, generally reopening from 4.00 pm. The larger stores do not close over lunch.

Bank opening times are generally 8.30 am to 2.00 pm from Monday to Friday, though some banks are open on Saturday mornings or on one afternoon per week. Restaurants are normally open between 1.00 pm and 4.00 pm and from 9.00 pm until late.

Chemists are usually open from 9.30 am to 1.30 pm and from 5.00 pm to 8.00 pm from Monday to Friday, and from 9.30 am to 1.30 pm on Saturdays. There is also a system of duty chemists open 24 hours a day, seven days a week. Most other businesses work from 9.00 am to 6.00 or 7.00 pm from Monday to Friday, with a two-hour lunch break.

Tipping

Most people leave a tip of up to 8% in bars, restaurants, cafés or taxis, though generally not more than 3 or 4 euros. Otherwise, tipping is not a common practice.

Living & Working in Spain
Our Top Ten Tips

Over the last 20 years, hundreds of our clients have gone to live or work in Spain. Most have made the adjustment very successfully. Some have failed. How do you make a successful move as likely and as easy as possible?

Do your Research
The first stage in the process should always be research about the areas where you are thinking of moving. Do your research *before* you go to look at any houses. It will save a lot of wasted time and money. Read magazines. Buy books. Use the internet. Attend seminars and conferences. All of these will cost you pennies compared with the cost of buying a home, moving or setting up in business.

Make a 'Life Plan'
Your life plan records, on paper, how you are going to deal with some of the key changes that will occur when you move to Spain. Where will you live? What will you do about health care? What will you do about your children's education? Which possessions will you take to Spain? What will you do with your pets? What will you do with your car? The contents will vary from person to person. This does not need to be a long or complicated document but, by putting it on paper, you will force yourself to address the key issues more thoroughly.

If you are going to start a business, make a written Business Plan
You will need this for your own use and also for production to your Spanish bank, particularly if you want to borrow the money. The format and the contents of a Spanish business plan are different from those found in England. And, of course, you will need a copy in fluent Spanish. Most businesses without any plan fail. You will probably need some help in doing this.

See your lawyer at an early stage - *before* you go to look at properties
Discuss all of the key issues – such as your life plan, your business plan, how to minimise your tax liabilities, what to do about your finances etc. Making the right choices here can save you lots of time and money later.

Sort out your finances

What are you going to do about your pensions? Where will they be paid? How much will you receive? Will you will need bridging finance to cover you until you sell your UK home? What are you doing about your investments? Remember that there will be many types of investments in Spain about which you will know nothing. You need good professional investment advice. You need it from someone reliable. Get recommendations.

Never plan to move into your property the day you buy it

Last minute changes to the date agreed for completion (signing the title deed and paying over the purchase money) are very common. Even if the property is transferred to you on the day agreed, it may not yet be connected to the water or electricity. Allow at least a week as a buffer – and a month if you can.

Make a local Will

This will save your heirs lots of trouble and money. Make a 'local' Will at the same time as you move. You will also need to modify your English will so that the two do not clash.

Don't be too British

You must learn to accept that things happen differently in Spain. Sometimes the system is better, sometimes it is worse. It is always different. If you adjust to this you will save yourself a lot of stress.

Learn Spanish

Everybody will tell you that you don't need to speak a word of the language. That may, technically, be true but your life will be a lot easier if you do and the more you speak the easier your life will become. We have many clients who have learnt to speak good Spanish at the age of 65. If you keep on plugging away at it, it will all suddenly fall into place.

Enjoy yourself

This is supposed to be fun.

John Howell & Co
Solicitors & International Lawyers
The Old Glass Works, 22 Endell Street, Covent Garden, London
WC2H 9AD
Tel: 020 7420 0400 **Fax:** 020 7836 3626
Email: info@europelaw.com

Up-to-date warnings!

The UK government website **www.ukinspain.com** has a regularly updated section containing advice on aspects of living in Spain, including warnings on such matters as personal safety and fraudulent practices. Go to Consular Services, then 'Be careful'. One of the most widespread fraudulent tricks relates to the Spanish lottery.

Investment scams

The website mentioned above contains more detailed warnings and information on what it terms 'Fly-by-night operations'. In brief, 'representatives' contact members of the public, usually by telephone, but sometimes by letter, often claiming to have inside knowledge about a particular share price. These swindlers present investment opportunities supposedly offering a high return. They often advertise in newspapers and magazines, supply professional-looking marketing material and rent expensive-looking offices to portray an image of success, acceptability and professionalism. To 'prime the pump' they often pay initial investors very good first returns in order to be able to use these people as witnesses to assist in their marketing.

The best approach to anyone offering a financial investment opportunity is this: assume that an opportunity that sounds too good to be true is probably *not* true. You will find that if you press these people with questions about their company and their product, those who are part of a fraudulent scam will probably back off, or be angry and annoyed. The above website pages include a list of helpful questions for you to ask. If you have any suspicions about people who have approached you, visit the website of the National Services Market Commission (CNMV) at **www.cnmv.es**.

Note that these crooks are usually Britons or other North Europeans rather than Spanish.

The police

There are three separate police forces in Spain: the *policía municipal*, the *policía nacional* and the *guardia civil*. All police officers carry guns. The *policía municipal* (blue uniforms with white bands on their hats and sleeves) are responsible for traffic regulation and investigating minor crimes. They have the power to impose on-the-spot fines. The *policía nacional* handle serious crime and carry sub-machine guns. It is the *policía nacional* who man the *comisaria de policía*. The *guardia civil* wear a green uniform and handle traffic accidents and are responsible for rural areas.

Corruption is not uncommon amongst police officers; it is endemic in Spanish society.

Emergencies

For the national police the telephone number is 091 and for the local police 192. For general emergencies, ring 112. The number to ring for the fire services differs from region to region, but is listed in the telephone directory. For ambulances, telephone 061. For assistance on the road, telephone 0900 12 35 05.

Crime

A major problem in some parts of Spain is theft from occupied vehicles stuck in stationary or slow-moving traffic. The offenders often operate in pairs. They approach a vehicle on a moped. One of them will jump off, open the car door and demand money or valuables, searching the occupants or threatening them with a knife. Once they have recovered enough they then speed off, leaving the unhappy motorist helpless to pursue. Even if the traffic in front starts to move off, the offenders will probably have jammed the car door lock so that it will not immediately close, thereby hampering any pursuit. Other motorists are tricked into stopping in the belief that there has been an accident, only to find themselves in turn attacked and robbed.

Another tactic, also often carried out with a moped, is to seize a woman's bag, or to cut the straps of the bag.

Accidents and criminal injuries

If you are involved in an accident or have been assaulted, you are under a legal obligation to report this to the police. This rule applies even to minor incidents. You should be given a copy of the report to provide to your insurer. You can make a *denuncia* (report over the telephone in Spanish or

English (tel: 902 10 21 12), or in Spanish via the internet at **www.mir.es/ policia/denuncia/denun_index.htm**. When you make a report by telephone, you should be given a reference number that enables you to obtain a copy of the report from your nearest police station.

Once you make a complaint to the police, they will take initial statements. These will then be submitted to an examining magistrate, who will decide on the appropriate course of action, including in relation to any arrest or examination of witnesses. If you have been injured as a result of a crime, you can claim damages in the criminal proceedings, or bring a separate civil claim. The time limit to make a claim within the criminal proceedings is two months from the incident.

There is a separate system of compensation for criminal injuries funded by the Spanish state. Applications must be lodged within 12 months of the incident, or within 12 months of the outcome of the criminal proceedings.

A separate civil claim can be made in the case of an assault, or in relation to any accident. The *general* time limit for a civil claim is 12 months from the incident.

You should take prompt legal advice as soon as practicable after the accident or assault, and also before you enter into any oral or written negotiations to settle your claim. Even if you believe that your claim may be out of time, obtain legal advice to verify that you are correct. There is a system of legal aid to cover the financing of legal assistance. People resident in the United Kingdom wishing to bring a claim in Spain should make enquiries of their local legal aid office, and take a look at the Legal Service Commission's website at **www.legalservices.co.uk**.

Accidents at work

There are no specific payments under the Spanish social security system in relation to work accidents or occupational diseases. You will need to claim one of the general benefits covering sickness, though where injuries result from accidents at work, or on the way to or from work, benefits are paid at a higher rate.

Consumer protection

The European Union has imposed its own regulations on consumer protection, and accordingly Spanish legislation on this is similar to that in other EU states. These regulations cover the purchase of goods and services, including timeshares (see further in Chapter 2). Your first port of call for any complaint is generally the store or person from which you purchased the goods or service. You should keep all correspondence, including copies of your own letters, and ideally make a note of details of any conversation (especially what was said by you and by the seller prior to any purchase) as soon as possible afterwards. Thereafter you can take up your complaint with the local *Oficina Municipal de Información al Consumidor*. Consumer information can be obtained from a website run by a consumers' association: **www.ocu.org**.

Trouble with the police and the courts

The police should report the arrest of foreign citizens to their nearest consulate. The UK authorities endeavour to have every arrested person visited by a consular officer within 72 hours. The person should normally either be released within 72 hours of his or her arrest, or be brought before an examining magistrate (*juez de instrucción*). Generally the arrested person will be entitled to access to legal representation. If a suspect does not have the means to pay for a lawyer, or declines to appoint one, a lawyer will be appointed.

You can obtain more information on this subject by requesting an information leaflet, 'Legal procedures in criminal cases', from the UK government website **www.ukinspain.com** (go to 'Consular Services – Living in Spain – legal').

Getting married in Spain

Those wishing to marry must be over 18. There is considerable paperwork involved before the ceremony can go ahead, and accordingly you will need to begin your application to marry in good time before the date on which you wish to marry. In theory, foreigners are permitted to marry without any condition of residence, but in practice it may be difficult to succeed in your application to marry if you or your partner has not been resident in Spain for two years or more.

The procedural requirements for religious marriages differ according to the region of Spain and the religious body concerned. While religious marriages are recognized by Spanish law, you will need to have your marriage registered with the civil authorities in order to receive an official marriage certificate, and for your marriage to be recognized in the United Kingdom. An application for civil marriage is made to the civil registry or town hall in the locality in which the marriage is to be celebrated. The application form can be downloaded from **www.mju.es/registro_civil/ c_matrimonio.htm**.

An alternative to marrying in Spain is to tie the knot in Gibraltar. For information, contact the Civil Status and Registration Office, Marriage Registry, 277 Main Street, Gibraltar (tel: 00 350 72289).

Deaths of British citizens in Spain

Details of official procedures are available on the UK government's website **www.ukinspain.com/english/ConsularServices/livingspain/deaths**, including the registration of deaths, repatriation to the United Kingdom, local burial and cremation, international funeral directors and representation in any legal proceedings. The site makes it clear that the Foreign and Commonwealth Office is willing to offer help and advice.

Voting in Spain

Non-Spanish EU residents are entitled to vote (and stand) in local and European elections. You will need to ensure that your name is on the *padrón municipal* (the register) at your local town hall, and to verify that your name is on the list of those eligible to vote. British residents in Spain are entitled to vote in the United Kingdom for up to 15 years. Forms are available from your local consulate or by downloading from **www.ukinspain.com/ English/ConsularServices**. Further information on voting in both Spanish and UK elections is to be found at **www.aboutmyvote.co.uk**.

Taking Spanish nationality

Before applying to become a Spanish citizen, ensure that you are fully aware of both the advantages and the disadvantages. Your country of origin will not be prepared to interfere with any demands made upon you by your adopted country, such as military service, or indeed conscription.

According to the Home Office, Her Majesty has no objection to British subjects applying for citizenship of a foreign state or states without losing their British nationality. Most English-speaking countries, including Ireland, the United States, Canada, Australia and New Zealand, take the same permissive stance. Spain, however, forbids dual nationality by requiring applicants to renounce their existing citizenship. If you are British, you will have to make a formal application to the British government to renounce your British citizenship.

Spain also insists on a period of 10 years' residency in Spain before a foreigner is entitled to become a citizen. This does not apply to those born in Spain, or who marry a Spaniard, and a shorter period is also applicable for citizens of South American countries.

If you do decide to take on Spanish nationality, remember that it comes with no guarantee of having a sense of belonging. When all is said and done, having a sense of being *at home* is perhaps the most important element of all.

Further information as to the obtaining of Spanish citizenship can be obtained from a Spanish consulate. Information on how this will affect your present national status can be obtained from your embassy in Madrid, or its local consulate. The procedure for obtaining citizenship takes about 12 months.

Local property tax

The local property tax (*impuesto sobre buenos inmeubles*, IBI) is levied annually on the *fiscal* value of a property. This is based upon various characteristics of the property and the area in which it is situated. It is similar to the old rateable value in the United Kingdom. The rate of IBI varies significantly and depends upon the facilities that the local council wishes to provide. It can be as high as 1.7 per cent. It is your obligation to pay this tax, irrespective of whether you are sent a bill. When you purchase, you should register with the local municipality; hefty surcharges and supplements are payable for late payment.

8 Education

The face of Spanish education has undergone a dramatic transformation in the past 10 years or so, with a substantial improvement in the standard offered by both private and state schools. Education is compulsory from the ages of 6 to 16. Many Spanish parents have become extremely keen on their children gaining academic qualifications.

Pre-school education (*educación infantil*)

Education does not become compulsory in Spain until children are six years old. Many parents of British and foreign children choose to send their children to Spanish nursery schools (*guarderías*), even though they may have already decided to opt for some form of English-speaking, bilingual or international school for the primary and secondary years. First, these nursery schools are not very expensive. Second, attendance enables children to learn to speak Spanish during the years when they are most receptive to acquiring a second language. A significant number of foreign parents keep their children at Spanish primary schools and make the move to an English/international education when the children are aged 12.

Education for under-sixes is divided into two cycles: up to three years old, and from age three to six. The institutions offering pre-school education are subject to control by the state, which sets down regulations governing what is taught and how the institutions are run. Some are state operated. Nursery school hours are usually from 9.00 am to 12.30 pm and 3.00 pm to 5.15 pm.

Choices for primary and secondary education

Your choices will depend very much on where you live. International, bilingual, British and US educational options are greater in and around Madrid, Barcelona, the Costa del Sol and the Costa Blanca. The larger towns and cities have a good range of private Spanish schools. Note that if you opt for a Spanish school, whether state or private, in a region in which Castilian is *not* the dominant language, your child will be educated in the local language. This is likely to place the child at a significant disadvantage in his or her general education unless you are in a position to provide him or her with considerable help and assistance with the local language. Furthermore, your child is unlikely to speak Spanish at the same level that he or she would have done at a Spanish school. It will also prove more difficult to ensure that his or her oral and written English are brought on to an acceptable level.

State schools

Education in state school (*escuela pública, colegio público*) is free, though parents are responsible for the cost of books and school materials such as exercise books, pens, pencils, crayons, and so on, as well as for the cost of extra-curricular activities. About two-thirds of Spanish children attend state schools, with the rest attending some form of private school.

As with all types of school, standards in state schools vary considerably. In some areas the presence of significant numbers of British or other foreign families is putting a considerable strain on school resources, and on the relationship between the foreigners and the local Spanish parents. Frequently the British children speak no Spanish on arrival in Spain, and Spanish parents are legitimately concerned about the disproportionate time spent by teaching staff in helping foreign children, and the detrimental effects on the progress of Spanish children. Amongst the children themselves, in some schools animosities develop between the Spanish children and foreign children, creating discipline problems. You may find that your child's progress, both in Spanish and across the board, is better in a state school where there are relatively few other English-speaking children. On the other hand, in some areas with large numbers of foreign residents, the local councils provide intensive Spanish lessons for foreign children.

If your child is to attend state school, it must be within a certain distance of your home. Accordingly, it would be wise to make enquiries about the local school and indeed see whether the headteacher is willing to meet you, *before* you choose your home.

In theory the procedure for admitting your child into a Spanish state school is somewhat complicated and long-winded, and should be put into motion before you leave the United Kingdom. Your child is supposed to be interviewed, and could be asked to complete an examination to assess his or her level of Spanish. A child's education records are 'supposed' to be translated into Spanish, a requirement that can be quite costly, and then 'convalidated' or assessed. I have seen it stated that a child will not be accepted until the convalidation papers have been issued.

In practice, however, the position is far more relaxed, and many parents state that they simply contacted the local school and spoke to the head-teacher. You will, however, need to provide your child's birth certificate or passport, proof of your child's immunization, and proof of residence such as a utility bill, rental agreement or *escritura*. Note, however, that in popular areas there is a risk that your child may not be admitted to your local school if the school is full. Enrolment usually starts from March/April for the September term.

Further information concerning state schools can be found on the website of the Spanish Ministry of Education, **www.mec.es/educacion**. In any event it would be wise to contact the Ministry's London office on 020 7727 2462 several months before you leave the United Kingdom.

Private Spanish schools

A large number of private schools (*escuelas privados, colegios privados*) in Spain are Catholic schools. Many private schools are assisted by the state (*colegios concertados*). The standard of education is generally higher than for state schools, and your child is more sheltered. Fees are lower than for the international schools, and in the areas most popular with foreign residents a significant proportion of children at these schools are foreign. A major advantage of sending your child to a private school is that he or she does not have to change schools if you move house, for example if you rent initially and only buy after living in the area for 12 months or so. There are relatively few boarding schools.

International private schools

International private schools are primarily day schools. They can be expensive, especially if you have more than one child. Fees for secondary education start from about 7,000 euros per annum, with the cost of primary education being somewhat lower. Discounts for second and third children are sometimes available. International schools usually require a registration fee (often around 600 euros per child). Most schools demand a full term's notice of leaving, or payment of a term's fees.

Some of these schools are essentially British, others are more US-orientated and yet others more internationally focused. The British-orientated schools tend to follow the UK curriculum (working to National Curriculum tests and GCSE O levels and A levels). The others prepare their students for the International Baccalaureate (in English). As with private schools in the United Kingdom and United States, extra-curricular activities are generally given far greater emphasis than in Spanish schools.

International schools generally start from nursery age and go all the way through to age 18. A list of international private schools can be found on several websites, including **www.ecis.org**, **www.nabss.org** and **www.ydelta.free.sp**. General guidance can also be obtained from ELSA-Spain (the English Language Schools Association). See also Chapter 1 for regional information. Another useful source of information is **www.spainexchange.com**.

The international private schools are generally fairly small, often with fewer than 500 pupils. Whilst this may be a great advantage in primary school and the early years of secondary school, it means that the choice of subjects that the schools can offer at GCSE and A level/Baccalaureate can be very restricted. Accordingly, if you have a choice of schools, and your child is likely to remain there during these examination years, you should enquire about not only which subjects are available, but also what the options are in terms of combining different subjects. Even though you may be happy with the range of subjects offered, it may not be possible to study certain combinations, owing to practical difficulties of timetabling and staffing.

The Spanish system: state and private

The school year runs from mid-September until the middle or end of June, with slight regional variations. For children at primary school the school day starts at 9.00 am through to 12.30 pm and 3.30 pm to 5.30 pm. At secondary school the day starts at 9.00 am and finishes at 4.00 pm with a lunch break of an hour during which a reasonably priced meal is provided, or a child can eat a packed lunch. However, more and more schools are deciding not to have a lunch break in favour of an early finish at 1.30 or 2.00 pm.

Primary education from ages 6 to 12 is divided into three cycles of two years each, with a foreign language introduced from age 8, generally English. Class size is usually limited to 25. The agenda for primary school is to achieve the socialization of children and their cultural inclusion, and to facilitate a progressive increase in their autonomy.

Secondary school compulsory education is divided into two cycles of two years each, ages 12–14 and 14–16. Maximum class size is intended to be 30. The last stage of secondary education, between 16 and 18, is not compulsory. Students still receive a general education intended to provide the basis for further studies, either at university or in vocational training.

Pupils who successfully complete the second cycle at secondary school are awarded the qualification of Graduate in Secondary Education. This entitles them to proceed to study for the Baccalaureate (*Bachillerato*) or be admitted to vocational training courses. In both primary and secondary schools, pupils who do not reach a given standard at the end of a cycle can be required to repeat a year. A pupil who repeatedly fails to reach a sufficient level can be repeatedly required to repeat a year.

Further information on the Spanish education system (including the private sector) can be obtained from the Spanish Embassy Education Office, 20 Peel Street, London W8 7PD (tel: 020 7727 2462; e-mail: consecuda.lon@dial.pipex.com.

Bilingual children

I have seen claims that children under the age of eight can acquire a competence in the language within three months and near fluency after six months, whilst at age 11 fluency can take up to a year. This is contrary to the views of many experts in this field. The Doman Institute in the United States, for example, claims that a child's capacity to acquire a second language is at its highest between the ages of three and five and drops dramatically from the age of six. In my experience the reality is somewhere in the middle, with complete fluency in two languages requiring considerable effort on the part of the child and his or her parents. If you do want your children to speak fluent Spanish, it would be advisable to seek out Spanish company as much as possible and, ideally, place them in a Spanish school rather than an international school.

Fluency is not automatic, and considerable effort is required on the part of parents, as well as children, to achieve it. Transferring from one language to another is a skill in itself that needs to be nurtured. Effort is also required to maintain your child's fluency in English – a language that many foreigners spend a great deal of time and money trying to acquire and that your child should not lose.

Bilingual summer camps

See **www.spanishsummercamp.com** for camps in Spanish and English for 9- to 16-year-olds in July and August. If Spanish is your priority, you will need to take care in your choice of camp, as in many of these camps English is or becomes the dominant language.

Dual qualifications

Under an agreement between the British Council and the Ministry of Education and Culture, students in some educational establishments can simultaneously obtain Spanish academic qualifications and those of the United Kingdom. For further information, contact the Centre for Investigation and Educational Documentation Innovative Programme, C/General Oraa 55, 28006 Madrid (tel: 91 745 94 00).

Table 8.1 shows the equivalent stages of education for Spain, the United Kingdom and the United States.

University education

There is a good selection of universities in Spain, including several Catholic and private universities. Whilst fees are low for both Spanish and EU nationals, the facilities are stretched to capacity. There is little in the way of extra-curricular activities, in contrast to the position in the United Kingdom and United States. Entrance is by examination, the *Selectividad*. A university education in Spain, however, takes longer than elsewhere in Europe, and for that reason many wealthy Spanish families send their children to universities abroad. Degrees in law, the sciences and humanities take four to five years; degrees in medicine, veterinary surgery and engineering take five to six years. The academic year runs from September to June, with examinations in February and/or July or at the end of June.

Spanish universities are under the jurisdiction of the *Ministerio de Educación, Cultura y Deportes* (MEC). If you wish to study for a degree in a Spanish university, you must first contact the Spanish embassy or consulate in your home country to validate (*convalidar*) your existing qualifications. You can then apply to take the university entrance examination. UK A levels are accepted for entrance to Spanish university, though a US high school diploma is generally not sufficient.

Table 8.1   Equivalent stages of education for Spain, the United Kingdom and the United States

Age	Spain	United Kingdom	United States
	INFANT		
2–5	Infant	Nursery	Nursery
5–6	Infant	Yr 1 (infants)	Kindergarten
	PRIMARY	PRIMARY	ELEMENTARY
6–7	Primary 1st cycle (1st)	Yr 2 (infants)	1st grade
7–8	Primary 1st cycle (2nd)	Yr 3 (junior)	2nd grade
8–9	Primary 2nd cycle (3rd)	Yr 4 (junior)	3rd grade
9–10	Primary 2nd cycle (4th)	Yr 5 (junior)	4th grade
10–11	Primary 3rd cycle (5th)	Yr 6 (junior)	5th grade
		SECONDARY	
11–12	Primary 3rd cycle (6th)	1st form	6th grade
	SECONDARY		JUNIOR HIGH
12–13	Secondary 1st cycle (1st)	2nd form	7th grade
13–14	Secondary 1st cycle (2nd)	3rd form	8th grade
			HIGH SCHOOL
14–15	Secondary 2nd cycle (3rd)		9th grade
15–16	Secondary 2nd cycle (4th)		10th grade
	BACHILLERATO		
16–17	Bachillerato (1st)	Lower 6th	11th grade
17–18	Bachillerato (2nd)	Upper 6th	12th grade

There is also the possibility of enrolling in a Spanish university as a visiting student for up to one academic year, although you cannot count these studies towards a degree in Spain should you later wish to continue your studies in Spain. You can obtain information from the *Vicerrectorado de Alumnos* or the International Relations office at each university.

Details of over 60 Spanish universities and schools of higher education, including business schools (with links to their websites and e-mail addresses) can be obtained from **www.spainexchange.com**. For further information on the Spanish University System, contact the Council for University Coordination, Ciudad Universitaria s/n, E-28040 Madrid (tel: 914 53 98 00; website: **www.mec.es/universidades/index.html**). Information on doctorates and postgraduate studies can be found at **www.mec.es/ consejou/cursodoc/index.html**.

Instituto de Empresa

The *Instituto de Empresa* is a private non-profit-making independent institute established for over 30 years that offers courses in business subjects, including MBAs, and is internationally recognized. The address is Instituto Empresa, Maria de Molina 11, E-28006 Madrid (tel: 34 915 68 96 00; website: **www.ie.edu/weben/insti/campus.html**.

Occupational training

Occupational training is subsidized by the Spanish state and the EU Social Fund, and available at Occupational Training Centres. It is free, and all those between 18 and 65 are eligible. Financial assistance is available in certain circumstances. In all, there are a total of 139 official qualifications.

The Open University

The Open University's distance learning programme is available in Spain, but the cost is substantially higher than in the United Kingdom. However, if you or your spouse pay UK income tax, you should be able to avoid paying the supplement. Information about the Open University's courses and the Open University Business School can be found on their respective websites: **www.open.ac.uk** and **www.oubs.open.ac.uk**.

Research

A researcher considering a move to another EU member state will find career opportunities and information and assistance from the European Commission's Mobility Portal, accessible via **www.europa.eu.int**.

Study abroad

The European Commission is keen to encourage studying in another country. It considers that this can be an invaluable experience for the individual as well as being beneficial to the European economy. Students learn from the different ways of formulating and solving problems.

Employers are increasingly keen to recruit people who not only speak other European languages but also have experience of interacting with nationals of other European countries and have the ability to adapt.

The Commission offers a service known as PLOTEUS (Portal on Learning Opportunities Throughout Europe) that provides information on education and training opportunities throughout Europe, such as websites of higher education institutions, databases of training courses, schools, etc. The PLOTEUS website is at **www.europa.eu.int/ploteus**. It includes details of national education and training systems, European exchange programmes and grants (from both your home and your host country) and contacts for further information. It is also worth taking a look at the home page of the Euroguide Network at **www.euroguidance.org.uk**.

The European Union now has a system for recognizing qualifications, namely its network of National Academic Recognition Information Centres (NARICs). See the website http://**www.enic-naric.net**.

Healthcare and the Spanish health system

Spaniards generally boast good health, primarily thanks to the climate and their diet. The average life expectancy for women is 80 years and that for men is 74, both amongst the highest in the world. Heart disease is nowhere near the health problem that it is in the United Kingdom. Two of the principal causes of illness are smoking and drinking.

The standard of healthcare in Spain has risen considerably over the past 20 years, and for the most part is of a reasonably high standard. There is a national health system, the *Instituto Nacional de Salud* or *Insalud* (Alcala 56, E-28014 Madrid; tel: 91 338 00 00; website: **www.msc.es/insalud**). Treatment and medication are free, or heavily subsidized, to those who contribute to the Spanish social security scheme, though a large number of Spaniards also take out private health insurance. About 75 per cent of the cost of most non-dental treatment is covered, with the balance being paid by the patient (except for retired or disabled people), or through private health insurance. Dental treatment is very limited (extractions only), though eye tests and prescriptions are free. US citizens are not entitled to cover under the Spanish health system, and must obtain private cover.

On the whole, doctors are well trained and hospitals have up-to-date medical equipment. The main shortcoming is in nursing care, and help for patients in the community, particularly the aged. Even in the private sector, there are, for example, very few retirement and convalescent homes, or homes for the terminally ill. Large numbers of Britons and other foreign residents who are no longer able to manage alone find themselves having to return home. Spain also lags considerably behind other West European countries in its provision of facilities, including access, for disabled people. You should note that severe strain is placed on public and indeed private health provision during August, when the holidays of medical staff coincide with peak demand in the tourist areas.

Your choice of doctor is determined by where you live and whether you are relying on the state system. In the most popular areas, such as the Costa del Sol, there is a wide choice of doctors available for those who are privately insured, or able to pay. Many of these doctors speak English, or are of British or other North European nationality. On the other hand, if you are using the state system you will initially be assigned to a general practitioner (*medico de cabecera*). You are entitled to change doctors, but your choices are restricted to another doctor in the same area whose list is not full. Almost certainly you will be consulting a Spanish doctor. You will not need to make any payment to a doctor under the state health scheme, but must present your social security card.

You do not need the referral of a general practitioner in order to consult a specialist, though you will if you wish the consultation to be paid for by the state. Similarly, many insurance policies will require a referral as a condition of paying for the fees of the specialist. The same general rule – obtain a referral if you are not paying yourself – applies to using the services of a nurse, physiotherapist or chiropodist. In public hospitals, private rooms are available on payment of a supplement.

In many towns there is a state-operated health centre, the *ambulatorio*, sometimes called the *consultorio*. You can attend the centre to register with one of the doctors there. You will be asked to show your social security card. These centres are generally quite well equipped. It is usually possible to have an X-ray taken there, or a blood sample taken for testing. Unfortunately, the centres are frequently very busy, and the system of queuing at times rather chaotic and disorganized.

Spain has a considerable number of private hospitals and clinics, with a particularly heavy concentration in the Costa del Sol, where residents also have the possibility of choosing the British-run Westminster Private Medical Clinic in Gibraltar.

Your rights to medical care in Spain

If you are going to Spain for a short stay only or as a student, obtain and complete a copy of form E111 from your local post office (it is attached to a guidance booklet). This will cover you for emergency treatment while in Spain for up to 90 days (pensioners are entitled to both emergency and routine treatment). You will be required to pay, but are entitled to recover most of the cost when you return to the United Kingdom. You will be left with having paid a modest contribution, as you would if you were living and working in Spain.

In the course of 2005 form E111 is to be replaced by a plastic card. This will enable nationals of EU member states to obtain not only emergency care (as in the past) but also *necessary routine and medical treatment* during a temporary stay of up to 12 months in another EU country. This will include, for example, ongoing treatment for a serious medical condition. The card will not enable EU nationals to *choose* to have treatment for a condition in another member state – this is possible, but only with the prior approval of the authorities in your home country. The card, which will avoid the necessity of obtaining a new form E111 for each trip abroad, should be available through post offices in the UK.

If you require a regular prescription and will need to obtain further supplies while in Spain, be sure to obtain form E112 and the generic name of the medication from your doctor. This will enable the Spanish chemist to identify the version of the drug available in Spain. Help and advice are available from the Overseas Section of the Department of Health (tel: 020 7210 4850).

If you are intending to retire to Spain, you should contact the Pension Service's International Pension Centre, which is part of the Department for Work and Pensions (tel: 0191 218 7777), or write to The International Pension Centre at Newcastle upon Tyne NE98 1BA. In Northern Ireland you should contact the Northern Ireland Social Security Agency, International Services (24–42 Corporation Street, Belfast BT1 3DR; tel: 028 9054 3245). In either case, ask for copies of the various leaflets applicable.

Those living and working in Spain are generally required to join the Spanish social security system governing pensions, sickness, unemployment and healthcare. If you are employed, your employer is required to register you with the social security authorities and to deduct social security contributions from your salary. You should receive your social security card (*cartilla de la seguridad social*) from your employer, to whom the authorities will send it. This is the proof of your entitlement, and the entitlement of your dependants, to medical cover, and will bear both your social security number and the name of the general practitioner to whom you will be initially assigned. You will be entitled to free hospital and medical treatment and 40 per cent of the cost of prescriptions.

Self-employed people are also required to make contributions, but the system is not identical to that applicable to salaried employees and you will need to check the up-to-date position. Medical and healthcare for your spouse and children are covered by your social security contributions.

If you are a UK national and have been sent to work in Spain by your employer, you should be entitled to cover under the Spanish health system whilst still paying your contributions to the UK system. If you are in receipt of a UK state pension, you are entitled to treatment under the Spanish health system without contribution. You will need to obtain form 121 to establish your entitlement.

Private insurance

A number of Spanish and foreign companies offer health insurance cover, including Sanitas, used by many Spaniards. BUPA and Danmark AS International Health Insurance are two other leaders in the field. Policies vary considerably in the cover provided, in particular in the degree of choice of doctors and hospitals and on matters that are excluded from cover.

Language difficulties

Many Spanish doctors claim to speak English, but relatively few speak it to a high standard. Assistance is available from various sources:

- The consulates of the various English-speaking nations that keep lists of English-speaking doctors.
- Private health insurance and travellers' associations – these often provide details of English-speaking doctors to their clients.
- British and US hospitals based in Spain.
- The English-language press (see Appendix 1) may be able to provide you with details. On the Costa del Sol, for example, many doctors and other medical professionals advertise in *Sur in English*.

Pharmacies

As in many other countries, *farmacias* have a green neon light outside their premises. In Spain you can obtain a considerable number of products over the counter without a prescription, including antibiotics. However, unless you have a prescription you will pay in full even if you are registered with the state health service (with a prescription, the cost of medication is 100 per cent recoverable in connection with work-related accidents, and 60 per cent in other cases). Chemists are usually open from 9.30 am to 1.30 pm and from 5.00 pm to 8.00 pm from Monday to Friday, and from 9.30 am to

1.30 pm on Saturdays. There is also a system of duty chemists open 24 hours a day, seven days a week. The address of the duty out-of-hours pharmacist is posted in the windows of pharmacies, and can also be found in the local newspaper.

Emergency treatment

For medical (and indeed all) emergencies, you should telephone 112. Those registered with the state health system do not pay for emergency ambulances; those who are privately insured will normally recover costs under their insurance policy. In addition, in most towns there are 24-hour private ambulance services. Private hospitals and clinics often have their own ambulances. Taxi drivers are legally obliged to take those in need of emergency treatment to hospital, if asked. They are entitled to payment. If you need to use a private vehicle to transport someone to hospital in an emergency, putting on the hazard lights and waving a white flag out of the window should make other drivers give you priority.

Emergency hospital care takes priority over means of payment, and so even if you are not able to prove that you have cover, or do not have cover, this is a matter for sorting out afterwards, and should not delay treatment.

Vaccinations

You are likely to be required to give details of vaccinations to your doctor, or your children's doctor, and indeed this is a condition of school entry. You should be given a vaccination record. The Spanish words for the diseases commonly vaccinated against are:

chickenpox – *varicela*
diphtheria – *difteria*
measles – *sarampión*
mumps – *paperas*
poliomyelitis – *poliomielitis*
rubella – *rubeola*
tetanus – *tétanos*
tuberculosis – *tuberculosis*
whooping cough – *ferina* or *convulsiva*

10 You and your car

Importing your car

EU citizens are entitled to bring their EU-registered car into Spain without completing any formalities. However, the car must not be used by its owner, or any other person, for more than six months in any calendar year. Broadly similar rules apply to boats. Those spending more than six months a year in Spain are deemed to be resident, and therefore must undertake the procedures involved in registering their vehicle in Spain. Traditionally the Spanish police have been very tolerant of those who continue to run their foreign-registered cars in Spain for prolonged periods. In recent years, however, foreigners have been increasingly stopped by the police and asked for proof that their car is only used for six months in any year. Accordingly, if you are a non-resident and run a car in Spain, you would be well advised to have your passport stamped, or to retain your travel documents so that you can prove how long you have been in Spain. If you are unable to provide this proof, you may be faced with fines in the region of 2,000 euros, and be required either to import the car formally into Spain, or to take it out of the country.

Non-EU citizens are also entitled to run their foreign-registered car in Spain for up to six months in a calendar year, but are required to undergo a 'sealing' procedure when the vehicle is not in use. You should notify the customs officials (the *aduana*) when a period of non-use is to begin. The civil guard will then come to put tape across the steering wheel, prohibiting its use. If you require the car for leaving the country, or become entitled to drive it again, you should contact the customs officials, who can then unseal it, and you can then drive it in Spain for a further six months. The costs involved in having your vehicle sealed and unsealed are modest.

For EU citizens there are no duties on cars purchased in EU countries. Non-EU citizens will not have to pay VAT either, provided they paid VAT in the country of origin and have owned the car for at least six months. They must start the procedure for importing the vehicle within one month of the issue of their residence card, and be able to prove residence in Spain. The latter can be done by making a declaration of intention to settle in Spain to the Spanish consulate in your home country, or to your own consulate on arrival in Spain. It is not unknown for people to receive their residence card some weeks after the date of its issue, and accordingly application for exemption from VAT should be made at the same time as the application for a residence card.

VAT of 16 per cent is payable on cars imported from outside the European Union (or purchased tax free within the European Union). A registration tax of 12 per cent of the vehicle's value at purchase, less a deduction for each year of its age, is also payable on cars on which no VAT has been paid. The rate is 6 per cent for smaller vehicles. Third, a 10 per cent import duty is payable on vehicles imported from outside the European Union for non-residents, again based on a combination of the original value of the vehicle and its age. Further information can be obtained from the website of the main *Dirección General de Tráfico*, **www. dgt.es**.

UK registration documents should be returned to the Driving and Vehicle Licensing Agency, from which a Certificate of Permanent Export (V561) should be obtained. You will need to obtain a roadworthiness certificate for a right-hand drive vehicle from a Spanish MOT centre (known as an ITV), and have your headlights adjusted.

If you are non-resident, then you can only obtain a car in Spain with temporary tourist plates that are valid for six months in any one year and are required to be renewed annually. The paperwork is substantial!

Traffic regulations

Traffic regulations now require drivers to keep certain equipment in their cars, namely a set of bulbs and a spare tyre, together with the tools required to replace them, and two warning triangles bearing a round symbol E9 and the code 27R03. A fine of about 90 euros is payable for failure to comply with this latter regulation. The use of mobile telephones is prohibited whilst driving. A completely hands-free set is permitted, but headsets are not. Radar detectors are also against the law. Speed limits are *slightly* higher than in the United Kingdom: 120 kph on motorways (80 kph if towing a caravan), 100 kph on dual carriageways, 90 kph on other main roads and 50 kph in built-up areas. Spanish law requires motorists to stop and assist in the event of an accident, a law that criminals have frequently abused by making the pretence of having been injured or otherwise involved in an accident, only to attack and/or steal from the person who has stopped to assist them. The Highway Code is known as *Código de la Circulación*.

Traffic police have the power to impose on-the-spot fines of up 300 euros, including for failure to carry a driving licence or wear a seat belt. Fines paid immediately are discounted by 30 per cent. Always obtain a receipt.

Driving licences

A UK driving licence (green), or other national driving licence is not accepted, save for tourists, who should obtain a translation in Spanish from the Spanish embassy in their home country. An EU licence (pink) issued in another member state is of course valid. Holders should register with the Provincial Traffic Headquarters (*Registro de Conductores y Infractores*) at the *Jefatura Provincial de Tráfico* in the provincial capital within six months of arrival in Spain, when they will be given details of when they must apply to renew their licence. For those over 70, a medical certificate will be required when they come to renew their licence, and annually thereafter.

In addition to completing an application form, you will need your existing driving licence, your current national identity document or passport, your foreigner's identity document (NIE) certifying your habitual residence or student status, together with copies of all three documents (the originals will be returned to you). You will also need two recent 35mm × 25mm photographs and written declarations confirming that you have not been banned or suspended from driving, and do not hold any other driving licence, Spanish or otherwise.

A Spanish driving licence is valid for 10 years for those under 45, three years for those aged between 45 and 70, and two years from age 70 onwards. These validity periods can be reduced if a person suffers from an illness or handicap that will probably worsen, even if it does not yet prevent him or her from driving. Once a driving licence has expired, the holder is no longer authorized to drive.

The minimum age for driving a car or motorcycle over 125 cc is 18 (16 for a motorcycle of 50–125 cc, and 14 for a moped up to 50 cc).

Non-EU nationals are required to apply for a Spanish driving licence on becoming resident. They must pass a driving test and a medical examination. Application forms are obtainable from the local provincial traffic department (*Jefatura Provincial de Tráfico*).

Insurance

If you are using your foreign-registered car in Spain, you need to extend your home-country insurance cover to Spain. The insurance company should issue you with a 'green card'. Those with Spanish-registered vehicles generally take out a policy in Spain. There are a number of differences between the regulations in the United Kingdom and those in Spain governing motor insurance. You should ensure that you fully understand the extent of the cover under any policy you are contemplating taking out. An important point is that even under apparently fully comprehensive policies (*responsabilidad civil voluntario* or *complimentario*), you will only receive a proportion of the vehicle's value should it need to be written off. Take care also that you comply with the conditions contained in the policy, including the time limits and other provisions for the reporting of claims. Insurance is considerably cheaper with a higher excess.

Insurance companies refuse insurance cover or offer only limited cover for older cars. Ensure that you will be able to insure a second-hand vehicle before you purchase one!

Third party insurance is compulsory. Ensure that you have sufficient third party cover (the minimum cover of 350,000–400,000 euros will be insufficient if a third party or parties were to suffer serious personal injuries). You will need separate cover for drivers and passengers. You can use your foreign non-claims bonus in Spain on production of a letter or other written proof from your previous or existing insurers.

If you have an accident, ensure that you obtain the name, address and insurance company of the other driver. Contact your insurance agent as quickly as possible (ie within 24–48 hours). You have two months in which to bring charges against the other driver.

Purchasing a car

Purchasing a new car in Spain is expensive, owing to the 12 per cent registration tax (*impuesto sobre la circulación*) combined with the VAT of 16 per cent. On the sale of a car the vendor is required to complete a transfer of ownership form in duplicate, one copy of which is registered with the *Jefatura Provincial de Tráfico*, the other given to the purchaser. A sales tax is payable amounting to 4 per cent of the fiscal value (based on the value of the car as new, discounted for its age). The vendor must pay this within 30 days of the sale to the provincial tax office. He or she must also take the transfer section of the car registration papers to the *Jefatura Provincial de Tráfico*. The buyer must then arrange for his or her ownership to be noted at the same office.

As part of its campaign to take old cars off its roads, the Spanish government grants a subsidy of up to about 750 euros off the car registration tax for those purchasing a new vehicle and scrapping their old car. The highest grants apply where the car to be scrapped runs on regular leaded petrol.

Annual vehicle tax and MOT

An annual vehicle tax is payable to your local council, based on the horsepower of the vehicle, with the tax payable starting from about 60 euros. The receipt for this tax should be kept in your car, together with the registration papers and insurance receipt to provide to the police if you are stopped.

All cars over four years old have to undergo a test, the *Inspección Técnica de Vehículos* (ITV), which is similar to the annual MOT in the United Kingdom, and thereafter must be tested every two years until the vehicle is nine years old, when the obligation becomes annual.

Drink-driving

New regulations came into force in October 2004. They are some of the severest in Europe. The general rule is a limit of 0.25 milligrams per litre of blood (compared to 0.4 in the United Kingdom, for example). Those who have recently obtained their driving licence, or drive as their profession, are subject to more stringent limits and should avoid any alcohol at all before driving. Punishments include very steep fines and driving bans of up to four years. Those who are found guilty of dangerous driving whilst under the influence of alcohol face up to two years in prison. You could find that your insurers do not cover you for claims (including claims against you) if you are involved in an accident when you are under the influence of alcohol.

Heating and utility bills

Choosing how to heat your home

Heating requirements vary greatly according to the location of your home, its type, size and insulation, whether you live at the property throughout the year and whether it is occupied during the day. In northern Spain the climate is wet and often as cold as in Northern Europe. Central Spain can be colder. Even slightly inland on the Costa del Sol you will definitely need heating in the winter months.

One disadvantage with many Spanish homes is that they are designed to remain cool during the hot summer season. In cold periods their tiled floors and concrete walls make your home seem particularly cold. In most Spanish homes you will need some form of heating facility. In deciding how to heat your home you have to consider the present heating system in the property, the costs of installing a new system, the life expectancy of a new system and your estimated consumption. In apartment blocks there is frequently a central gas-fired under-floor heating system, which is paid in whole or in part through your community fees.

Electricity

Electricity is a convenient form of heating, especially for smaller flats and coastal properties in the south, where your heating requirements will be modest. It has the great advantage of being easy and inexpensive to install, so it is often the choice of landlords. The disadvantage of electricity, however, is that the running costs are high.

Gas

The advantages of gas are that it is clean and relatively economical. However, for the most part only properties in the main towns and larger cities are connected to the gas mains. Elsewhere, bottled butane gas is commonly used, especially for cooking. This is relatively economic, and in most areas bottled butane can be delivered to your home by Repsol Butano. Canisters of 23.5 kilograms cost about 10 euros, with a deposit for the bottle of about 20 euros. You should keep a spare full bottle, as it is difficult to determine when a bottle is likely to run out. It is wise to check the rubber tubing regularly (it should have an expiry date on it).

One disadvantage of gas is that it can be dangerous if any gas-run apparatus is not functioning properly. Accordingly, a word of caution is appropriate: beware carbon monoxide poisoning. It is likely that the problem is in fact quite widespread, with many people being unaware of their exposure and the cause of symptoms from which they are suffering. Symptoms resemble those associated with flu: headache, fatigue, nausea and problems with vision and hearing.

Carbon monoxide is a colourless, odourless gas associated with gas- and also oil-, wood- and coal-burning appliances. Almost invariably the problem arises from a faulty or incorrectly used appliance. Appliances should be regularly serviced and replaced when appropriate. A faulty appliance is not only dangerous, but is inefficient and accordingly more expensive to run.

Solar energy

Solar energy is renewable, clean, silent and free. Moreover, a system that uses solar energy requires very little maintenance and should last 20 or 30 years. Solar energy is particularly popular for heating water in Austria and Germany. Spain has rather more hours of sunshine and so solar energy is capable of meeting the majority of your needs for the heating of both your rooms and your water. A major disadvantage is the relatively high installation cost. A second drawback is that you will need a back-up system (although portable electric radiators may suffice).

Air-conditioning

Increasingly, modern buildings have the benefit of air-conditioning, a great relief during the height of summer. If the property is without this facility, it may be worthwhile obtaining an estimate, especially if you are purchasing a new home. Note that for older people, some form of system for lowering the temperature is likely to be essential, and if there is no central air-conditioning, serious consideration should be given to obtaining a portable gas cooler.

Electricity bills

Electricity bills are issued every two months in Spain, rather than quarterly. Your bill will consist of a subscription for the service paid in advance, plus an amount depending on the quantity of electricity consumed. For most of Spain, electricity supplied is at 220 volts, which is compatible with 240-volt appliances purchased in the United Kingdom but not with equipment purchased in the United States. US-purchased appliances that have a motor are designed to run at 60 Hz and may be unsuitable in Europe where the frequency is 50 Hz (check the label on the back of the equipment).

If you are proposing to purchase an old property you will need to check the voltage, as it may be wired for the older 110-volt system formerly in use.

When registering, you will need to take your title deeds or rental agreement, your NIE number, and the last receipt of the previous occupier. You must also decide the level of kilowatt-hours (kWh) of your electricity supply. This will determine the tariff applicable to your supply. The wattage you require can range from as little as 3.3 kWh if your needs are limited to lighting and running such electrical appliances as a television, refrigerator and vacuum cleaner. If you wish to be able to run a washing machine, dishwasher and electric cooker, you will probably need a supply of between 9 and 18 kWh. Many property owners opt for tariff 2.0 (up to15 kWh), for which the current rate is 0.086 euros per kWh. For homes with numerous electrical appliances likely to be switched on at the same time or with an electric system for heating rooms or water, you should discuss your needs with a representative of the electricity company.

If you need to connect your property to the electricity supply, you should apply to do this well in advance, as there can be considerable delays in being connected.

The appliances that place the greatest demands in kilowatts on your system are as follows (figures indicate the maximum the appliances would use):

- water heater – 4,500;
- cooker's hotplates – 4,000;
- dishwasher – 3,000;
- washing machine – 3,000;
- tumble-dryer – 3,000;
- electric kettle – 1,800;
- oven –1,200;
- iron – 1,100;
- hair-dryer – 1,100.

Accordingly, a family household in which a water heater, kettle, washing machine, oven and hairdryer could well be operated simultaneously would require up to 11.6 kilowatts without taking into account the less hungry items such as lighting, televisions, computers, fridge, freezer, and so on.

Note that power cuts are a common hazard in Spain, especially during torrential rain, and you should consider fitting an uninterrupted power supply with a backing battery. You should also consider purchasing a power surge protector (at a cost of about 18 euros) to avoid damage to electrical appliances during storms.

You can opt for a night tariff. The standing charge is slightly more than with the standard tariff, but electricity consumed between 11.00 pm and 7.00 am (for both times one hour later in the summer) is at under half that of the normal tariff.

When a bill remains unpaid the electricity company should send you a warning letter stating that the supply will be cut off if the bill is not paid, before which your supply should not be cut off.

Water bills

Whilst water is in plentiful supply in the north of the country, the hottest and most popular tourist areas suffer from water shortages, often severe. In rural areas, *fincas* may be some distance from the mains supply, and so have to be supplied from tankers, causing an added expense. If the property boasts a well in the garden, you will need to check whether others have rights to use it, and also the quality of the water and whether it dries up during the summer.

For the most part, mains water supplies in Spain are metered. Prices vary according to the region, but bills can be quite hefty. An average family can easily use about 500 litres of water per day. About 60 per cent of an average family's consumption relates to the taking of baths and showers and the flushing of the toilet. Accordingly, substantial reductions in consumption can be made by taking showers instead of baths and choosing the toilet cistern carefully; more modern cisterns use a third or less of the amount used by older toilets.

Always check where the main stop-valve or stopcock is located in case you need to turn off the water supply in an emergency.

In some developments there are no individual meters, and occupants simply pay a proportion of the whole community's water bill. In others the water supply is dependent upon an electric pump, and accordingly your water will be cut off when the power supply is interrupted.

You will need to register your occupancy, and can do this by taking a copy of your title deeds or rental contract, your NIE number and the previous occupant's last receipt to the local office of the water company. Your water supply can be cut off for non-payment of your water bill.

Note that in some regions, including Andalusia, the water is very hard.

The telephone

To have a line installed you will need to visit your local office of Telefonica. Always enter into a new contract with a new telephone number, rather than continue with the previous occupier's number. Following installation of your line, your number is included in the next edition of the local white pages, unless you opt for your number not to be listed (*no registrado*). You can find out the address of your local Telefonica office by telephoning 1004, and if you wish, you can start your application over the telephone. To subscribe, you will need to show your residence card or passport, proof of residence such as a recent utility bill, and your *escritura* (or rental contract) if your home is rented. It can take up to 10 days to be connected. Information about Telefonica is available on its website, **www.telefonica.es**, where you can also fill out an application form. Telefonica is reputed to have the highest charges and you should consider using another telephone company for your calls.

It is possible to have your line temporarily disconnected for up to three months per year, for example if you are away from the property. For further information about telephones, see Chapter 7.

Direct debit

There is much to be said for paying utility bills by direct debit, particularly if you are away from the property for extended periods.

Spanish inheritance laws and the taxation of capital

When you purchase a property abroad, you *must* give consideration as to the effect that your purchase is likely to have on the passing of your estate, and in particular as to how it will affect your spouse and children. In theory the situation is complex. Spanish law states that the disposal of a foreigner's property (even where the foreigner is resident in Spain) shall be in accordance with that person's own national law, ie UK law in the case of a UK citizen. The law of England and Wales, however, states that the passing of property should be in accordance with the rules of the country in which *the property is situated*! Whilst the 1989 Hague Convention provides that citizens of Europe can *choose* that the national laws of their home country should apply to their estate, the United Kingdom has not ratified the convention.

With Swedish law there is no difficulty, as this provides that a Swedish national's assets should be distributed *in accordance with Swedish law*, even where the person is living abroad and his or her assets are situated abroad. Norwegian law adopts a third position: that the distribution of assets should be in accordance with the law of the country in which he or she is living.

You really need to take legal advice from a lawyer with knowledge of the law in both your home country *and* Spain, and taking into account your particular circumstances and testamentary intentions.

Spanish rules of succession

The rules mentioned above are in theory important, because in Spain, as in other continental European countries, such as France, succession law restricts your freedom to dispose of your estate on your death. In brief, if your property is subject to Spanish succession rules, you are obliged to leave a proportion of your estate to your children, with some (rather limited) provision for your spouse. Accordingly, where a deceased has children, the *Ley de Herederos Forzosos* stipulates that:

▌ A third must be left to the surviving children (or other issue) in equal shares.

▌ A second third must also be left to the children (or grandchildren), although in relation to this third you may distribute this how you like amongst your issue, perhaps leaving it only to your grandchildren. This third, however, is subject to a life interest in favour of your surviving spouse: that is, the spouse has the income from this third until his or her death.

▌ In relation to the last third, you retain complete control, and accordingly you may leave this third completely to your spouse.

As is apparent, the surviving spouse receives little obligatory protection (with no protection at all for a common law partner), and a person is significantly restricted in the protection that he or she can provide to his or her spouse. Clearly, if a property (or other asset) is owned jointly, the surviving spouse will retain his or her half of the property, and the above inheritance rules will only apply to the share of the person who has died. The position of the surviving spouse is also alleviated by the fact that in Spanish law a spouse is entitled to 50 per cent of assets that have been acquired by the couple during the marriage (though wealth inherited by one spouse remains the sole property of that spouse).

A working solution

It is currently common practice for British citizens to make a *Spanish* will declaring that your national law provides for freedom of disposition of property on death, and to leave your Spanish property to the person you wish. The Spanish authorities have accepted this to date, and properties have simply been transferred into the names of the beneficiary stated in the will. What would happen, however, if a disinherited child wished to challenge the will, on the basis that part of the estate should have passed to him or her in accordance with Spanish law, remains to be seen.

Whilst your UK will can be effective to pass property in Spain in accordance with UK rules of succession, the procedures are somewhat long-winded. Furthermore, a UK will may not have been drafted with Spanish inheritance tax in mind, and the consequences may be rather draconian for the beneficiaries of your estate.

Note that if you do not make a will, in practice your estate will be distributed in accordance with Spanish succession law for intestacy. This means that your estate will be divided equally between your children, though subject to a life interest in favour of your spouse: that is, the spouse is entitled to the income from your estate, or, for example, can occupy the family home, until his or her death. As elsewhere, the estate of someone who dies intestate generally takes more time and expense to wind up. Accordingly, you should seriously consider making a Spanish will, in addition to your UK will. The latter may well require updating to take account of your testamentary plans for your Spanish property. You should also note that if you emigrate to Spain and have no remaining assets in the United Kingdom, your UK will may prove ineffective and fail to regulate the distribution of your entirely Spanish estate on your death.

Inheritance tax (*impuesto sobre sucesiones y donaciones*)

Inheritance tax applies irrespective of whether your property is to be disposed of according to Spanish law, or the law of your home country. Your family will not be able to gain access to your Spanish estate until the tax is paid, and accordingly it is advisable to have a life policy that is sufficient to cover the tax that will be due, and indeed any outstanding mortgage. There is no exemption for a family home, and, subject to a modest allowance, transfers on death to a spouse are taxed. All legacies to direct descendants and ascendants under 16,000 euros are exempt, as are legacies up to 8,000 euros to brothers and sisters, uncles, aunts, nephews and nieces. Accordingly, less tax is payable where a modest estate is widely distributed. There are also exemptions of up to 48,000 euros for legacies passing to children, brothers, sisters and also spouses under the age of 21.

The amount of the tax is determined by three factors:

▪ the amount received by each beneficiary (*not* by the size of the total estate);

▌ the relationship of the beneficiary to the deceased;
▌ the existing financial circumstances of the beneficiary.

The system of taxation is intended to encourage the passing of estates to close family members, with the lowest rates applicable to children, spouse or parents and the highest rates to those to whom you are unrelated, including a common-law or same-sex partner. A common-law partner will pay tax at twice the rate of a married spouse. This does not apply in Andalusia and Madrid, where the authorities now apply the same rules to unmarried as to married couples, and in some circumstances to same-sex couples, though it is necessary to register a relationship to benefit from this.

Note that inheritance tax scales in some regions (eg Madrid, Valencia and Catalonia) are different from those applicable in the rest of Spain.

As to the existing wealth of the beneficiaries, a recipient who already has net assets above 400,000 euros pays a higher rate of tax.

The complexities are such that advice should be sought from an expert. There is double taxation relief, so that inheritance tax paid in Spain is taken into account in calculating liability for UK inheritance tax, and vice versa.

For those resident in Spain for at least three years, there is a 95 per cent exemption up to about 120,000 euros in relation to property that has been your principal residence for at least three years. This exemption applies where the property is left to a spouse or to children, or to a sibling aged 65 or above who at the date of the death had been resident in the property for two years. In all cases the beneficiary must not sell the property for 10 years, or he or she will be liable to pay the tax that would have been due on the inheritance. In Andalusia this exemption has been increased to 99.9 per cent. Tax relief is available if you leave a business to your spouse or children. In brief, if the beneficiaries continue to operate the business for at least 10 years, then no inheritance tax is payable.

The rate of tax for close family members rises to 34 per cent for amounts in excess of 800,000 euros. The tax take on a taxable transfer (after exemptions) of 120,00 euros is about 15,600 euros, rising to 40,000 euros for a taxable transfer of 240,000 euros, 80,000 euros for a taxable transfer of 400,000 euros, and 200,000 euros on a taxable transfer of 800,000 euros. The marginal rates for a wealthy beneficiary who is not a close member of the deceased's family are 2.4 times higher, giving a marginal rate of 81.6 per cent for sums in excess of 800,000!

You should note that all property is taken into account, based on its market value at death. Personal effects in a home are valued at 3 per cent of the value of the home, but if they include items of substantial value such as antiques, it is likely that they will be included on the basis of their market value. Life insurance is also included, with a modest exemption if it is in favour of a child. Payments on policies in favour of a spouse are in part taxed as income.

Inheritance tax is payable within 6 months of death (it is possible to obtain an extension), or within 16 months in the case of a death abroad.

Note that in cases where the deceased's debts exceed the value of his or her assets, the beneficiaries should consider refusing the inheritance in order to avoid taking on the deceased's debts. If you think that this may be the case, you should consult a lawyer as soon as possible and *before* you deal with *any* of the deceased's property in *any* way.

Avoiding Spanish inheritance tax

There are a number of ways lawfully to reduce the liability of your successors to pay inheritance tax, including the creation of a family trust to own property. On the death of a member of the family, there is no transfer of ownership as the property remains vested in the trust and hence there is no liability to pay the tax. Another option is to sell your property to your heirs, but reserving the right to live in it for life. If you are a non-resident, you could consider purchasing your property via an offshore company. When you die, the shares of the company will be disposed of according to the will you made in your own country, and there is no Spanish inheritance tax payable as there is no transfer of the Spanish property, which is still owned by the company. Offshore companies owning property in Spain, however, are subject to an annual 3 per cent tax on the value of the property. If your estate is likely to be significant, you need to obtain expert tax advice at the outset.

Lifetime transfers are treated in the same way as transfers on death. The tax is payable within 30 days of the transfer.

Making a will

You would be well advised to make a Spanish will dealing with land and property that you own in Spain if you are not resident there, or dealing with your entire estate if you are a Spanish resident. Reliance solely on your will from your home country can have disastrous consequences, in terms of both inheritance rules and taxation. Your existing will may need to be amended, for example to exclude your Spanish property.

There are three types of Spanish will. The most usual is the *testamento abierto* ('open will'), drawn up by a notary or lawyer. The lawyer and the person making the will both sign the document, and details of the will are registered with the *Registro de las últimas voluntades*. On your death a search will be made of this register before assets are distributed, and accordingly your wishes will be ascertained even if your copy of the will has been lost. If the notary is unable to understand the language in which the testator wishes to express his or her will, then the services of a translator will be required.

A second type of will is the *testamento olografo* (handwritten will). This must be completely written in the testator's own hand, signed by him or her and dated. The main problem with this type of will is that it can be lost, although of course that applies to all wills in England and Wales, and other jurisdictions in which there is no system for registering wills.

The third kind of will is a *testamento cerrado* (a closed will). In this case the testator writes his or her will and encloses it in a sealed envelope. A notary and five witnesses then sign the envelope, the contents of which remain secret until the testator's death.

By virtue of the Hague Convention of 1961, a will is valid if it is signed in accordance with the requirements either of the country in which it is signed or of those of the testator's home country. Accordingly, an English person can sign a will in accordance with the formalities of English law: that is, that the will is signed in the presence of two witnesses, who each sign that they have attested the will. A witness to a will cannot inherit under the will, nor can a member of his or her family.

You should keep a copy of your will and leave a copy with your lawyer or executor. The most recent will takes complete precedence over previous wills, provided that it indicates clearly that all previous wills are revoked. It is not usual to appoint executors to a will in Spain.

Under no circumstances use a home-made will of the type that you can buy in the high street. Such wills are often unclear and are far more prone to result in protracted and expensive litigation than a will drafted by a competent lawyer.

Capital gains tax (*impuesto sobre el incremento patrimonial*)

Residents (generally those living in Spain for more than 183 days a year) pay a maximum rate of 18 per cent on capital gains. It is included in their income tax bill, and accordingly you do not have to declare the gain until the date for filing of the next income tax return. There are a number of exemptions, including the following:

▊ Residents over 65 are completely exempt from capital gains tax on their *principal* residence, provided they have lived in it for more than three years.

▊ The sale proceeds from the sale of a *principal* residence are completely exempt if the vendor has lived in it for at least three years, and the proceeds are used entirely to purchase another principal residence in Spain, or the vendor plans to do so within three years of the sale. If only part of the sale proceeds are used to purchase the new principal residence, the balance is liable for capital gains tax.

▊ A person who is over 65 and who sells his or her home in return for the right to live in it for life and receive an income is exempt from tax on any gain on the sale.

Gains on property purchased prior to 1987 are not subject to the tax. Properties purchased after 1988 but before 31 December 1996 are subject to the tax, but there is sliding scale reduction. The effect of this is that there is no capital gains tax on these properties after they have been owned for more than 10 years. This applies to residents and non-residents alike.

The above exemptions aside, both residents and non-residents can set off their costs of purchase against the tax, and both benefit from an annual inflation allowance that is applied to the purchase price and reduces the gain. Non-residents pay a uniform rate of 35 per cent, and the tax should be declared within a short time of the sale. In relation to sales of property, the purchaser will, of course, retain 5 per cent of the sale proceeds that he or she pays to the tax authorities on account of the tax, and the non-resident vendor must apply for any refund of overpaid capital gains tax within three months. Non-residents, including UK residents, may be liable in their home country for the gain on their Spanish property. Fortunately, a double taxation agreement with Spain means that you will not have to pay the full tax twice.

You can set off your capital losses against your capital gains and you can carry capital losses forward for up to five years to set off against future capital gains.

The *plus valía* tax (*arbitrio sobre el incremento de valor de los terrenos*)

This tax is payable by the vendor on the increase in the *catastral* value (not the market value) from the time of purchase to the sale. Although a liability of the vendor, sale contracts increasingly provide that this is to be paid by the purchaser. If this tax is to be paid by the vendor, but he or she fails to pay, the tax can still be levied against the property itself, despite the transfer to the purchaser. The *plus valia* tax should not be confused with the capital gains tax payable by a vendor on his or her true gain on the sale, which remains normally payable by the vendor.

The rate of the *plus valia* tax varies between 10 per cent and 40 per cent, depending on the time since the last sale, and the location of the property. Where a property has not been sold for some time, and includes much land, the tax can be substantial. The *catastral* value at the date of the vendor's purchase, and the current rate can both be obtained from the local tax office.

Wealth tax (*impuesto sobre el patrimonio*)

Both residents and non-residents are required to pay a tax on their capital assets. If you are resident, the tax is based on the *market* value of *all* your *worldwide* assets. That means anything and everything of value, save for reasonable home furnishings, objets d'art, rights in pension plans and copyright. Mortgages and other debts are deducted from the total value of your assets, as is any similar tax that you are required to pay abroad. Residents benefit from an allowance of about 110,000 euros. There is also an exemption of 150,000 euros per person for one's principal residence.

Accordingly, a couple resident in Spain with a property valued at 500,000 euros, a mortgage of 100,000 euros and other assets totalling 120,000 euros would pay no or very little tax. A couple *not* resident in Spain with the same assets would each pay wealth tax on half of the net value, ie 260,000 euros, and accordingly their joint wealth tax bill would be significantly higher.

The tax rate on the first 170,000 euros or so of taxable wealth is 0.2 per cent, rising to a marginal rate of 2.5 per cent for those with assets over 10.7 million euros. The following table gives examples of the approximate wealth tax bill to be paid by a couple resident in Spain and owning a principal residence worth in excess of 300,000 euros:

Net joint assets (euros)	Approximate joint annual tax (euros)
860,000	650
1,220,000	1,700
2,220,000	7,500

The wealth tax declaration must be made at the same time as the income tax declaration, ie 1 May to 20 June, on form 714, available from your local tax office or from a tobacconist. Not surprisingly, a non-resident is only required to include his or her assets in Spain, but clearly there can be no principal residence exemption. Non-residents must make annual declarations.

In recent years the autonomous regions, including Andalusia and the Canary Islands, have been given the right to fix their own rates of wealth tax, and accordingly rates may well vary depending on your region.

Imputed income tax

The Spanish tax authorities impute an income to your property (other than your principal residence, which is exempt) generally calculated at 2 per cent of the *valor catastral*. The sum is included as income in your income tax declaration, and then taxed at the individual's rate of taxation. For non-residents the tax is fixed at 25 per cent, making a tax of 0.5 per cent of the *catastral* value.

Appendix 1: Useful addresses

See also regional information in Chapter 1. In the *Yellow Pages*, embassies and consulates are listed under *Embajadas*.

British embassy and consulates

British Embassy
C/de Fernando el Santo 16, 28010 Madrid
Tel: 91 319 02 00
e-mail: presslibrary@ukinspain.com
www.ukinspain.com. The website contains a considerable deal of useful information on a wide range of subjects.

Alicante
British Consulate, Plaza Calvo Sotelo 1–2, 03001 Alicante
Tel: 965 21 61 90
e-mail: enquries.alicante@fco.gov.uk

Barcelona
British Consulate-General, Avenida Diagonal 477-13, 08036 Barcelona
Tel: 93 366 62 00

Bilbao
British Consulate-General, Alamada de Urquijo 2–8, 48008 Bilbao
Tel: 944 15 76 00

Madrid
British Consulate-General, Centro Colón, Marques de la Ensenada 16, 28004 Madrid
Tel: 91 308 52 01

Málaga
British Consulate, Edificio Duquesa, Duquesa de Parcent 8, 29001 Málaga
Tel: 952 35 23 00
e-mail: malaga@fco.gov.uk

Palma de Mallorca
British Consulate, Plaza Mayor 3D, 07002 Palma de Mallorca
Tel: 971 36 33 73
e-mail: consulate@palma.mail.fco.gov.uk

Las Palmas
British Consulate, Edificio Cataluña, Luis Morote 6-3, 35007 Las Palmas,
Gran Canaria
Tel: 928 26 25 08
e-mail: LAPAL-consular@fco.gov.uk

Santa Cruz de Tenerife
British Consulate, Plaza Weyler 8–1, 38003 Santa Cruz de Tenerife
Tel: 922 28 68 63

Santander
Honorary British Consulate, Paseo de Pereda 27, 39004 Santander
Tel: 942 22 00 00

Other embassies

Australia
Pasco de la Castellana 143, 28046 Madrid
Tel: 91 579 04 28

Canada
C/Nuñez de Balboa 35, 28001 Madrid
Tel: 91 431 43 00

Denmark
C/Claudio Coello 91, 28006 Madrid
Tel: 91 431 84 45

Germany
C/Fortuny 8, 28010 Madrid
Tel: 91 319 63 10

Ireland
C/Claudio Coello 73, 28001 Madrid
Tel: 91 576 35 09

Netherlands
Avenida del Comandante Franco 32, 28016 Madrid
Tel: 91 359 09 14

New Zealand
Plaza de la Lealtad 2, 28014 Madrid
Tel: 91 510 31 16

Norway
Paseo de la Castellana 31, 28046 Madrid
Tel: 91 310 31 16

South Africa
C/Claudio Coello 91, 28006 Madrid
Tel: 91 435 66 88

Sweden
C/Caracas 25, 28010 Madrid
Tel: 91 308 15 35

United States of America
C/Serrano 75, 28006 Madrid
Tel: 91 577 40 00

Spanish embassies and consulates

United Kingdom

The Spanish Embassy, 39 Chesham Place, London SW1X 8SB
Tel: 020 7235 5555
e-mail: embespuk@mail.mae.es

The Spanish Consulate-General, 20 Draycott Place, London SW3 2RZ
Tel: 020 7589 8989
e-mail: consplon@mail.mae.es

The Spanish Consulate Manchester, Suite 1A, Brookhouse, 70 Spring
Gardens, Manchester M2 2BQ
Tel: 0161 236 1262
e-mail: conspmanchester@mail.mae.es

The Spanish Consulate Edinburgh, 63 North Castle Street, Edinburgh EH2 3LJ
Tel: 0131 220 1843
e-mail: cgspedimburgo@mail.mae.es

Ireland

The Spanish Embassy, 17a Merlyn Park, Ballsbridge, Dublin
Tel: 353 1 269 1640
e-mail: embespie@mail.mae.es

United States

The Spanish Embassy, 2375 Pennsylvania Avenue NW, Washington, DC 20037
Tel: 202 452 0100
www.spainemb.org

Consulates-General (Washington, DC, New York, Boston, Chicago, Houston, Los Angeles, Miami, New Orleans and San Francisco). All accessible via the embassy website, **www.spainemb.org**.

Canada

The Spanish Embassy, 74 Stanley Avenue, Ottawa, Ontario K1M 1P4
Tel: 613 747 2252
www.embaspain.ca

Australia

15 Arkana Street, Yarralumla, ACT 2600 (postal address: PO Box 9076, Deakin, ACT 2600)
Tel: 02 6273 3555
e-mail: embespau@mail.mae.es
www.embaspain.com

Consulate-General, Level 24, St Martin's Tower, 31 Market St, Sydney, NSW 2600
Tel: 02 92 61 24 33 (there is also a Consulate-General in Melbourne)

Spanish tourist offices

United Kingdom

22–23 Manchester Square, London W1M 5AP
Tel: 020 7486 8077
www.tourspain.co.uk

Ireland

PO Box 10015, Dublin 1

United States

666 Fifth Avenue, New York, NY 10103
Tel: 212 265 8822
www.okspain.org

8383 Wilshire Boulevard, Suite 960, Beverly Hills, CA 90211
Tel: 323 658 7188

Also offices in Miami and Chicago. The website for all offices is accessible via the Embassy website, **www.spainemb.org**

Canada

2 Bloor Street West, 34th Floor, Toronto, Ontario M4W 3E2
Tel: 416 961 3131
www.tourspain.toronto.on.ca

Australia

541 Orchard Road, 09-04 Liat Tower, Singapore 228881
Tel: 65 67373008
www.spain.info

The British Council

The British Council, Plaza Santa Barbara 10, 28010 Madrid
Tel: 91 3191 250

www.britishcouncil.co.uk. Includes information on education and equivalence of qualifications.

British Chamber of Commerce in Spain

Barcelona (main office)
Camara de Comercio Británica, Calle Bruc 21, 1º 4º 08010 Barcelona
Tel: 93 317 32 20
Fax: 93 302 48 96
e-mail: britchamber@britchamber.com
www.britishchamberspain.com
Director: Sarah-Jane Stone

Madrid
Roger Fry, OBE, Maestro Lassalle 46, 28016 Madrid
Tel: 91 345 63 44
Fax: 91 359 27 67
e-mail: moreno@kingsgroup.com

Bilbao
British Chamber of Commerce Association en Bilbao, Ercilla 24, 2º dpto 19, 48011 Bilbao
Tel: 944 15 93 99
Fax: 944 79 09 22

Aragon
Graham Rhodes, Plaza del Carmen 1, 1ª 50004 Zaragoza
Tel: 976 22 93 14
Fax: 976 22 93 14
e-mail: grahamis@teleline.es

American Chamber of Commerce in Spain

The American Chamber of Commerce in Spain, Tuset, 8 entlo 3ª, 08006 Barcelona
Tel: 34 93 415 99 63
e-mail: info@amchamspain.com
www.amchamspain.com

There is also an office in Madrid with the same website and e-mail address.

Accountants

Ernst & Young
Avenida de Sarriá 102–106, Edificio Sarrià Fórum, 08017 Barcelona
Tel: 93 366 37 00/38 00
Fax: 93 405 37 84
www.ey.com/es

Banks

Barclays Bank

www.barclays.es

Madrid
Plaza de Colón 1, 28046 Madrid
Tel: 91 336 13 15/10 00
Fax: 91 336 12 22

Barcelona
Paseo de Gracia 45, 08007 Barcelona
Tel: 93 481 20 00
Fax: 93 215 85 72

Bilbao
Alameda de Recalde 36, 48009 Bilbao
Tel: 944 23 64 86
Fax: 944 24 44 21

Seville
Tetuán 32, 41001 Sevilla
Tel: 954 22 09 90
Fax: 954 21 26 45

Valencia
Barcas 4, 46002 Valencia
Tel: 963 52 30 85
Fax: 963 51 17 81

Lloyds TSB

www.lloydtsb.es

Madrid
Serrano 90, 28006 Madrid
Tel: 91 520 99 00
Fax: 91 577 28 10

Barcelona
Calvet 16–22, 08021 Barcelona
Tel: 93 362 45 10
Fax: 93 362 45 14

Bilbao
Gran Vía 64, 48011 Bilbao
Tel: 944 39 31 12
Fax: 944 41 28 53

Canary Islands
Avenida de Anaga 37–39, 38001 Santa Cruz de Tenerife, Islas Canarias
Tel: 922 53 36 00
Fax: 922 28 39 16

Majorca
Paseo de la Mallorca 4, 07012 Palma de Mallorca
Tel: 971 21 37 90

Navarra
Avenida Roncesvalles 11, 31002 Pamplona, Navarra
Tel: 948 20 69 70

Seville
Plaza Nueva 8, 41001 Sevilla
Tel: 954 50 15 46

Business

British and American Chambers of Commerce in Spain (see above).

Commercial lawyers

Monero, Meyer & Marinel-lo Abogados SL, Passeig de Gràcia 98, 4º 2ª,
08008 Barcelona (with offices in Madrid and Majorca)
Tel: 93 487 58 94
Fax: 93 487 38 44
www.mmmm.es

Churches and mosques

A comprehensive list of Anglican churches throughout Spain can be
accessed from **www.anglicansonline.com**, or alternatively via **www.
anglican-mallorca.org**. For the latter site, go to 'dioceses in Europe' at the
foot of the homepage, and then to 'location'.

An extensive list of English-speaking churches on the Costa del Sol
(including Anglican/Episcopal, Roman Catholic, Presbyterian, Methodist
and Evangelical and non-denominational) is to be found on the website
www.surinenglish.com, which also has details of mosques.

English bookshops

The Spanish Bookshop
80 High St, Winchester, Hants SO23 9AT
Tel: 01962 773055
e-mail: Info@thespanishbookshop.com
www.thespanishbookshop.com

The Shakespeare Second Hand Bookshop
Calle Lagasca, 69 San Pedro de Alcántara, Costa del Sol

Bookworld España (six branches)
e-mail: bookworld@in.es or mailorder@bookworldespana.com
www.bookworldespana.com

San Pedro: Las Palmeras 25, San Pedro Alcántara
Tel: 952 78 63 66

Fuengirola: Avenida Jesús Santos Rein, Fuengirola
Tel: 952 66 48 37

Puerto Banús: Numero 15 local 1 y 2, Marina Banús, Marbella
Tel: 952 81 60 84

and branches also in Guadalmina, Jávea and Calpe.

Bookseller SA
José Abascal, 48 28003 Madrid
Tel: 91 442 79 59
e-mail: booksellers@wanadoo.fr

Hemmingway & Co
Maestra Concepción, Guidet 6, Los Boliches, Fuengirola
Tel: 952 58 83 58

Chapter & Verse
Central Commercial, Las Rampas, Fuengirola
Tel: 952 47 4411
www.chapterandverse.bizhosting.com

The English Bookshop City
Barcelona postal address: Entença 63
Tel: 93 425 44 66

Come in – English bookshop
Provença 203, 08036 Barcelona
Tel: 93 453 12 04

FNAC
Centre Comercial L'Illa, Avinguda Diagonal 555–559, 08028 Barcelona
Tel: 93 444 59 00

Happy Books
Passeig de Gràcia 77, 08008 Barcelona
Tel: 93 487 95 71

English-language newspapers and journals

Absolute Marbella
Office 21, Edificio Tembo, C/Rotary International s/n, Puerto Banús, Marbella
Tel: 952 90 86 17
e-mail: info@absolute-marbella.com
www.absolute-marbella.com

Costa del Sol News
Apartado 102, 29630 Benalmádena Costa, Málaga
Tel: 952 44 92 50
e-mail: costasol@dragonet.es

Costa Blanca News
Apartado 95, 03500 Benidorm, Alicante
Tel: 966 81 28 41
www.costablanca-news.com

Costa Blanca Weekly Post
www.cbweeklypost.com

The Island Gazette
C/Iriate 43–2, Puerto de la Santa Cruz, Tenerife

The Mallorca Daily Bulletin
Sam Feliu 25, Palma de Mallorca, Majorca
e-mail: master@majorcadailybulletin.es

Sur in English
Avenida Doctor Marañon 48, 29009 Malaga
Tel: 952 64 97 41
e-mail: sureng@surinenglish.com
www.surinenglish.com

El Sun
Tel: 952 59 94 41
e-mail: sunnews@idecnet.com

The Broadsheet (Madrid)
e-mail: frontdesk@thebroadsheet.com

See also **www.spainview.com** for information on English-language newspapers.

Estate agents

Numerous estate agents have websites that are easily accessible, including via a number of information websites, as listed below.

Spanish Property Centre
2 Alva Street, Edinburgh
Tel: 0131 226 6633

Anglo Continental Properties
Tel: 01926 401274
www.anglocontinental.co.uk

Other property sites

www.Iwanttobuyapropertyinspain.com

www.anadalucia.com

www.apartmentspain.co.uk

www.buyspanish.co.uk

www.propertyfinance4less.com

www.spanishproperty.com

Expatriate websites

There are very many such sites, some of which are listed (with links) at the Back in Blighty website under 'Expat Links' (see **www.backin blighty.com**). See also the website of the British Expats Association Spain (**www.ukgovabusesexpats.co.uk**), which campaigns against injustices against expats by the UK government.

Financial advice

Blevins Franks International
Barbican House, 26–34 Old Street, London EC1 9QQ
Tel: 020 7336 1022; in Spain, tel: 952 79 97 52
e-mail: infolondon@blevinsfranks.com
www.blevinsfranks.com

Siddalls International
Tel: 01329 288641
e-mail: investment@johnsiddals.co.uk

Information

Many of the sites listed in this Appendix, such as those of the British Embassy in Madrid and the Spanish Embassy in London, contain information on Spain. See also:

www.surinenglish.com (for information on the Costa del Sol).

www.sispain.org – a site with information on Spanish culture, language and history with other useful links. In Spanish and English.

www.spainnet.net – provides information on property, the regions, travel, etc in English and Spanish.

www.spaininfo.com – a tourist site in English.

www.spainabout.com – in English.

www.tuspain.com

The *Instituto de la Juvendad* specifically provides information to young people in Spain. The address is Instituto de la Juvendad, Servicio Voluntario Internacional España, Marques de Riscal 16, Madrid
Tel: 91 347 77 00
e-mail: svi@mtas.es
www.mtas.es/infojoven

The *Instituto de la Mujer* provides advice and assistance to women. The contact details are Instituto de la Mujer, C/Condesa de Venadito n. 34, 28027 Madrid
Tel: 91 347 80 00
e-mail: inmujer@mtas.es
www.mtas.es/mujer/principal

Legal contacts

United Kingdom

Fernando Scornik Gerstein, Holborn Hall, 193–197 High Holborn, London WC1V 7BD
Tel: 020 7404 8400
e-mail cedillo@scornik.co.uk
Offices in Madrid, Barcelona, Gran Canaria, Lanzarote and Tenerife

Baily Gibson, 5 Station Parade, Beaconsfield, Bucks HP29 2PG
Tel (UK): 01494 672661
e-mail: susanad@bailygibson.co.uk

Michael Soul & Associates, 16 Old Bailey, London EC4M 7EG
Tel: 020 7597 6292
e-mail: mailbox@spanishlawyers.co.uk
www.spanishlawyers.co.uk
Offices also in Marbella and Madrid

Bennett & Co, 144 Knutsford Road, Wilmslow, Cheshire SK9 6JP
Tel: 01625 586 937
e-mail: internationallawyers@bennett-and-co.com
www.bennett-and-co.com

Edgar Wagner: Anglo-Spanish Law, 6 Lower Birch Road, Eyam, Hope
Valley, Sheffield S32 5QF
Tel: 01433 631 508
e-mail: anglospanishlaw@legalisp.net

J Palanco Abad & Asociados, Heal House, 375 Kennington Lane, London
SE11 5QY
Tel: 020 7377 8088
e-mail: demigpol@aol.com

Spain

Several of the firms listed under the United Kingdom also have offices in
Spain.

Costa del Sol

Esther Wilkie, Plaza Abogados, Puerto Sotogrande, Edificio C Puerta 2,
11310 Sotogrande
Tel: 956 79 02 80

Carlos Llanos & Francisco Dopico, Plaza Abogados, Edificio Puerta del
Mar, Oficina B1, TVA de Carlos Mackintosh s/n, Marbella, Málaga
Tel: 952 82 93 93

Costa Brava

Aurelia Fortuny, De Fortuny Abogados, Calle Aragon no. 235 Pral. 2a
ESC.DCHA, 08007 Barcelona
Tel: 93 487 26 79

Costa del Almería

Michael John Davies, Parque Comercial 50, Mojácar, Almería
Tel: 950 47 27 75

Canary Islands

Santiago Martin Helva, Apartado de Correos 105, Los Cristianos, Arona
386400, Tenerife
Tel: 922 75 23 43

Balearic Islands

Caballero Lafuente Mercadal Abogados Asociados, Calle Norte 12, Mahón,
Menorca
Tel: 971 35 25 72

Note: You may be able to obtain initial advice on an aspect of Spanish law
from the Spanish Legal Forum, hosted by lawyers from Albertoa Mondine
Abogados in Marbella on the website **www.tuspain.com**. Questions are
published anonymously and answered on the website.

You can find a list of British and English-speaking lawyers in Madrid
on the website **www.ukinspain.com** (go to consular information – living
in Spain – legal advice).

Removal firms

Allied Pickfords
Tel: 0800 289 229

Bishop's Move
Tel: 0800 616 425
www.bishopsmove.com

Overs International
Tel: 0800 243433
www.overs.co.uk

World Wide Shipping & Airfreight Co
Tel: 02380 633 660
www.worldfreight.co.uk

See also the website of the International Federation of Removers: **www. fidi.com**.

Schools

See the website of the British Council: **www.britishcouncil.co.uk**. Click on 'Education' for details of the Spanish education system. See also other addresses and websites referred to in Chapter 8.

Spanish: learning the language

Instituto Cervantes
102 Eaton Square, London SW1W 9AN
Tel: 020 7235 0353/0329
e-mail: cenlon@cervantes.es
www.cervantes.es

326–330 Deansgate, Campfield Avenue Arcade, Manchester M3 4FN
Tel: 0161 661 4200/4203
e-mail: cenman@cervantes.es

58 Northumberland Road, Ballsbridge, Dublin 4
Tel: 353 1 668 29 36/353 1 668 84 16
e-mail: cendub@cervantes.es

First established in 1991, Instituto Cervantes now has over 40 centres worldwide, including in New York, Chicago and Albuquerque in the United States. A full list can be seen on the website **www.cervantes.es** by clicking on '*IC en el mundo*'. At the time of writing there were no centres in Canada, Australia, New Zealand, South Africa or any of the Scandinavian countries.

The Hispanic and Luso-Brazilian Council
Canning House, 2 Belgrave Square, London W1X 8PJ
Tel: 020 7235 2303
e-mail: hlbclibrary@btinternet.com

The Council is a non-profit-making organization that seeks to foster good relations between the United Kingdom and Spain, Portugal and Latin American countries. It organizes courses and examinations in Spanish, provides information on employment, work experience placements and cultural events, keeps lists of other organizations that provide help and advice, and provides information to British businesses about Spain, Portugal and Latin America.

Europa Pages
www.europa-pages.co.uk/spain/

A directory of schools, colleges and universities offering Spanish-language tuition in Spain.

People Going Global
www.peoplegoingglobal.com

A directory of universities and other establishments where one can study Spanish in Spain, and access to the Newcomers Club Directory for Spain.

Timeshares

Timeshare Consumers' Association
Tel: 01909 591100
www.timeshare.org.uk

Organisation for Timeshare in Europe
www.ote-info.com

See also the website **www.guidetotimeshares.com**.

Transport

Airlines

For airlines serving the United States, see Appendix 2C, and for the Netherlands and Scandinavia, see Appendix 2B.

Air Scotland
Tel: 0141 222 2363
www.air-scotland.com

Avro
Tel: 0870 458 2847
www.avro.co.uk

British Airways
Tel: 0845 773 3377
www.britishairways.com

BMI Baby
Tel: 0870 607 0555
www.flybmi.com

Britannia Airways (for holiday flights)
Tel: 0870 607 675
www.britanniaairways.com

City Jet
Tel: 00 35 318 700 200
www.cityjet.com

easyJet
Tel: 0870 600 0000
www.easyjet.co.uk

EU Jet
Tel: 08704 141414
www.eujet.com

Globespan
Tel: 0870 056 6611
www.globespan.com

GB Airways
Tel: 0870 850 9850
www.gbairways.com

Iberia
Tel: 0845 850 9000
www.iberia.com

Jet 2
Tel: 0870 737 8282
www.jet2.com

Monarch
Tel: 0870 040 6300
www.flymonarch.com

MytravelLite
Tel: 08701 564 564
www.MyTravelLite.com

Ryanair
Tel: 0871 246 0000
www.ryanair.com

Spanair
www.spanair.com

Thomsonfly
Tel: 0800 000 747
www.thompsonfly.com

See also:
www.cheap-flights-to-spain.co.uk
Tel: 0870 990 8009

www.skyscanner.net

British Airways Authority: **www.baa.co.uk** (links to Aberdeen, Edinburgh, Glasgow, London Gatwick, London Heathrow and Southampton airports).

Pets

www.airpets.com
Tel: 0800 371554 or 01753 685571 (boarding, kennels, flights)

Ferries

Brittany Ferries
Tel: 0870 556 1600
www.brittany-ferries.com

Condor
Tel: 0845 345 2000
www.condorferries.co.uk

Hoverspeed
Tel: 0870 240 8070
www.hoverspeed.com

Irish Ferries
Tel: 0870 517 1717
www.irishferries.com

Norfolkline
Tel: 0870 870 1020
www.norfolkline.com

P&O Ferries
Tel: 0870 600 0611
www.poferries.com

P&O Portsmouth
Tel: 0870 242 4999
www.poportsmouth.com

SeaFrance
Tel: 0870 571 1711
www.seafrance.com

Transmanche
Tel: 0800 9171201
www.transmancheferries.com

Rail

Eurotunnel
Tel: 0870 535 3535
www.eurotunnel.com

French Motorail
Tel: 0870 241 5415
www.frenchmotorail.com

Spanish National Railways
Tel: 902 24 02 02
www.renfe.es

Rail Europe
Tel: 0870 584 8848
www.raileurope.co.uk

Road and route planning

AA
www.theaa.com

Mappy
www.mappy.com

RAC
www.rac.co.uk

Appendix 2A:
Direct flights from the United Kingdom and Ireland to Spain

The details given below will obviously be subject to change and should be checked with the operator concerned. The flight routes listed include the Balearic Islands and Canary Islands.

United Kingdom

From	To	Airline
Belfast	Alicante	easyJet
	Barcelona	Jet 2
	Málaga	easyJet
Birmingham	Alicante	BMI, MyTravel Lite
	Almería	MyTravel Lite
	Arrecife	MyTravel Lite
	Barcelona	BA, Iberia, Ryanair, MyTravel Lite
	Gran Canaria	MyTravel Lite
	Ibiza	MyTravel Lite
	Madrid	BA
	Majorca	BMI, MyTravel Lite
	Málaga	BMI, MyTravel Lite
	Minorca	MyTravel Lite
	Murcia	MyTravel Lite
	Tenerife	MyTravel Lite
Blackpool	Barcelona	Ryanair
Bristol	Alicante	easyJet
	Barcelona	easyJet

From	To	Airline
	Bilbao	easyJet
	Málaga	easyJet
	Madrid	easyJet
	Majorca	easyJet
	Valencia	easyJet
Cardiff	Alicante	BMI Baby
	Majorca	BMI Baby
	Málaga	BMI Baby
Coventry	Alicante	Thomsonfly
	Ibiza	Thomsonfly
	Majorca	Thomsonfly
	Málaga	Thomsonfly
	Valencia	Thomsonfly
Doncaster/Sheffield	Alicante	Thomsonfly
(from spring 2005)	Barcelona	Thomsonfly
	Ibiza	Thomsonfly
	Majorca	Thomsonfly
	Málaga	Thomsonfly
	Valencia	Thomsonfly
East Midlands	Alicante	easyJet, BMI Baby
	Barcelona	BMI Baby, easyJet
	Ibiza	BMI Baby
	Majorca	BMI Baby
	Málaga	BMI Baby, easyJet
	Murcia	BMI Baby
Edinburgh	Alicante	Monarch, flyglobespan
	Barcelona	flyglobespan
	Madrid	BA
	Majorca	BMI, Monarch, flyglobespan
	Málaga	BMI, Monarch
	Tenerife	BMI, Monarch
Exeter	Alicante	Flybe
	Málaga	Flybe
Glasgow	Alicante	flyglobespan
	Barcelona	BA, Ryanair, flyglobespan
	Majorca	flyglobespan
	Málaga	flyglobespan
	Murcia	Ryanair
	Tenerife	flyglobespan

From	To	Airline
Kent	Faro	EUJet
	Girona	EUJet
	Ibiza	EUJet
	Madrid	EUJet
	Majorca	EUJet
	Málaga	EUJet
	Murcia	EUJet
Leeds/Bradford	Alicante	Jet2
	Barcelona	Jet2
	Ibiza	Jet2
	Málaga	Jet2
	Majorca	Jet2
	Murcia	Jet2
Liverpool	Alicante	easyJet
	Barcelona	easyJet
	Girona	Ryanair
	Madrid	easyJet
	Majorca	easyJet
	Málaga	easyJet

Ryanair plans to operate routes to Reus, Murcia and Granada.

London City	Málaga	Cityjet
London Gatwick	Alicante	easyJet, BA, GB Airways, Iberia, Monarch
	Barcelona	easyJet, BA
	Bilbao	easyJet
	Gran Canaria	GB Airways
	Ibiza	easyJet
	Madrid	easyJet
	Majorca	easyJet, Monarch, GB Airways, Iberia
	Málaga	easyJet, GB Airways, Monarch
	Minorca	GB Airways
	Murcia	BA, GB Airways
	Seville	GB Airways
	Tenerife	GB Airways, Iberia
	Valencia	easyJet
London Heathrow	Barcelona	Iberia
	Bilbao	Iberia

From	To	Airline
	Madrid	BA, British Midland, Iberia
	Majorca	British Midland
	Málaga	GB Airways, Iberia
	Santiago de Compostela	Iberia
	Valencia	GB Airways
London Luton	Alicante	easyJet, Monarch
	Barcelona	easyJet
	Gran Canaria	Monarch
	Lanzarote	Monarch
	Madrid	easyJet
	Majorca	easyJet
	Málaga	easyJet, Monarch
	Minorca	Monarch
	Murcia	Ryanair
	Reus	Ryanair
	Tenerife	Monarch
London Stansted	Alicante	easyJet
	Almería	easyJet, Ryanair
	Barcelona	easyJet, Ryanair
	Bilbao	easyJet
	Ibiza	easyJet
	Jerez de la Frontera	Ryanair
	Majorca	easyJet
	Málaga	easyJet
	Murcia	Ryanair
	Santander	Ryanair
	Seville	Ryanair
	Valencia	Ryanair, easyJet
	Valladolid	Ryanair
	Zaragoza	Ryanair
Londonderry (Derry City Airport)	Alicante	Falcon
	Málaga	Falcon
Manchester	Alicante	Monarch, BMI Baby
	Barcelona	Iberia, BMI Baby, Monarch
	Ibiza	BMI Baby
	Majorca	Monarch, BMI Baby, Excel

From	To	Airline
	Málaga	Monarch, BMI Baby, Jet2
	Murcia	BMI Baby, Jet2
	Tenerife	Monarch
	Valencia	Jet2

GB Airways plans flights from Manchester to Málaga and Tenerife, and Britannia has recently announced plans for flights to Alicante, Almería, Fuerteventura, Ibiza, Las Palmas, Minorca, Málaga, Majorca and Tenerife.

Newcastle	Alicante	easyJet
	Barcelona	easyJet
	Majorca	easyJet
	Málaga	easyJet
Sheffield – see under Doncaster/Sheffield		
Southampton	Alicante	Flybe
	Málaga	Flybe
	Murcia	Flybe
Teesside	Alicante	Flybe
	Majorca	Flybe
	Málaga	Flybe

Ireland

From	To	Airline
Cork	Alicante	Aer Lingus
	Barcelona	Aer Lingus
	Málaga	Aer Lingus
Dublin	Alicante	Aer Lingus, Spanair
	Barcelona	Aer Lingus, Iberia, Ryanair
	Bilbao	Aer Lingus
	Lanzarote	Aer Lingus
	Madrid	Aer Lingus, Spanair
	Majorca	Aer Lingus
	Málaga	Aer Lingus, Ryanair, Spanair, Cityjet
	Murcia	Ryanair
	Reus	Ryanair

From	To	Airline
	Tenerife	Aer Lingus
	Valencia	Aer Lingus
Shannon	Ibiza	EUJet
	Málaga	EUJet
	Murcia	EUJet

Note that north-western Spain is accessible from Biarritz, north-eastern Spain from Perpignan and Montpellier in France, and southern Spain from Faro in Portugal and from Gibraltar.

Gibraltar	London Gatwick	GB Airways
	London Luton	Monarch
	Manchester	Monarch
Faro	Birmingham	MyTravel Lite
	Bristol	easyJet
	Cork	Aer Lingus
	Dublin	Ryanair, Aer Lingus
	Leeds/Bradford	Jet2
	East Midlands	easyJet, BMI Baby
	Edinburgh	BMI Baby, Monarch, flyglobespan
	Exeter	Flybe
	Glasgow	flyglobespan
	London Gatwick	easyJet, Monarch
	London Luton	easyJet, Monarch
	London Stansted	easyJet
	Manchester	Monarch, Jet2
	Shannon	EUJet
Biarritz	London Stansted	Ryanair
Perpignan	Birmingham	Flybe
	London Stansted	Ryanair
	Southampton	Flybe
Montpellier	London Stansted	Ryanair

Note

▋ Iberia Airlines flies to all main Spanish locations, and operates from Aberdeen, Birmingham, Cork, Dublin, Edinburgh, Glasgow, Manchester, Newcastle and Shannon, often with changes at London. See **www.iberia.com**.

▋ Excel, voted the Telegraph Best Charter Airline 2004, has flights from Belfast, Bristol, Birmingham, Nottingham, Glasgow, London Gatwick, London Stansted, Manchester and Newcastle to 11 Spanish destinations. See **www.excelairways.com**.

▋ Britannia, a leading holiday airline, has flights to Spain from 20 UK airports. See **www.britanniaairways.com**.

▋ Avro, a leading charter airline, flies to destinations in Spain and to Gibraltar. See **www.avro.co.uk**. Air Scotland also has flights to Spain. See **www.air-scotland.com**.

Details of airline telephone numbers and websites can be found in Appendix 1.

Appendix 2B:
Flights to Spain from the Netherlands and Scandinavia

Denmark

Billend	Alicante, Gran Canaria, Lanzarote, Málaga, Palma (Majorca), Tenerife
Copenhagen	Barcelona, Gran Canaria, Lanzarote, Madrid, Palma (Majorca), Tenerife

Finland

Helsinki	Barcelona, Faro, Gran Canaria, Lanzarote, Madrid, Málaga, Murcia, Palma (Majorca), Tenerife

Netherlands

Amsterdam	Almería, Alicante, Barcelona, Gran Canaria, Ibiza, Lanzarote, Madrid, Málaga, Palma (Majorca), Seville
Eindhoven	Gerona, Gran Canaria
Enschede	Palma (Majorca)
Groningen	Faro, Palma (Majorca)
Maastricht	Faro, Gran Canaria, Málaga, Tenerife
Rotterdam	Alicante, Faro, Málaga, Palma (Majorca)

Norway

Bergen	Alicante, Málaga, Murcia
Oslo	Alicante, Barcelona, Faro, Gran Canaria, Madrid, Málaga, Murcia, Palma (Majorca)
Oslo Topp	Alicante
Trondheim	Alicante, Murcia
Stavanger	Alicante, Murcia

Sweden

Gothenburg	Alicante, Faro, Madrid, Málaga, Palma (Majorca)
Stockholm	Alicante, Barcelona, Bilbao, Gran Canaria, Ibiza, Madrid, Málaga, Palma (Majorca)

Airlines

www.basiqair.com
www.braathens.no
www.finnair.com
www.iberia.com
www.klm.com
www.scandinavian.net
www.spanair.com
www.sterlingticket.com
www.flysnowflake.com

For a full list of airports, airlines and destinations, see **www.skyscanner.net**.

Appendix 2C:
Direct flights from the United States to Spain

From	To	Airline
Atlanta	Madrid	Delta
Chicago O'Hare	Madrid	Iberia
Miami	Madrid	American Airlines, Iberia
New York (JFK)	Madrid	Delta, Aircomet, Iberia
	Barcelona	Delta
	Málaga	Aircomet
	Santiago de Compostela	Aircomet (summer only)
New York (Newark)	Madrid	Continental, Europa

Airline contact details

www.aircomet.com; tel: 877 999 7587
www.aa.com; tel: 800 433 7300
www.continental.com; tel: 800 231 0856
www.delta.com; tel: 800 241 4141
www.iberia.com; tel: 800 772 4642
www.air-europa.com

Appendix 3:
Pet travel scheme – approved routes and carriers to Spain

By sea

Route	Ferry company
Portsmouth to Santander	Brittany Ferries (winter only)
Plymouth to Santander	Brittany Ferries (summer only)

Channel crossings to France include from Portsmouth, Dover, Plymouth, Poole and Newhaven – see contact details of ferry companies in Appendix 1.

By air

Spain

To	From	Airline
Alicante	London Gatwick	Britannia Airways, Excel Airways Cargo, GB Airways, Monarch
	London Heathrow	British Midland
	Manchester	Britannia Airways, Monarch
Almería	London Gatwick	GB Airways, Astraeus Cargo,
	Manchester	Britannia Airways

To	From	Airline
Arrecife	London Gatwick	Britannia Airways, Excel Airways Cargo
	Manchester	Britannia Airways
Barcelona	London Gatwick	British Airways, Excel Airways
	London Heathrow	KLM Cargo (via Amsterdam)
	Manchester	Monarch
Fuerteventura	London Gatwick	Britannia Airways, Excel Airways Cargo, MyTravel
	Manchester	Britannia Airways
Girona	London Gatwick	GB Airways
Ibiza	London Gatwick	Britannia Airways, GB Airways
	Manchester	Britannia Airways
Lanzarote	London Gatwick	GB Airways
	Manchester	Excel Airways
Las Palmas	London Gatwick	Britannia Airways, Astraeus Cargo
Madrid	London Heathrow	British Midland, KLM Cargo (via Amsterdam), BA
Mahón	London Gatwick	Britannia Airways, GB Airways, Excel Airways Cargo
	Manchester	BA
Málaga	London Gatwick	Britannia Airways, GB Airways, Monarch Airlines, Excel Airways Cargo
	London Heathrow	GB Airways
Murcia	London Gatwick	GB Airways
Palma (Majorca)	London Gatwick	GB Airways, Britannia Airways, MyTravel
	London Heathrow	British Midland
Seville	London Gatwick	GB Airways
Tenerife North	London Gatwick	GB Airways
	London Heathrow	British Midland
	Manchester	Britannia Airways
Tenerife South	London Gatwick	Britannia Airways, GB Airways
	London Heathrow	British Midland
Valencia	London Gatwick	GB Airways

Portugal

To	From	Airline
Faro	London Gatwick	Britannia Airways, GB Airways, Monarch
	Manchester	Britannia Airways, Monarch

Gibraltar

To	From	Airline
Gibraltar	London Gatwick	GB Airways

The above information is subject to variation, so you should check before making your travel plans. Transport companies may also have their own conditions of travel. Pets travel as cargo, though on a small number of flights guide dogs are permitted in the cabin. See the Defra website (details below).

Further information

Pets helpline (Defra)
Tel: 0870 241 1710 (Monday–Friday, 8.30 am to 5.00 pm, UK time)
e-mail: helpline@defra.gsi.gov.uk
www.defra.gov.uk

See also **www.airpets.com**, which provides boarding facilities and flights.
Tel: 01753 685571 and 0800 371554
e-mail: info@airpets.com

Appendix 4:
Non-EU nationals – acquiring the right to live and work in Spain and the European Union

Citizens of the various English-speaking countries may well be entitled to live in any country of the European Union, including Spain, by virtue of their Irish roots. Americans, Canadians, South Africans, Australians, New Zealanders and those of any other nationality who can establish that they have one grandparent who was both an Irish national and born in either the Republic of Ireland or Northern Ireland have the right to an Irish passport. No period of residence in Ireland is required. In addition, a person whose great-grandparent was born in Ireland or Northern Ireland may also obtain Irish citizenship, but only if that person's parent had registered in the Foreign Births Register before the person's birth.

Irish citizenship of course brings with it entitlement to live and work anywhere within the European Union. You can register at the Foreign Births Registry at an Irish embassy or consulate, or at the Department of Foreign Affairs in Dublin.

Department of Foreign Affairs
72–76 St Stephen's Green
Dublin 2
Tel: 353 1 478 0822

Irish embassies

United States
Embassy of Ireland
2234 Massachusetts Avenue NW
Washington, DC 20008-2849
Tel: +1 202 462 3939
Fax: +1 202 232 5993
e-mail: embirlus@aol.com
www.irelandemb.org

Canada
Embassy of Ireland
Suite1105
130 Albert Street
Ottawa K1P 5G4
Tel: +1 613 233 6281

Australia
Embassy of Ireland
20 Arkana Street
Yarralumla
ACT 2600
Canberra
Tel: +612 6273 3022, +612 6273 3201

New Zealand
Embassy of Ireland
6th Floor
18 Shortland Street
1001 Auckland
Tel: 0064 9 977 2252

Appendix 5: Scandinavian and Dutch resources

Information websites

See the Scandinavian portal **www.costadelsol.st** (in Norwegian and Swedish).

Newspapers and periodicals

Costa Blanca

Aktuelt Magasin
03580 Alfaz del Pi (Alicante)
Tel: 965 88 99 05
e-mail aktuelt@wanadoo.es
www.aktuelmagasin.com

Costa del Sol

Det Norske Magasinet and **La Danesa**
Centro Idea
Ctra de Mijas km 3,6
29650 Mijas (Málaga)
Tel: 952 58 15 53
e-mail: hello@norrbo.com
www.norrbom.com

De Vliegende Hollander
Avenida ús Cautivo 44
Ed Jupiter local 6
29640 Fuengirola
Tel: 953 56 90 07
e-mail: info@nederlandseclub.com
www.nederlandseclub.com

Solkysten
Edificio Tres Coronas A 103
Avenida Suel 4
29640 Fuengirola (Málaga)
Tel: 952 47 22 48
e-mail: solkysten@solkysten.net
www.solkysten.net (with links to other Swedish, Danish and Norwegian sites)

Spaniaweb
Urb. Puebla Lucia
Local 7/21-9
29640 Fuengirola (Málaga)
Tel: 952 46 70 79
e-mail: info@spaniaweb.net
www.spaniaweb.net (with an internet bookshop)

Svenska
Calle Quemada No 6
29640 Fuengirola (Málaga)
Tel: 952 58 18 19

Hallo
Partida El Planet 156K 03590 Altea Aptdo 212
03581 Albir
Tel: 965 84 58 18
www.haloweekblad.com

Appendix 6: Clothes sizes

Women (coats, dresses, skirts)

UK	8	10	12	14	16	18	20	22
US	6	8	10	12	14	16	18	20
Spain	34	36	38	40	42	44	46	48

Women (blouses and jumpers)

UK	31	32	34	36	38	40	42 (inches)
US	6	8	10	12	14	16	18 (size)
Spain	81	84	87	90	93	96	99 (cm)

Women (shoes)

UK	3.5	4/4.5	5	5.5	6	6.5	7
US	5	5.5/6	6.5	7	7.5	8	8.5
Spain	36	37	38	39	39	40	41

Men (suits)

UK/US	36	38	40	42	44	46	48
Spain	46	48	50	52	54	56	58

Men (shirts)

UK/US	14	14.5	15	15.5	16	16.5	17	17.5
Spain	36	37	38	39	41	42	43	44

Men (shoes)

UK	6	7	8	9	10	11	12
US	7	8	9	10	11	12	13
Spain	39	41	42	43	44	45	46

Children (clothes)

UK	16/18	20/22	24/26	28/30	32/34	36/38
US	2	4	6	8	10	12
Spain	92	104	116	128	140	152

Children (shoes)

UK	2	3	4	4.5	5	6	7	7.5	8	9
US	2	3	4	4.5	5	6	7	7.5	8	9
Spain	18	19	20	21	22	23	24	25	26	27

UK	10	11	11.5	12	13	1	2	2.5	3	4
US	10	11	11.5	12	13	1	2	2.5	3	4
Spain	28	29	30	31	32	33	34	35	36	37

Appendix 7: Useful Spanish words and phrases

English to Spanish

General

Good morning	Buenos días
Where do you come from?	¿De dónde eres?
I am from. . .	Soy de. . .
Are you staying long in Spain?	¿Te vas/Se va a quedar mucho tiempo en España?
I am staying for three months	Me voy a quedar tres meses
nationality	la nacionalidad
I am English/Scottish/Welsh/ Irish/American/Australian	Soy ingles/inglesa; escocés/escosesa; gales/galesa; irlandes/americano/a; australiano/a
What's your name?	¿Como se llama usted?
Are you married?	¿Eres/estás casado/a?
In which year were you born?	¿En qué año naciste?
I was born in 1984	Nací en mil novecientos ochenta y cuatro
What is your birthday?	¿Cuándo es tu/su nacimiento?
My birthday is the 30 June	Mi cumpleaños es el trenta de junio
What is your address?	¿Cual es tu/su dirección?
surname	el apellido
welcome	bienvenido

Can you repeat that?	¿Me lo puede repetir?
How do you spell that?	¿Cómo se escribe?
Is that spelt with or without an 'h'?	¿Se scribe con 'h' o sin 'h'?
I think that there is a mistake	Creo que hay un error
May I see your passport	¿Puedo ver su passaporte?
What is today's date?	¿Qué fecha es hoy?

Jobs and employment

I want to find a job	Quiero encontrar un trabajo
I am looking for a job	Busco un trabajo
occupation	la profesión
work record, background	los antecedentes
I am a teacher	Soy profesor/a
student	estudiante
waiter	camarero/a
secretary	secretario
journalist	periodista
gardener	jardinero
I work in a shop	Trabajo en une tienda
Where's the job centre?	¿Dónde esta la oficina de empleo, por favor?
Please will you fill in this form?	¿Quieres/Quiere rellenar el forumlario, por favor?
I saw your advert in the newspaper	Vi su anuncio en el periódico
Please can you give me some details about the job?	¿Puede dame detalles sobre el empleo?
Can you send me an application form, please?	Puede enviarme un impreso de solicitud, por favor?
Where is your office?	¿Dónde está su oficina?
What work have you done before?	¿Qué trabajo has/ha hecho antes?
Why did you decide to apply for this job?	¿Por qué decidiste/decidio solicitar este trabajo?
Have you worked in an office?	¿Tienes/Tiene alguna experiencia de trabajo en une oficina?

I have worked in an office	He trabajo en una oficina
I have worked in a supermarket	Hice practicas en un supermercado
to be unemployed	estar en paro
workplace	el lugar de trabajo
When can you start?	¿Cuándo puedes/puede empezar?
I can start whenever you want	Puedo empezar cuando quiera
full time, part time	a tiempo completo, a tempo parcial
permanent job	trabajo fijo/permanente
temporary job	el trabajo temporal
fixed-term contract	contrato a plazo fijo
permanent contract	contrato par tiempo indefinido
Are you prepared to work on Saturdays?	¿Estás/Está dispuesto a trabajar los sabados?
How much do you earn an hour?	¿Cuánto ganas por hora?
I earn. . .	Gano. . .
Do you speak other languages?	¿Hablas otros idiomas?
I speak German	Hablo alemán
I have a driving licence	Tengo carnet de conducir
At what time do you start work?	¿A qué hora comienza a trabajar?
At what time do you finish work?	¿A qué hora termina de trabajar?
on the dot	en punto
late	tarde
training	formación
in-house training	el formación en la empresa
job/employment	el empleo
interview	la entrevista
to select	seleccionar
experience	la experiencia
salary	el salario
competitive salary	el salario competitivo
desired salary	pretensiones de renta
'Company requires teacher'	'Empresa require profesor'
qualification	titulación
knowledge of French	conocimientos de francés
to write	escribir
to repeat	repetir
to answer	contestar

to send	enviar
to study	estudiar
to sell	vender
the director	el director
personnel manager	el jefe/la jefa de personal
company	la empresa

In the office

computer	el ordenador
stamp	el sello
switchboard	la centralita
to type	escribir a máquina
mobile phone	el movil
pack of paper	el paquete de papel
ballpoint pen, Biro	el bolígrafo
letter	la carta
compact disk	el disco compacto
laser printer	la impresora laser
telephone/fax number	el numero de telefono/de fax
Dear	Estimado/a
Kind regards	Un cordial saludo
Good luck	Bueno suerte
Data base	la base de datos
Printer	la impresora
Keyboard	el teclado
Word processing	el tratamiento de texto

Internet

to open (file)	abrir
@	arroba
dot	punta
hyphen	guión
toolbar	barra de herramientas
search engine	buscador
to exit	cerrar
to copy	copiar
e-mail	el correo eléctrico, un emilio, un email

attachment	datos adjuntos
e-mail address	dirección de correo electrónico
my new e-mail address is. . .	mi nueva dirección de correo electrónico es. . .
to delete	eliminar
to save as	guardar cómo
to print	imprimir
online	en línea
screen	pantalla
dotcom	punto com
website	sitios web
to download	transvaar
www	uve doble, uve doble, uve doble

Renting

deposit on renting	fianza
furnished apartment	apartamento amueblado
furnished	amueblado
landlord	casero
lease	contrato de arrendamiento
notice	casa preaviso
rent	arrendamiento
for rent	se alguila
to rent	alquilar
tenant	inquilino

Utilities

electricity supply	suministro de electricidad
gas	gas
meter	contador
standing charge	abono
utility bills	gastos excluidos
water supply	suministro de agua

Dealing with the authorities

citizenship	ciudadananía
native country	país de origen
police station	la comisaría
registration (car)	matrícula
residence permit	permiso de residencia
town hall	municipalidad

Miscellaneous

bank	el banco
cat	el gato
dentist	el dentista
doctor	el médico
dog	el perro
fuse	plomo
GP	médico de medicina general
money	el dinero
pharmacist	farmacéutico
the chemist opens at. . .	la farmacia se abre a. . .
post office	la casa de correos
prescription	receta

Spanish to English

Financial, legal, property transactions

asegurar	to insure
banco	bank
cuenta corriente	current account
derecho	a right
entidad	lender
gastos	expenses
impuesto sobre bienes inmeubles (IBI)	property tax
impuesto sobre el patrimonio	wealth tax
pagar a plazos	to pay by instalments
prestamo	loan

recibo	receipt
seguro de hogar	household insurance
tipos de interés	interest rate
abogado	lawyer, solicitor
administrador de fincas	licensed property manager
arras	deposit paid on a contract
arrendamiento	sitting tenant
cargos	charges
certificado de matrimonio	marriage certificate
ciudadanía	citizenship
complejo residencial	housing complex
comprar	to purchase
comprar al contado	to pay cash
contable	accountant
contrato	contract
contrato de arrendamiento/ alquiler	rental agreement
contrato de compraventa	sales contract
cosas comunes	common parts (of a block of flats)
demandar	to sue
desocupado	vacant
estado de cuenta	bank statement
firma	signature
arantizar	to guarantee
gestor	licensed professional who acts for individuals in their dealings with the state
honorarios	fees
impuesto sobre actos jurídicos documentados	stamp duty on transfer of property
ley	a law
llave	key
llave en mano	ready for immediate occupation
mudanza	removal
multa	fine, penalty
notario	public notary who oversees property transactions
poder	power of attorney
precio	price

préstamo	loan
presupuesto	estimate/quote
promotor	developer
reformar	to refurbish
reparación	repair
en ruinas	in ruins
sala de estar	sitting room
salón	living room
sanción	penalty, fine
techo	ceiling
tejado	roof
urbanización	purpose-built housing development
valorar	to value
vendedor	seller
vista	view
vivenda secundaria	second home

Types of property

adosado	semi-detached, often in modern developments
apartamento/piso	apartment
apartamento de lujo	exclusive apartment
apartamento de vacaciones	holiday apartment
apartamento duplex	duplex apartment
buhardilla	top-floor flat under eaves
casa	house, home
casa de época	old house, period home
casa rural	rural home
casa sensorial	exclusive property
casa urbana	urban home
caserio	country house
chalet	detached villa, house
chalet semi-adosado	semi-detached house
complejo residencial	residential complex
cortijo	country house/farmhouse
estudio	studio flat
finca	estate or farm (including its land)
finca urbana	urban estate

granja	farm
masia	type of farmhouse in Catalonia
multipropiedad	timeshare
piso	apartment, flat
rascacielos	skyscraper
solar	building plot
último piso	top floor

Property descriptions, condition of the property and estate agents

accesorios	fittings
aire acondicionado	air-conditioning
alfombra	carpet
alicatado	tiling (walls)
amiante	asbestos
anexos	building extensions
antena	aerial
aparcamiento	car park
arboles	trees
arquitecto	architect
arroyo	stream
ascensor	lift/elevator
azotea	flat roof
azulejos	tiles
balcón	balcony
bañera	bath
barrio	neighbourhood/suburb
barro cocido	terracotta
basura	rubbish, garbage
bien situado	good location
bodega	cellar (for storage or wine)
bombona	gas bottle
bosque	woods/forest
bricolage	DIY
caldera	water heater, boiler
calefacción general	common heating system
calefacción	heating
calle (c/)	street

canaleta	gutter (on roof)
carpintero	carpenter
césped	lawn
cielo	ceiling
clavo	nail
cocina americana	fitted kitchen
cocina comedor	kitchen-diner
cocina	kitchen (or cooker)
comedor	dining room
construcción	building
constructor	builder
cuarto de baño	bathroom
cuarto	room
dependencia	outbuildings
depósito de agua	water tank
desván / altillo	attic/loft
dintel	lintel
dirección	address
doble cristal	double-glazing
dormitorio	bedroom
ducha	shower
edificio	building
electrodomésticos	domestic appliances
enchufe	electric socket
entrado	entrance
escalera	ladder
establo	stable
estado	condition, state
estancia	room
estante	shelf
estructura	structure
fantaneria	plumbing
fosa séptica	septic tank
garaje	garage
garanizar	to guarantee
granero	barn
grava	gravel
habitable	habitable
hormigón	concrete
humedad	dampness

impermeable	waterproof
inspección	survey
instalación de agua	plumbing
interruptor	switch
ladrillo	brick
lavabo	wall
leña	firewood
llave	tap
mantenimiento	maintenance
martillo	hammer
membrana aislante	damp course
metros cuadrados	square metres
mobiliario	fixed furnishings
moqueta	fitted carpet
obra	work, construction
ocasión	bargain
parabólica	satellite dish
pared de cargo	supporting wall
persianas	blinds
pestillo	bolt
piedra	stone
pintoresco	picturesque
pintura	paintwork
piscina	swimming pool
planta	floor, storey
planta baja	ground floor

Appendix 8:
Public holidays

1 January	New Year's Day (*Año Nuevo*)
6 January	Epiphany (*Reyes Magos*)
19 March	San José (*Día de San José*)
Easter Easter Monday	*Semana Santa*
1 May	Labour Day
Pentecost	Second Monday after Ascension
May/June	Corpus Christi, second Thursday after Whitsun Ascension Day (*Ascensión*), 40 days after Easter
15 August	Assumption of the Virgin (*Asunción*)
12 October	Virgin of Pilar
8 December	Immaculate Conception (*Inmaculada Concepción*)
25 December	Christmas (*Navidad*)

Appendix 9:
Further reading

A search of Amazon UK gives a substantial number of books relating to Spain, including the following:

Davey, Charles (2004) *The Complete Guide to Buying Property in Spain*, Kogan Page, London

Ellingham, Mark and Fisher, John (2004) *The Rough Guide to Spain*, Rough Guides, London

Hampshire, David (2003) *Living and Working in Spain*, Survival Books, Fleet

Hobbs, Guy (2004) *Starting a Business in Spain*, Vacation Work Publications, Oxford

Searl, David (2004) *You and the Law in Spain*, Santana Books, Fuengirola

Stewart, Chris (1999) *Driving over Lemons: An optimist in Andalucía*, Sort of Books, London

Driving over Lemons is a delightful and entertaining account of a family moving to the foothills of the Sierra Nevada.

You and the Law in Spain is particularly useful for those already living in Spain, though it is nearly 400 pages long, and retails at about £20.

Appendix 10:
Advertisers' contact details

Acdemia Andaluza
Confederacio 13
E-11140 Concil
Spain
Tel: 956 44 05 52
Website: www.academia.andaluza.net

Associated Foreign Exchange
Berkeley Square House
Berkeley Square
Mayfair
London W1 J 6BD
Tel: 0870 735 8486
Website: www.afex.com

Blauverd Habitat UK
126 Wigmore Street
London W1U 3RZ
Tel: 020 7224 2202
Website: www.blauverd-habitat.com

Bluecosta Property Services
19 Ashlea Meadow
Bishops Cleeve
Cheltenham
Gloucestershire GL52 7WG
Tel: 07968 234 010
Website: www.bluecosta.co.uk

Catalunya Property Services
Apartode Correps 13
43780 Gandesa
Tarragona
Spain
Tel: 977 49 36 07
Website: www.catalunyapropertyservices.com

CJ Spanish Homes
Avenida De Murcia
03503 Benidorm
Alicante
Spain
Tel: 0871 218 0820
Website: www.cjspanishhomes.com

Currencies Direct
Hanover House
73–74 High Holborn
London WC1V 6LS
Tel: 020 7813 0332
Website: www.currenciesdirect.com

EXTRASPAIN CONSULTANTS
Apartado de Corroes 8
10190 Casar de Caceres
Extremadura
Spain
Tel: 927 29 02 88
Website: www.extremadura-country-homes.com

Fuenplaza Group
Avienda Alcade Clemente
Diaz Ruiz
Locel 16 Pueblo Lucia
29640 Fuengirola
Spain
Tel: 0871 910 3555
Website: www.fuenplaza.com

Galicia Paradise
C/Orense 59
27430 Ferreira de Panton
Lugo
Spain
Tel: 982 45 54 37
Website: www.galiciaparadise.com

Gil Stauffer
Chase Road
Park Royal
London NW10
Tel: 020 8965 4560
Website: www.gil-stauffer.com

John Howell & Co
The Old Glass Works
22 Endell Street
Covent Garden
London WC2H 9AD
Tel: 020 7420 0400
Website: www.europelaw.com

Moneycorp
100 Brompton Road
London SW3 1ER
Tel: 020 7589 3000
Website: www.moneycorp.com

Offshore Money Managers
Urb. El Rosario 2
29600 Marbella
Málaga
Spain
Tel: 952 83 09 16
Website: www.offshoremoneymanagers.net

Residential Mortgage Collection
The Old Bakery
Golden Square
Petworth
West Sussex GU28 0AP
Tel: 01798 344930
Website: www.overseaspropertyfinance.me.uk

Spanish Inland Properties S.L
Ave Nicasiu Tomas, 12
1880 Glera
Greneda
Spain
Tel: 958 73 90 32
Website: www.spanish-inland-properties.com

Spanish Mountain Property
Immo Fuente Highuera Molinicos
0440 Elche De La Sierra
Albacete
Spain
Tel: 690 73 04 70
Website: www.spanishmountainproperty.com

Sunshine Lodges
Priory Farmhouse
Braiseworth
Eye
Suffolk IP23 7DS
Tel: 01379 871383
Website: www.sunshinelodges.com

TK Movers
Tel: 0800 328 4378
Email: sales@tkmovers.co.uk
Website: www.tkmovers.co.uk

Torre Alicante Grupo
Ste. Lo Torrent nº 3
Bajo
Edificio Parque I
03690 San Vicente del Raspeig
Alicante
Spain
Tel: 965 66 53 47
Website: www.grupotorrealicante.com

Utopian Properties
23a Castle Street
Cirencester
Gloucestershire GL7 1QD
Tel: 01285 644 247
Website: www.utopian-properties.com

WASINSPAIN
Cordwainors
The Street
Longstratton
Norfolk NR15 2AH
Tel: 01508 530622
Website: www.wasinspain.com

Index